D0995324

Ha Bloody Ha

William Cook was born in London, and educated at
Sidcot School and Keele University. He is comedy critic
of the *Guardian* and television editor of the *Modern
Review*. He also writes for the *Scotsman*. He is married,
and lives in London.

02

LIVERPOOL JMU LIBRARY

3 1111 00791 3062

William Cook

Ha Bloody Ha

Comedians Talking

FOURTH ESTATE

LONDON

First published in Great Britain in 1994 by
Fourth Estate Limited
289 Westbourne Grove
London W11 2QA

Copyright © 1994 by William Cook

The right of William Cook to be identified as the author of this work
has been asserted by him in accordance with the Copyright, Designs
and Patents Act 1988.

A catalogue record for this book is available from the British Library.

ISBN 1–85702–180–0

All rights reserved. No part of this publication may be reproduced,
transmitted, or stored in a retrieval system, in any form or by any means,
without permission in writing from Fourth Estate Limited.

Typeset by York House Typographic Ltd.
Printed in Great Britain by Cox & Wyman Ltd., Reading, Berks.

For Sophie

'Two babies are born in hospital on the same day. They put them in the same room. They lie there looking at each other. The two families come along, and take their babies away. Eighty-five years later, by a bizarre coincidence, the same two babies end up in the same hospital room, on their death beds, looking at each other. One of them says to the other one, "So, what did you think?" ' – Steven Wright

Contents

Introduction

In the summer of 1979 two events occurred which were to shape British cultural life throughout the 1980s. Mrs Margaret Thatcher became Prime Minister of Great Britain and Northern Ireland, and the Comedy Store – the UK's first Alternative Comedy club – opened in an attic above a Soho strip club. Today there can be little doubt which of these two events was the most enduring. Baroness Thatcher has been booted upstairs to the sleepy torpor of the House of Lords, while her successor is busy dismantling all the institutions she erected.

Meanwhile the Comedy Store (now housed in an expansive basement between Piccadilly Circus and Leicester Square) still packs in the punters seven nights a week. Its success has spawned dozens of imitators in London alone, while its (mainly pseudo-) proletarian crack comic troops have seized the Light Ent means of production at BBCs 1 and 2, Radios 1 and 4, and (above all) the TV station that invented the eighties – Channel 4. Within a decade and a bit, Alternative Comedy has become Britain's mainstream Light Entertainment genre – and its pioneers have established themselves as showbusiness celebrities at home and, occasionally, abroad. Countless comics have followed in their wake and the services of Ben Elton, Dawn French, Jennifer Saunders, Lenny Henry and the rest of the Alternative Comedy Royal Family are a central plank of Alan Yentob's bid to claw back the peak-viewing millions lost to ITV in the small screen ratings war. Alternative Comedy is dead. Long live the alternative.

The advertising industry has become a comedic safari park, with Jack Dee, Paul Merton, Mel Smith and Harry Enfield all fronting recent ad campaigns. Political parties (well, pink and yellow ones at any rate) have become happy comic hunting grounds, with comedians rubbing shoulder pads with MPs at election rallies. There's even a charitable conglomerate – Comic Relief – devoted to tongue-in-cheek fundraising, although perhaps as Alexei Sayle observed, 'The people who benefit most from Comic Relief are the comedians.' Whether it's soap, shares or famine relief, comics make superb campaigners – because nowadays, unlike MPs or thesps, we actually know who they are.

   As pop music retreats into a self-referential netherworld of cover versions, remixes and reissues (as epitomised by tribute bands like Abba impersonators Bjorn Again), comedians command a cross-market appeal that rock music used to monopolise but now can only mimic. The implosive pop scene has disintegrated into a series of isolated ghettos, and most tabloid rock megastars (Elton John, Phil Collins, Mick Jagger, Eric Clapton et al.) are balding and middle-aged, like suburban dads at a teenage disco, while teenaged kids (the natural market place of pop) look away with embarrassment. Consequently, the coast is left clear for a clutch of comics to seize the peak viewing time initiative. 'Come on in!' you can almost hear them holler. 'The mainstream water's lovely!' Alternative Comedy began as a clique. No longer. Its protégés confound the narrow stereotype of the ranting foul-mouthed radical. Jack Dee is popular with punters twice his age (hence his success at hawking John Smiths bitter) while Rob Newman and David Baddiel are idolised by fans half theirs. Many of Julian Clary's nationwide TV and live audiences aren't homosexual men, but prim and proper (and devoutly heterosexual) matrons. Yet despite such astonishing success, most people know comparatively little about the mechanics of Alternative Comedy – about the network of ad-hoc comedy clubs in function rooms above suburban pubs and the up-and-coming comedy agents, several of whom are even more colourful than the comics they manage. The underbelly of open mike nights and open spots, the first booking and the fiercest heckle – these are the things that make or break a stand-up comic, and the things that make up this book.

   In spite of comedy's explosive renaissance, there's a remarkable paucity of decent literature on the subject. John Connor's *Comics: A Decade of Comedy At The Assembly Rooms* (Macmillan) is an amusing ragbag of Edinburgh Festival anecdotes. Connor was the first journalist to start listing London's Alternative Comedy clubs, in *City Limits*, the radical listings magazine that's now sadly defunct. Contrary to popular belief, *Time Out*'s Malcolm Hay actually followed in his wake, while Connor's journalistic innovation helped to put the Alternative Comedy circuit on the map. Connor now produces The Cutting Edge – a stand-up/impro hybrid which has a weekly residency at the Comedy Store, in which a rolling cast of five comics perform topical, off-the-cuff material. Yet Connor's book is virtually the sole exception to a disappointing rule. The only comprehensive history of Alternative Comedy is *Didn't You Kill My Mother-In-Law?* by Roger Wilmut and Peter Rosengard, who was instrumental in setting up the Comedy Store. Published by Methuen, its exhaustive index and inspired title more than make up for its prosaic style. However, five years after publication, it's already out of date – a telling indication of the New Comedy's continued fertility.

One reason for this is that – as with all new movements – most publishers don't take Alternative Comedy at all seriously. Paradoxically this has probably been its saving grace. Oxbridge adulation sank the Beatles and Redbrick Radical Chic scuppered Punk, but the Elvis myth thrived and prospered on a hi-cholesterol diet of junk journalism. It wasn't until the sixties that pop music was shoplifted as a suitable subject for broadsheet pontification and dinner party debate, and the dreaded gatefold concept album was the inevitable result. Mercifully, stand-up has been similarly slow to filter through into print.

The result is a dearth of decent comedy journalism, which has much to do with the marked disinclination of most arts editors to pay more than lip service to the most dynamic and influential development in the performing arts since Punk Rock. I reviewed countless fringe plays for the *Independent*, where the first night audience numbered barely a dozen. Yet these same productions were often also reviewed by the *Guardian*, the *Daily Telegraph* and *The Times*. Meanwhile a nearby comedy club would pack in an audience of hundreds, and all it merited was a two-line listing in *City Limits* or *Time Out*. Fans of third-division football must feel similarly frustrated when their favourite broadsheet prints lengthy reports of Rugby Union matches whose attendances amount to only a few hundred. The reason for this imbalance is impure and simple: class.

The *Guardian* has been one of the few national newspapers brave enough to peep above the parapet, and is the first one – to my knowledge – to have appointed a comedy critic. Jocelyn Targett, the paper's innovative arts editor, and his successor, Ian Mayes, both gave me a unique opportunity to learn about comedy on the paper's time and money, and without their foresight and patience, this book probably still would have been written – but almost certainly by someone else. Allen Wright, arts editor of the *Scotsman*, also gave me an invaluable early break. But the real reason I wanted to compile a book about comedians is that I've always found them fascinating. Most of the actors I've met have displayed a marked disinclination to discuss their craft – and those who do usually descend into the sort of self-regarding waffle encapsulated in *Private Eye*'s 'Luvvies'.

An actor inhabits two separate worlds – within the theatre and without it – but for a stand-up comic, art doesn't imitate life, it duplicates it – and behind the mike or back in the dressing room (in most comedy clubs, a public toilet) their dialogue drips with excruciating yet hilarious anecdotes about their on- and offstage lives. Most of these tales are too unwieldy to be accommodated in the bite-sized McNuggets which make up so much of our increasingly unpopular press. Hence the motivation for *Ha Bloody Ha*.

Stand-up comedy is probably the least fictional of all the performing arts – and a comedian's best routines are almost always rooted in real life. Since the craft consists of telling stories to an audience, rather than interacting with other performers behind an imaginary fourth wall, comics are much closer to performance mode in interviews than actors – and so it's a lot easier to squeeze their art inside the covers of a book. No esoteric agonising is required as to how a comedian's background relates to their art because the evidence is all there, upfront in the kiss-and-tell material that comics share with their audience from the Punk pulpit of the stage. And although Alternative Comedy owes much to Punk, comedy is *not* the new rock 'n' roll and comedians are *not* rock stars. Rather, comedy feeds off pop's subject matter, and reinterprets it onstage with a dynamic relevance that modern theatre has manifestly failed to replicate. So the contemporary comic is both star and actor – reuniting two disparate audiences. Brixton Academy meets the Royal Court in the comedy clubs of the nineties.

Most of the comedians I've met are misfits. Few of them grew up with any powerful sense of vocation, and many stumbled into comedy by accident. Jack Dee's début stemmed from a chance trip to the Comedy Store, and many comics since have followed his mongrel example. Jonathan Ross is one of several celebs who had an uncertain stab at stand-up before finding a cosier format for his Viscose talents. And for a few years Jim Tavare – now a celebrity in America and Australia – was known throughout London as the worst stand-up comedian on the circuit. Tavare says he could have been a tramp if he hadn't become a comic, and I've heard the same thing said of that wayward Glaswegian-Jewish genius, Gerry Sadowitz. Sadowitz started out by busking magic on the street – the comedy came second. Today his humour has mutated into a mental zimmer frame, a loathsome yet indispensable device for hauling himself along life's shit-strewn pavements. 'This album is sincerely dedicated to all those to refuse to hold *anything* sacred, since life is absolutely fucking shite,' reads the sleeve of his LP, which he subsequently withdrew for fear of libel. For Sadowitz, stand-up is a way of staying upright, rather than a way to get ahead. Even those career-minded comedians who do fit in offstage often cultivate an assiduous misfit image on it. Actors are orchestral players; comedians, one man bands. More than any actor, a comic is someone who can't or won't conform.

The artform itself is an affront to most people's perceptions of work, or even entertainment. 'I can stand up here,' declares the comic, 'and amuse you without props, stunts or special effects – merely by the sheer magnetic force of my personality.' This is the type of challenge that bare-knuckle boxers issue to their fairground punters, and it's no coincidence that when comics fumble for the words to frame their work, their metaphors so often return to the three-roped ring, rather than the stage. Heckling is not an aberration, but the natural state of stand-up – and the successful comic is someone who somehow defies its gravitational urge, that insatiable desire to drag the smart-arse on the stage back down to earth, where the rest of us belong. That somehow is apposite – because the one thing this book will not do is to try and describe why audiences laugh, and how comedians make them. Freud was the most famous writer to wrestle with this conundrum – and whatever psychological discoveries he may have made, his results were spectacularly unfunny. Subsequent commentators have made less sense, and even less laughter. 'A joke's a joke,' declares Sadowitz (whose *Gobshite* LP carries the warning: 'This album contains material that is offensive to everyone'). 'Art has no rules, and nor does comedy.' Pre-alternative comics like Billy Connolly have

LIVERPOOL JOHN MOORES UNIVERSITY
LEARNING SERVICES

railed against those who seek to legislate against ideologically un-sound humour, but contrary to mainstream folklore, no alternative comic has ever sought to censor – they simply demanded the same stage time for jokes that attacked the strong instead of the weak.

The one thing I can say of all stand-up comedians is that no two are alike. It would be a cruel exaggeration to say that all actors are identical but, as in other professions, they do have certain characteristics in common; hence the success of satires like *I, An Actor* by Nicholas Craig (aka ex-Young One Nigel Planer). No such text exists about stand-up, and nobody seems to know how many comics it takes to change a light bulb . . . (Incidentally, it takes two actors: one to change the bulb, the other to say, 'It should have been me up there'.) Stock types are the bread and butter of the theatre trade, from character roles via romantic leads to spotty juveniles. There's even a theatrical agency which specialises in ugly thesps. Conversely, stand-up comedy is allergic to types and aspiring comics are mercilessly punished for conforming to any recognisable norms. The downside is that the circuit tends to reward shallow novelty acts with a short shelf life – at the expense of more substantial, though superficially less original comics.

The plus is that the best comics are forced constantly to comb their new material for any gag that's even remotely derivative. Jack Dee's wife rejects all new jokes which sound too much like Steven Wright. The establishment of the comic as sole author and rightful owner of his own material is Alternative Comedy's most important achieve-ment – and a far more profound conceptual leap than the rank rejection of sexist and racist humour – although, given the synchronicity of so much topical material, this new ethic can be difficult to enforce.

The one stereotype that sticks is that all comedians are melan-choly drunkards. Evidence suggests that the reverse is more often the case. I have rarely met a comic who drank anything either before or during a show and more than several of the most notorious (Skinner, Dee, Sadowitz, Charlie Chuck) are virtual teetotallers. The tabloid 'MY BOOZE HELL' legends probably stem from the sort of places where stand-up comedy happens and the illusory hi-octane euphoria that it strives to evoke, but it's a fallacy to assume that a drunken audience laughs longer or louder. Punters (as well as

Introduction7

performers) lose their comic timing when they've had a skinful and legless spectators range from surly to downright narcoleptic.

If there are any common traits that unite successful stand-ups, they seem to be: a distant father (but not a clinging mother); a comprehensive school education; an adolescent appetite for horse-play (but not a history as a class clown); mediocre exam results; a string of dull dead-end jobs, and an insatiable thirst for ironic introspection. Contrary to popular belief, it isn't only children so much as youngest ones who (whether as an attention-seeking device, or a way of pricking the pomposity of elder siblings) seem to enjoy the greatest propensity for stand-up comedy. It usually takes a pretty awful event to push someone into contemplating, let alone embarking on, a career as a stand-up – when you've got nothing, you've got nothing to lose – but despite all the Hancockian 'heaven knows I'm miserable now' mythology, the prevailing mood in most stand-up dressing rooms I've invaded is reserved and businesslike rather than flamboyantly maudlin.

Many of Britain's best comedians grew up in some of its bleakest small towns. John Hegley comes from Luton, Mark Lamarr was born and bred in Swindon and Stu Who hails from the spartan Scots New Town of Cumbernauld. When Stu started his own comedy club there he thought he was on to a winner. After all, the only competition was the local disco and chip shop. He reckoned without Cumbernauld's spectacular capacity for superhuman apathy. The disco–chip shop coalition won – Stu's club closed down.

Perhaps a provincial upbringing breeds an appreciation of the absurd, coupled with a desire to belong to something bigger. But it's probably more to do with the fact that cosmopolitan big city types tend to take themselves so bloody seriously. One constant theme on the London circuit is the out-of-town comic (who has usually had to move to London to make his living) telling his audience (increas-ingly made up of folk who've also moved to the capital to find work and can't wait to leave it every weekend) what a miserable shit-hole their adopted city is. This is in stark contrast to trad comics whose winsome celebrations of their economically devastated hometowns constitute the cornerstones of their shamelessly parochial acts. Alternative comics loathe London, but at least they don't come on all cutsie-pie about their small-town origins. Thankfully they've nous enough to know that narrow streets breed narrow minds.

The comics in this book all appear in the first person. This is because almost all of what they have to say stands up perfectly well without any spurious interruptions, and most of the stuff that does need clarifying probably isn't worth printing anyway. I reckon that if a stand-up comic can construct a seamless hour of uninterrupted live banter, he'll probably stand up on paper without too much help from me.

In short, this book comes straight from the horses' mouths. It is a collection of intimate (and I hope entertaining) anecdotes about the business of being a stand-up comic, and if it doesn't make you laugh out loud a few times at least, it will have failed. It is my belief that there is colossal substance behind this laughter – but onstage, the laughs come first, and *Ha Bloody Ha* isn't any different. If you want hifalutin theories about the sociology of stand-up comedy, look elsewhere.

The comics I've chosen all have one thing in common. They've all appeared on television or radio, but they're all still working in front of live audiences on a regular basis. Although some comics now appear solely on T V (and do excellent work there) it's a much more insular and self-absorbed arena. I've never heard a funny story about a comic shooting his or her own T V show.

Primarily, *Ha Bloody Ha* is about comedians on the up – those new wave acts who you may have heard on the radio, or seen on T V once or twice, but who still have a foot in the grass roots of the profession, where most of the interesting things in comedy still happen. And with a few notable exceptions, they all fall under that increasingly large and unshapely umbrella otherwise known as Alternative Comedy – although the second generation alternative stand-ups ('post alternative' for want of a better term) are almost as different from their Alternative Comedy forefathers as the first alternative comics were from the pre-alternative comics who preceded them. This book contains both teams.

The most exciting thing about Alternative Comedy is that anyone can do it. Or rather, anyone can try. Like the girl in the nursery rhyme, when it's good, it's very good – but when it's bad, it's bloody awful. Traditional comics are forever harping on and on about the importance of learning the ropes, whereas Alternative acts wallow in their naked amateurism. Jack Dee spent five years trawling the circuit before securing his own T V show – but that's a quarter of the time it took for many mainstream acts of yesteryear, which is perhaps why so many of their sets sound so mindnumbingly similar. Alternative Comedy is a resolutely 'can do' artform – and in this respect, it's a natural (thought somewhat belated) child of Punk Rock – another movement born in London. Liverpudlians and Glaswegians are famous for their sense of humour (both share the same inheritance of Irish immigration, shipbuilding, hardship, docks, dole, religious bigotry and militant socialism), but the Big Smoke is where they go to get it honed. Like Punk, alternative and post-alternative humour have also fed a plethora of artforms beyond their original boundaries: theatre, music, fashion and comic books to name a few. Like early seventies supergroups, theatre and conventional variety are comparatively closed shops, seemingly confined to those in the know with the proper backgrounds and connections (nepotism's fine and dandy, so long as you keep it in the family).

In their joyous destruction of this regulated universe, of time serving and eternal apprenticeships that kept comedians off the goggle box until they were as clapped out and conventional as their menopausal viewers, the Alternative Comedians of the eighties unwittingly imitated strike breakers at Wapping and Orgreave. Rupert Murdoch and Ben Elton have much more in common than they realise (well, more than Elton realises – I don't suppose that Murdoch gives a damn), which is why both men are images, albeit mirror ones, which sum up the volatile spirit of those times. Elton and his showbiz brothers back Labour and the unions, but they made it big by short-circuiting the system rather than juggling gerbils in front of kindergarten kids in a grovelling attempt to get an Equity card and paying their dues on the windswept seaside circuit.

There's a seminal fanzine scribble (recently reprinted in *England's Dreaming*, Jon Savage's meticulous if pompous history of the Sex Pistols and Punk, published by Faber) which depicts three guitar chords, scrawled out hastily in a crude anarchic hand. Beneath them is the slogan 'Now Form A Band'. This is the Alternative Comedy ethos in a nutshell and the theatre's attempts to respond to this revolution, either in performance style or scriptual substance, have always seemed muted and apologetic by comparison. (It's not for nothing that the current crop of comics constantly refer back to the halcyon days of Punk with ill-concealed longing – even if Rob

Newman needed to tell his Wembley audience who Crass were. Alan Parker Urban Warrior – Simon Munnery's satire on adolescent anarchic angst – is a simultaneous send-up of Alternative Comedy and Sham 69.) One notable exception is Trevor Griffiths' *Comedians*, a play that anticipated – with astonishing foresight – the coming of Alternative Comedy. However even Griffiths dared not address the theatre's endemic problem, that a large proportion of its potential audience was drinking in the pub next door. Alternative Comedy wasted no time trying to coax these truant punters back into the theatre. Instead it cut out the middle man and set up shop slap bang in the middle of the saloon bar.

In London, an average fringe theatre (i.e. a pub attic with a few rows of raked seating and an antique lighting rig) costs upward of £600 a week to hire. Then there's posters, fliers and advertising – all at your own expense. Write your own play (with no props) and don't pay your cast (aka 'profit share') and you may be able to mount a three-week run for a little less than £3000. Blag an open spot at a comedy club and you won't get paid, but then again, you won't have to fork out for the privilege of being booed off either. The club hires the room, foots the bills, and provides you with a much bigger audience than most fringe theatre companies can muster. And if your open spot wins you a paid booking, then you're already making a profit.

Ironically, it was Thatcherite cuts in arts funding which made fringe theatre so prohibitively expensive – and pushed aspiring show-offs into the agit-prop arena of stand-up comedy. A further irony is that the alternative comedian is the quintessential Thatcherite small-businessman, ploughing a lone furrow through the badlands of the free market, without the back-up of bosses or unions. Many comedians even started out courtesy of Maggie's own Enterprise Allowance Scheme: £40 a week for a year, no questions asked. Several (Julian Clary, Jack Dee . . .) now own their own TV production companies. Jeremy Hardy only became a comedian, he says, because during the recessionary early eighties, he couldn't find himself a 'proper' job. There are few professions as entrepreneurial, as on-yer-bike, as stand-up.

Alternative Comedy was founded on the twin axioms of non-sexism and non-racism. Its early acts and audiences were predominantly left-wing, though this aspect of Alternative Comedy has since been simplified and exaggerated. Suffice to say that almost all early performers and punters disliked the Conservative government intensely. In addition, some felt that Labour (or even Militant) would be a distinct improvement, and few felt they could be any worse. However this seismic shift wasn't so much political as practical. Punters weren't so much shocked by sexist and racist material as bored rigid by its monotony and repetition. Punters were voting with their feet, not for fear of being outraged but because (to butcher Morrissey) pre-alternative comedians said nothing to them about their lives. Alternative Comedy's success can be measured in pounds sterling, and even resolutely anti-alternative comedians such as Jim Davidson now pay lip service via lengthy apologias and disclaimers, translating unsound gags into indirect speech and occasionally even reinventing racist gags as cultural critiques. These basic tenets have restored the significance of comedy and brought audiences back in droves.

Much has been made of the anti-alternative backlash among contemporary comedians, and it is true that today's comics eschew a lot of the right-on causes which Alternative Comedy helped to resuscitate, then strangle – such as Strikers' Benefits, Nicaragua and Red Wedge. Compere's compere Arthur Smith (who went on to co-write the West End hit *An Evening With Gary Lineker*) remembers playing Red Wedge gigs in six marginal constituencies during the run up to the 1987 general election. The gigs all sold out, but Labour lost each seat by more or less the same number of votes as there were voters at each gig. Most comedians treat Labour with contempt (a far more damning indictment than their hatred of the Tories) and the more left-wing a comic is, the more likely he is to loathe the People's Party.

However, today's comics are no more enthusiastic about the Conservative government. If anything, their antipathy towards them is more sophisticated and deep-seated. What has changed is that the level of enthusiasm for a left or left-of-centre opposition has dropped off dramatically. Nevertheless, even the most apolitical post-alternative acts (like David Baddiel and Rob Newman) steer a wide berth of sexist and racist humour and in this area (as in many others) they have more in common with the alternative acts of the early eighties than the frilly-shirted stand-ups ousted by the alternatives fifteen years ago.

One aspect which has changed is the pleasant blur between stage and stalls which was the hallmark of the New Comedy. Even during the mid-eighties, today's audiences were often tomorrow's acts. Glaswegian-Jewish comic Arnold Brown was in the audience (and onstage for an entire thirty seconds before he got gonged off) on the opening night of the Comedy Store. Vic Reeves (real name Jim Moir) plucked his partner Bob Mortimer and sometime support act Simon Day (aka Tommy Cockles) out of the audience at his original Big Night Out. In this respect, the New Comedy is a victim of its own success. Whereas comperes were once eager to enlist fledgling funnymen from the front few rows, the supply and demand seesaw has now swung firmly the other way. In big halls the gap between stand-up and sit-down participants is even bigger – and at Jongleurs Camden Lock (Britain's first purpose-built Alternative Comedy venue) heckling is actually prohibited. One punter was even ejected for flouting this draconian rule.

Nevertheless, the Alternative Comedy hierarchy remains remarkably fluid, and new acts can still rise through the ranks in an incredibly short space of time. Harry Hill was a junior doctor when he started out as a solo stand-up in 1991. Within a year he had been snapped up by Avalon – arguably the country's top comedy agency – and his first solo show at the Edinburgh Festival Fringe won him the inaugural Perrier Award for Most Promising New Performer. He's since appeared on several TV shows, and has recorded his own radio series.

More dispiriting is the sad fact that although Alternative Comedy has always attacked sexism and racism, it has ignored its own inherent elitism – and consequently the vast majority of alternative comics and white middle-class men. Alternative Comedy clubs can still seem uninviting to black acts (and audiences), and while women are enthusiastic punters, they still get a far rougher ride onstage. The legacy of the stand-up comic as the bloke who comes on between strippers is mighty hard to shake off. Even mainstream comics like Jim Davidson started out bringing on exotic dancers in a pub in the Old Kent Road.

Maybe that's why female comics like Brenda Gilhooley and Caroline Aherne are in the forefront of the new wave of character comedy: a hybrid of acting and stand-up that's not historically intertwined with the masculine aesthetic. Gilhooley's page three girl cum pop star (Gayle Tuesday) and Aherne's agony aunt (Mrs Merton) and nun (Sister Mary) ridicule man-made female stereotypes far more effectively than some holy stand-up rant. Of thirty comics in this book, only three are female – but this reflects the one in ten ratio of women to men on the circuit. Significantly, on open mike nights that ratio is far higher. This suggests that it's not that fewer women attempt stand-up, but that fewer stay the course. And after hearing some of the fiercely personal abuse that men have heaped on Jo Brand and Donna McPhail (two of our best comics of either sex) I can't blame them. Even more significantly, Jenny Eclair has been attacked twice on the way home from the gigs she does to pay for her daughter's nanny. Meanwhile a black circuit – inspired by African-American comics such as Richard Pryor and Eddie Murphy, rather than white British stand-ups – is gathering steam in clubs up and down the country, particularly at the Hackney Empire. Here, Curtis Walker has established himself as a comic compere *par excellence*, while the Empire's rowdy 291 Club has made a highly successful transition to TV. Like women, black comedians have often had more success working outside the rigid boundaries of stand-up. The Posse (an eight-strong troupe of black actors) virtually reinvented the sketch show in *Armed & Dangerous* at the Theatre Royal Stratford East, which was subsequently filmed (remarkably faithfully) for Channel 4.

Some new wave comics have even benefited from the cross-traffic between the mainstream and alternative traditions. Comedians from outside London (like Birmingham's Frank Skinner) cut their teeth on a more mixed circuit and their humour is more egalitarian as a result. Skinner's unpretentious persona and warm rapport with his audience pay testament to this provincial apprenticeship. Lee Evans hails from a vaudeville family, a legacy that's reflected in the universal physicality of his act. Another comic offshoot of this osmosis is John Thomson's Bernard Right-On, a caricature of Bernard Manning after a damascene conversion to Alternative Comedy. This hilarious device mocks both the blinkered if seductive bigotry of the northern working men's club comic, and the po-faced cant of Alternative Comedy's most self-righteous wags.

The results of this crossover can be less attractive. Bob Mills (presenter of In Bed with Me Dinner) is a child of the alternative boom – but you wouldn't believe it if you saw the way he talks to

women in his live audiences. Perhaps that's why camp acts like Clary
are so popular with women, because all their comic scorn, which
most stand-ups reserve for women, is inverted and boomeranged
back at men. Other alternative comics tell racist jokes about
Americans and Germans and audiences laugh, even though they'd
boo the same gags if told about blacks or Asians. Alternative
Comedy, argues Stewart Lee, has merely swapped Pakistanis for
Tories and mothers-in-law for Margaret Thatcher.

It's currently considered chic to sneer at politically correct
comedy. And indeed in its worst form, it's unbearable (and unfunny
to boot). Just as every journalist knows that news is something
someone somewhere doesn't want printed, so virtually every joke is
something somebody doesn't want told. But modern audiences
forget the inherent violence of racist and sexist humour. The nicer
gags claim that women, blacks and Asians are all as stupid as each
other. The nastier ones end in rape and murder. Hear the one about
the Paki who applied for a job as a conductor? They nailed him to a
chimney in Oldham. Or the one about the guy who raped a deaf and
dumb girl and then cut off her fingers so she couldn't tell her folks
who did it? You don't have to go to a miners' club to hear these
'outrageous' and 'uncensored' one-liners. The former was broadcast on primetime network TV (albeit back in the seventies), while
the latter is freely available for hire or purchase from the comedy
shelf of your local video store. PC humour may tend too often
towards two-faced piety, but there's nothing so hilarious about the
comedy it replaced.

Alternative Comedy has always struggled to secure a foothold in
the regions – but this is not down to a lack of comic talent or even
audiences so much as a lack of business accumen. Since Billy
Connolly forsook folk rock for stand-up back in the seventies,
Scotland has become a cornucopia of revolutionary rather than
alternative stand-up comedians (Arnold Brown, Craig Ferguson,
Fred MacAulay, Bruce Morton, Gerry Sadowitz, Parrot, Phil Kay,
Stu Who) but even a huge city like Glasgow (which has spawned the
vast majority of Scotland's comics) has been unable to sustain a top
class comedy club. The showbiz magnet that is London is still as
powerful as ever, and even Frank Skinner – who created the hugely
successful Four X comedy club in his native West Bromwich – has
since migrated south. Part of the problem is that, even though they

despise it, provincial audiences are far too reverential about London. Until he moved to London, Gerry Sadowitz couldn't get gigs – not only in London, but even in his native Glasgow. A comic isn't accepted as a proper star in the provinces until he's made it in the Big Smoke, and this perverse logic even applies to such Irish comics as Sean Hughes and Michael Redmond.

In London, Alternative Comedy is now the norm – but in pubs and clubs around the country traditional humour prevails. There are more trad clubs in Sheffield alone than there are alternative clubs in London. Some acts from this circuit, like ex Butlins Redcoat Boothby Graffoe (the only comedian named after a market town in Lincolnshire), bring fresh candour to the alternative scene, but many northern clubs deny full membership to women, and there are rumours of unofficial colour bars. However, Alternative Comedy has even had an influence on the closed shop of the trad circuit. The recent revival of *The Comedians*, the ITV pot-pourri of working men's one-liners was heralded as a renaissance of a genre that had been killed off by the university-educated Young Turks of the alternative boom. In fact *The Comedians* died a natural death (before its nineties resurrection) in 1975, a full four years before the opening of the Comedy Store – and far from returning to a tried and trusted old-fashioned formula, Granada's self-censorship was far more stringent this time around.

Yet the biggest advance since 1979 has been in form, not content. On the trad circuit, comics bought jokes by the hundred and, once told, a gag became public property to be rehashed by anonymous stand-ups time and time again. They gave away nothing of themselves. Their humour was fickle fiction, their routines endless strings of standard one-liners, impersonal and interchangeable, If you'd heard it once, you'd heard it a thousand times, from a hundred different yet indistinguishable comics. Authorship, not ideology, is Alternative Comedy's lasting achievement. Just as The Beatles began a pop music revolution by writing their own songs, alternative comedians kick-started a stand-up renaissance by writing and performing their own jokes which were particular to their own personalities and experiences.

Alternative Comedians dare to direct their humour inwards instead of outwards at an absent minority. They tell tales about

themselves, and by extension, their audience. This humour celeb-
rates similarity, rather than condemning difference. The best of it
hits hard and it hurts, but it's philanthropic not misanthropic, a
bridge and not a wall. Above all Alternative Comedy reveals, via
laughter, something of the real life of the comedian. Since 1979 a
laugh has become a means and not an end.

⌐ Will there be a backlash against New Comedy? In the press it's
highly likely, since journalism exists to build phenomena up in order
to knock them down. But it's precisely because of this that hatchet-
job journalism actually constitutes a backhanded compliment. If
New Comedy has become big and bold enough to merit knocking
copy then it really has arrived. Next year, stand-up probably won't
still be the Sunday colour supplement darling that it was last year,
but audiences will keep growing, regardless of what Hampstead and
Highgate says. Do Take That care that the broadsheet critics don't
hold them in high esteem? The day the heavies started taking
Madonna seriously, she stopped being hip and the kids stopped
dancing. Dance and laughter have a lot in common. They're both
joyous, they're both instinctive – and neither of them gives a damn
what anybody else says.

Biographies

David Baddiel

'My grandad died tragically on his ninety-second birthday. That was a shame, because we were only half way through giving him the bumps.'

Alongside Rob Newman, David Baddiel is probably the most popular post-alternative comedian in Britain. He made his name with *The Mary Whitehouse Experience*, Radio 1's first comedy show, whose phenomenal popularity soon secured an even more successful transfer to BBC TV. This sketch/stand-up hybrid was rigorously committed to 'yoof' obsessions like pop music and dating, in stark contrast to the thirtysomething preoccupations of most alternative comics. It also exhibited a precocious flair for coining compulsive catch-phrases, the most memorable being 'That's You, That Is' (from that seminal spoof History Today) which has since entered common usage.

They're not a double-act, but Newman and Baddiel compliment each other like a comedic Lennon and McCartney, and Baddiel's solo excursions, like *A Shot in the Dark* (on Channel 4) have been significantly less successful. His cocktail of smart-alec backchat and playground banter has attracted an enthusiastic teenage audience, yet he's fiercely – and rightly – defensive of his youthful fans. Stuck-up pundits forget that kids are usually the most astute comedy critics, and for the most part, Baddiel is this maxim's living proof. But his laconic stand-up routines can also be as informed as befits somebody who holds a double first from Cambridge University. With Newman he has made another TV series, *Newman & Baddiel In Pieces*. Maybe this imaginative outing missed the slick MOR input of their MWE partners, Punt and Dennis, yet such short-comings have done nothing to put the brakes on his ascent to superstardom. Last year Baddiel and Newman made comic history when they rounded off their UK tour with the first ever comedy gig at Wembley Arena (capacity 12,000).

Barely a few hours before that seminal show, Newman and Baddiel announced that they were parting company, and while some commentators (including myself) initially dismissed this untimely declaration as one more shameless publicity stunt, it does seem, for the time being at least, as if they'll be going their separate ways.

Will Baddiel ever recapture that ecstatic synchronicity between stage and stalls – the rapturous collective laughter of recognition? His first vehicle since the split – *Fantasy Football League* on BBC2, alongside his flatmate Frank Skinner – is a solid, no-nonsense showcase for his laddish flair. But although it's entertaining enough (in a pissed-up, affable, Friday night sort of way), it's not a patch on the empathetic *Meisterwerks* that marked the heyday of *The Mary Whitehouse Experience*, and smart-alec that he is, in his heart of hearts, he must know it. Whether he's slipped into a safe (if successful) career on late-night telly, or is merely taking a well-earned breather in preparation for a fresh assault remains to be seen.

Jo Brand

'Civil war in Yugoslavia? That's not going to get the washing up done or the beds made.'

Jo Brand conforms to one of traditional comedy's most insidious stereotypes – she's a fat woman who doesn't duplicate the page three convention of beauty. And as a consequence of this simple fact of physiology the best new female comic in the country has been on the receiving end of an astonishing amount of abuse. That she has withstood this torrent of bilious hatred is due to a unique combination of thick skin and sharp tongue: Jo can dish it out, but she can take it too, and a great deal of her humour is self-inflicted. 'I'm not an opera singer,' she says. 'I just look like one.' When it comes to masochistic comedy, the buck stops with Brand.

She was a relatively late convert to stand-up, doing her first gig at the advanced age of twenty-nine and quitting her day job (as a psychiatric nurse) eighteen months later. She built up a rock-solid reputation on the club circuit, but her big break, and subsequent transition to peak-time TV and national touring, came five years later after she was shortlisted for the 1992 Perrier Award. Her breakthrough was a surprise, since Edinburgh tends to elevate newer names than her to overnight stardom, and doubly so since Brand remains an unashamedly left-wing benefit-friendly comedienne, defiantly out of step with the apolitical nihilism of these post-alternative times. Her act is especially popular with those female comics who remain woefully under-represented behind the mike – despite forming half of Alternative Comedy's audience. However, her act is also accessible to men – most of whom are happy to laugh at themselves, or their more misogynistic alter-egos. She owes much of her inherent toughness to her previous career, and she admits that she never hears anything as awful from her audience as she did from her patients. Now aged thirty-six, her egalitarian act embraces a range of audiences whose ages span twenty years either side of hers – and it's Brand who best encapsulates the difference between alternative and post-alternative comedy: alternative comics don't buy South African fruit, post-alternative comics don't buy any fruit at all.

Arnold Brown

'When I was about ten, some guy told me that all Jewish people were wealthy. Even now, I remember running home to break the news to my mother and father. We spent the weekend taking up the floorboards.'

Arnold Brown is probably Britain's cleverest comedian, but in a culture where the word 'clever' is less of a compliment than a coded insult it is precisely this quality which has stood between him and the wider audience that his ingenious wit so richly deserves. However his is not the cold cunning of the English intelligentsia, but the humanitarian insight common to all the finest Celtic comics. Brown was born in Glasgow, the son of a Jewish fruiterer, and migrated to London in his twenties to work as a chartered accountant. His humour represents a constant tug of war between these two contradictory influences.

He wrote sketches for Radio 4's *Weekending*, but he was already in his forties when he first stepped onstage to defend a friend besieged by hecklers. Later that year, he was gonged off on the opening night of the Comedy Store. He subsequently teamed up with The Comic Strip, but was dropped, like a stand-up Pete Best, just before they made the big time. He won the Perrier Award in 1987 and had cameos in a couple of British movies, *Comfort and Joy* and *Personal Services*. A couple of Radio 4 series – *Arnold Brown & Company* – attracted a cult following, but the national acclaim that stems only from sustained T V exposure has always eluded him.

This is chiefly due to the idiosyncratic nature of his comedy, which doesn't adopt popular postures or court fashionable causes. His delivery is low-key, his material unpredictable and yet Brown's offbeat observations unearth the marvellous within the mundane.

His soft, smoky style masks an uncompromising set of convictions which have proved remarkably prophetic. In the early eighties, he wrote a joke for *Not the Nine O'Clock News* about Mrs Thatcher encouraging prisoners to buy their own cells. It pre-empted prison privatisation by the best part of a decade. And despite the apolitical spirit of the nineties, he remains true to his socialist roots, turning down the chance to lend his lilting brogue to an advertising campaign for the privatisation of Scottish Water, reputedly worth around £50k.

He lives in Hampstead, as he puts it, 'N W Twee – headquarters of the campaign for real champagne, where even people who live in council houses have another council house in the country that they go to at weekends'. However, he receives the warmest welcome from punters back in his native Scotland, which remains his spiritual homeland. In 1993, he supported Steven Wright at London's Dominion Theatre, but his proudest moment came in 1991 when he opened for Frank Sinatra at Ibrox Stadium – the soccer mecca of Glasgow Rangers FC.

Charlie Chuck

*'. . . and a slice of that there
cake!'*

Charlie Chuck is a coarse and ugly cuckoo in the neat and cosy nest
of New Comedy. He broke on to the post-alternative circuit a couple
of years ago, after two decades on the mainstream scene as a
piecemeal entertainer at traditional clubs like Butlins (including a
spell as a drummer with a band called the Amazing Bavarian
Stompers). He might well have sunk back into total obscurity, had it
not been for Vic Reeves and Bob Mortimer. Vic and Bob were
among a single-figured audience who watched his first solo show on
the Edinburgh Festival Fringe. They subsequently enlisted him as a
cameo act for their anarchic TV series *The Smell of Reeves &
Mortimer* where his autistic antics make even Vic and Bob seem
sane.

Absurdist is too tame a term for Chuck's horribly compulsive act,
which hangs on a string of incomprehensible yet addictive catch-
phrases. He spits these bizarre buzzwords into the stalls like a
cantankerous old coffin-dodger confronted by a baying mob. His
disciples bay them back at him, with the relish of newfound converts
while the unconverted look on in dumbstruck disbelief, like
Victorian missionaries who've stumbled upon a savage ceremony,
performed by the witch doctor of an ancient heathen tribe. At forty-
eight, with a face that's creased and battered like a bare-knuckle
boxer's, and a huge mane of frizzy hair, he looks and plays the part of
the maestro turned madman, complete with a dishevelled dinner
jacket and a moth-eaten bow tie.

His act is far too limited to sustain an entire evening (as he revealed at the Shaw Theatre in 1993), and his surreal signature jokes are undermined by an unsavoury appetite for archaic Irish gags. However, he's a welcome antidote to the neo-conservative conventions of Alternative Comedy, and the ritualistic destruction of his drum kit – performed in perfect four-four time with a mis-shapen plank – remains the most invigorating curtain-raiser that I've ever seen.

Julian Clary

'Is that a pistol in your pocket, or is your penis engorged with blood?'

Julian Clary has done more than any other comedian to drag gay humour out of the closet and into the living room. His act is a lewd but pleasant pot pourri of Butlins bonhomie, seaside smut and Christmas panto amateurism, and yet the tension he sustains between polite syntax and pornographic subtext is often reminiscent of the dramas of spunky sixties playwright Joe Orton. His pre-prepared material is politically and artistically unpretentious, but his comic trump card is his prodigious talent for off the cuff put-downs and *double entendres*. One of this early musical numbers was called 'The Man With the Swollen Head', and his Channel 4 sit-com, *Terry and Julian*, was originally entitled *Stick Your Hand Up*.

Clary's comedy feeds off his audience, and this can manifest itself in pranks which performed by any other comic would appear exceptionally malicious. During his West End extravaganza, *Camping At the Aldwych*, a female punter in the front row made the mistake of visiting the toilet during one of his routines. By the time she'd returned, the entire audience was intimately acquainted with the contents of her handbag. Yet Clary's splendidly anarchic game show, *Sticky Moments*, never patronises its contestants. Surprisingly, his audience is predominantly female. Maybe that's because, as a queen in control, straight men are his stooges. Russell Churney, his pet pianist, is billed as the only heterosexual in showbiz.

The youngest son of a policeman and a social worker and with three elder sisters, Clary hails from the stockbroker belt suburb of

Teddington and attended a boarding school run by Benedictine
monks. He studied drama at Goldsmiths College, University of
London, whereafter he plied his trade as a singing telegram (and
sometime nappygram) whose speciality was a character called Gay
Tarzan. Maybe this disparate education accounts for his unpar-
alleled success in reinventing vaudeville as a Light Ent vehicle for
the nineties.

His participation in *Carry On Columbus*, an insipid revival of the
Carry On genre, wasn't a great success. Yet had he seen him on the
stage or on the small screen, Kenneth Williams, for one, would have
surely laughed and laughed. His instinctive talent for stealing the
limelight was epitomised by his performance at the 1993 Comedy
Awards, where he upstaged Jonathan Ross and all the celebrity
guests at this sycophantic and self-serving televisual non-event, by
cracking a joke about former Chancellor of the Exchequer (and
fellow guest) Norman Lamont, which the *Sun* deemed too obscene
to be printed in a family newspaper but which nevertheless delighted
millions of live viewers throughout the land. It took true alternative
grit to reveal this advertorial as a masturbatory snore.

Initially billed as Gillian Pieface, and then as The Joan Collins Fan
Club (until Joan's solicitor threatened to sue), Clary's own name is
now the one that sticks to the wall of comedy's hall of glorious
infamy. The Queen of Camp is alive and kicking. Long may he
reign.

Steve Coogan

'Bag O' Shite!'

An instinctive talent for mimicry is a poisoned chalice for a comedian. It ensures swift initial exposure, and opens the door to a lucrative if anonymous career in advertising voice-overs on TV and radio. However, it's a gift that goes nowhere unless it's adapted and applied to fit a set of targets more elusive than the current crop of peak-time TV celebs.

Coogan's prodigious flair for impressions is second to none and not even Rob Newman can match his effortless ability to capture the fundamentals of a public persona in a few choice phrases. Yet despite pursuing a profitable side-line in advertising, he has balanced this workaday hackery with a series of remarkably creative radio shows. If *On the Hour* was the most richly textured radio comedy since the Goons, then his solo spin-off, *Knowing Me, Knowing You* was certainly the funniest. These seminal shows have spawned a string of iconoclastic and provocative caricatures which draw on Coogan's talent for instant imitation, but isolate contemporary social types rather than parodying individuals. In this respect, Coogan bears comparison with Harry Enfield. His most popular character, sexist student-bashing drunkard, Paul Calf, can lay claim to being a Loadsamoney for the nineties. Indeed, it's appropriate that Calf has become a totem for the Mancurian beer boys that he satirises much as Loadsamoney became a hero of the cockney barrow-boys who were the target of Enfield's cultural critique. However, while Loadsamoney was arguably Enfield's most sophisticated creation, Paul and Pauline Calf are probably Coogan's crudest. His eye is much more acute than Enfield's, and he sketches each new stage persona in far greater depth and detail. Ernest Moss, a terminally boring safety inspector, and Duncan Thickett, a chronically inept apprentice stand-up, are both hilarious archetypes, but his finest creation is Alan Partridge, a slippery sports presenter who epitomises the suburban insincerity, sycophancy and philistinism of populist broadcasting. In 1992 he won the Perrier Award (with John Thomson), for a character-based show which began the long march away from the dramatically sterile stand-up of the eighties back towards the performance-based precepts of traditional variety. Indeed, the show's compere, John Thomson's Bernard Right-On, could well become post-alternative comedy's new mascot.

His latest vehicle is *The Day Today*, the BBC 2 current affairs satire that does to *Newsnight* what *On the Hour* did to Radio 4's *PM*. Although comedy purists may decry this descent into broad parody (*On the Hour* was a subtle pastiche which was often almost subtle enough to masquerade as a bona fide current affairs programme), there's little doubt that this crude yet effective showcase is the crowbar with which Coogan will prise open the door marked stardom.

Jack Dee

'People stop me in the street and say, "You're not as big as you are on the telly!" ' I Say, "How big's your telly?" '

Terms like deadpan, dour and downbeat cling to Dee's name like limpets, but to dismiss him as a 'bulldog on valium' is to tell only half the story. Dee's miserable bastard persona was a useful tool with which to establish his identity amid a phone directory of anonymous white male stand-ups, but he's subsequently evolved into a remarkably expressive performer with a polished set of stage skills and a versatile vocal range. He's an eloquent mimic, and far from remaining straight-faced throughout his act, his face and often his body are enlisted to punctuate his routines. When he slips into his comic alter-ego – a spoilt whinging brat – he doesn't grin so much as gurn.

Dee's perspective is that of an everyday bloke adrift in an exceptionally mixed up world. Farmers ('nature's Nazis'), teachers ('don't mention the holidays') and ante-natal classes are all assassinated with citric contempt, but he's the only wag I know who can talk about parenting without coming over either whimsical or worldweary. Dee is a pessimist – however, his profound love of family life keeps his caustic tongue in check, and fatherhood actually sharpens his crueller witticisms by providing them with a soft-focus contrast.

His suburban observations still sustain an undercurrent of sedate menace due to the dark shadow that his brooding delivery casts over the most innocuous one-liners. Dee actually looks a lot like Jack Nicholson (like Nicholson, his eyes are too close together), and there are occasions when an axe-wielding madman threatens to burst out, *Shining* style, from within his dapper bespoke suit. Dee has lived a little and after toiling for most of his twenties in the hectic netherworld of London's bars and restaurants, his cod-cynicism is underpinned by the seasoned perspective of real-life experience.

Jenny Eclair

*'Marriage is a dirty job, but
somebody's got to do it – which
is why I hired a maid.'*

Jenny Eclair is probably the most frightening and alluring comedienne on the alternative circuit. Her addictive cocktail of
revulsion and attraction makes her stand-up act an intoxicating and
compulsive pleasure. A bug-eyed, peroxide prima donna, she
doesn't crack jokes so much as shriek them – locking her
amphetamine glare on to any punter unlucky enough to intercept
her gaze. Despite weathering such a battering, shell-shocked
audiences are invariably seduced by the sheer power of her
personality, which swallows up men and women alike. Her
explosive stage persona is that of a fucked-up and fading beauty
queen, screaming her selfish protests, *Sunset Boulevard* style, into
the teeth of encroaching middle age. Although the insults she
cackles into the stalls are shamelessly savage, her unflinching self-
criticism is by far the cruellest aspect of her act.

Indeed, it's this raw honesty which endows her bitchy set with its
huge horsepower. The force and velocity of her delivery often
obliterate her subtler sexual observations, but the nervous energy
that fuels her assaults is pure and undiluted. She was a military baby,
raised on anonymous army bases, and perhaps this dislocated
upbringing has added to her hysterical, neurotic muse. She was a
pioneer of sit-down comedy/stand-up drama – that hybrid of cabaret
and theatre which spawned showbiz mongrels like Arthur Smith's
Live Bed Show and Robert Llewelyn's *From Volvo to Vulva*. She co-
wrote and co-performed *Thirtysomehow*, in 1990 with Julie Balloo

and Maria Callous, and scribbled her own one woman melodrama, *Mummy's Little Girl* – a penny dreadful which premiered at the Edinburgh Festival in 1992. She appeared in two Channel 4 series: *Packet of Three* and *Packing Them In*, with Frank Skinner and Henry Normal. However her extrovert introspection is best enjoyed on the live stage where her gynaecological shock-treatment is underscored by acute insights into the private hell of manic depression.

Lee Evans

'I lost my dog, so I put an advert in the paper – it said, "Here boy!"'

Like traditional British actors, most new comedians perform only from the neck up. Lee Evans is an ecstatic exception to this miserable rule of thumb. His father was an old-time variety entertainer, his elder brother worked as an acrobat, and his physically fraught one-man show marries modern stand-up with vintage silent movie acting. Evans combines two comic devices which often thrive apart but are rarely seen together: acute observation and instinctive mimicry and mime. Consequently, he can extract extraordinary details from everyday experiences and expand them into volatile dramatic tableaux of comic coincidences and cock-ups.

His little-boy-lost persona and his appetite for slapstick have bracketed his name with Norman Wisdom's – yet his influences go far further back. He admires Laurel and Hardy's physicality and Bob Hope's honed one-liners, but his style most closely resembles a hybrid of Harpo and Chico Marx. There are echoes of George Formby and Frank Spencer in his egalitarian urban landscape but only an entertainer as original as Evans would inspire so many comparisons. Although he cut his teeth in working men's clubs, his early try-outs on the trad circuit were all unmitigated disasters. Indeed, it was only after he stumbled on to the alternative circuit, after a chance visit to the Comedy Store, that the vaudeville skills he'd acquired began to work to his advantage. Ironically, the core of his act consists of an inspired parody of an inept apprentice stand-up – a lampoon on the hostile reception he endured in holiday camps and seaside towns up and down the land. Evans won the Perrier Award in 1993, and not since Arnold Brown has there been a more popular winner. A universal comic, with proven international appeal as far afield as France and Canada, his bantamweight talent shouldn't remain hidden for much longer from the mainstream.

Graham Fellows

*'My wife died in nineteen
seventy/ peacefully, in her sleep
. . .'*

Graham Fellows is better known to a generation of late twentysomething and early thirtysomething pop fans as Jilted John – writer
and performer of the novelty hit 'Gordon Is A Moron' in 1978. The
record sold half a million copies, and reached number four in the
British charts, although Fellows has since observed that, given the
dramatic decline in singles sales in subsequent years, the same sale
today would probably keep him at number one for several months.
Pop slump has coincided with comedy boom, so it's apposite that
he's since migrated from the music market to the cabaret circuit.

His current reincarnation is John Shuttleworth, a meticulously
drawn character which sustains a strength and depth that sets him
above the crude caricatures of other character-comics in his field.
Shuttleworth is a redundant security guard, attempting to reinvent
himself as a menopausal pop-star – a role for which he's chronically
unsuited. His cringeworthy stabs at pop, performed on a gimmick-
laden Yamaha keyboard, are appropriately embarrassing, but it's
his boundless optimism which is most gut-wrenching, and the tiny
details of his daily life which continue to enthral. In 1992 his first full
show as Shuttleworth was shortlisted for the Perrier Award –
winning him a slot on Jonathan Ross's *Saturday Zoo* on Channel 4.
Fellows' delicate satire was too subtle to be chopped up into bite-
sized chunks (he fared better in his own series on Radio 4) but he
nevertheless won a cult following on the comedy and rock circuits,
where he once supported rock legend Robert Plant.

Jeff Green

'A message to all women in the audience: this [makes vigorous masturbating motion with his right hand] *hurts!'*

The word 'likeable' has hung around Jeff Green's neck like the proverbial millstone ever since he entered stand-up – and it's this ambivalent tag, more than any other, that has prevented him from becoming a household name. He enjoys the dubious honour of being probably the best comedian not to make the shortlist for the 1993 Perrier Award, when he was left off a bloated and uneven bill of seven. He's carved himself a neat little niche on the London club circuit, but his lack of big-time success (so far) begs the question: Why shouldn't comics be likeable? And – even more perversely – why do we refuse to like them when they are? True, a comic's job is often to say the unsayable – but there's no reason why their stage personae should be as unpalatable as their opinions.

Green's subject matter is unexceptional – but he has a cartoonist's eye for the absurdities of everyday situations, and in a class-bound culture his identity is refreshingly egalitarian. He has shown an irritating disinclination to ditch old material and his first solo show, in Edinburgh last summer, was weighed down with some very familiar ballast. Yet these weaknesses are redeemed by his naturalistic delivery and laddish charm, which found its finest focus supporting Jo Brand on tour last year. Green is not an innovative performer, nor a prolific writer, but, blessed with the instinctive *bonhomie* and pin-up good looks of those boy-next-door teenyboppers that used to fill the pages of *Jackie* and *Blue Jeans*, he has all the makings of a top class TV presenter.

Malcolm Hardee

'Oi, oi!'

Malcolm Hardee is the patron sinner of Alternative Comedy – indeed, he was one of its prime exponents before the phrase was even coined. Born and (in)bred in Sarf East London, he played harmonica with Neil Innes' Bonzo Dog Doodah Band and spent most of the seventies (seven years all told) as a guest of Her Majesty for several fraud and theft offences, most notably stealing Conservative cabinet minister Sir Peter Walker's Rolls Royce. After his release, he performed a pornographic Punch & Judy show with his anarchic soulmate Martin Soan around the West Country, before dreaming up The Greatest Show On Legs – a novelty act performed by half a dozen distinctly unattractive nude men plus a dozen balloons. This post-modern Edwardian fan dance provoked a flurry of complaints when it was performed on TV, and even inspired a leader page cartoon in the *Sun*. His annual pilgrimages to Edinburgh are always punctuated by outrageous pranks, and his most recent Festival Fringe show consisted of a string of reminiscences entitled (entirely truthfully) *I Stole Freddie Mercury's Birthday Cake*.

However, his most important contribution has been as a pioneering promoter. His first venture was the notorious Tunnel Club in Greenwich, which developed a fearsome reputation for energetic heckling and became a graveyard for countless open-mikers. Since the pub that housed it was raided by the police, Hardee has migrated to Up the Creek – a converted snooker hall and sometime Seamen's

Mission a spitting distance from Deptford Creek, affectionately referred to by locals as Shit Creek, as in 'up shit creek without a paddle'. Rarely can a comedy club have had a more appropriate location. Marginally better behaved than the Tunnel (but not that much), it remains a happy hunting ground for hecklers, and the sternest sink or swim test for any aspiring comedian.

Hardee's own *coup de grâce* is an impersonation of General de Gaulle using only his penis and a pair of spectacles, which prompted Waldemar Januszczak to observe in the *Guardian*: 'Hardee has unfeasibly large testicles. I should know – I watched them dangling in front of me in the early hours of Sunday morning. They didn't drop – they abseiled.' Hardee could scarcely have written himself a more suitable tribute.

Jeremy Hardy

'When you're over thirty, you still want the same things – you just want them delivered.'

Jeremy Hardy was once described in a national newspaper as 'the most left-wing man in Britain'. This tag – which stemmed from a mauled and mangled quote – is a gross exaggeration. Yet due in part to the grain of truth that it contains it has plagued him and his stop-start career ever since. Hardy probably isn't even the most left-wing comedian in Britain, but more than any other stand-up, apart from Ben Elton, he epitomises that fast-talking brew of anti-racist, anti-sexist banter which characterised the salad days of Alternative Comedy. Hardy won the Perrier Award in 1988 (after being shortlisted in '87) during an era when his dogmatic school was still in the ascendant. However, since then too much of his time and energy has been eaten up by abortive TV pilots and in his five-year absence from the forefront British comedy has moved on.

Since 1988 the alternative boom has bred a leaner, meaner breed of post-alternative comic, such as David Baddiel, Jack Dee, Rob Newman and Frank Skinner, whose nihilistic backchat is far better suited to the cooler climate of the nineties. Alternative Comedy was the most energetic artistic response to the assault of Thatcherism – but in a less polarised era, such unsophisticated agit-prop usually sounds trite and out of step. That Hardy has survived at all is a testament to his user-friendly technique rather than the socialist purity of his politics. His harmless stage persona has won him appearances on mainstream chat-shows like *Wogan*, which remain out of bounds to left-wing comedians whose delivery mirrors the dogmatic perspective of their material more faithfully.

Along with Stephen Frost, Ben Keaton, Alan Marriot and Hardy's wife, American comedienne Kit Hollerbach, he formed South of the River? You Must Be Joking! (latterly known as Holstein Impro), an improvisation troupe who toured extensively around the college circuit. He's the author of a lighthearted book about parenting, *When Did You Last See Your Father* and recorded a series of mock-polemical lectures for Radio 4 (*Jeremy Hardy Speaks to the Nation*), also published in book form.

John Hegley

*'Don't give me the third degree/
About the two of us/ Or the one
of me.'*

John Hegley is the most prolific member of that motley crew of
comic poets or poetic comics (who also include Henry Normal and
Attila the Stockbroker) who followed in the innovative wake of
seventies Punk poet John Cooper Clarke. This mongrel genre is a
hybrid of pop poetry, stand-up comedy and rough and ready rock 'n'
roll – and since Clarke's eclipse, Hegley has become its most
intelligent exponent. He comes from Luton, supports Luton Town
F C and bears an uncanny resemblance to the 'before' bloke in those
old Bullworker ads – but his stage persona lampoons the po-faced
attitudes of Faber's Oxbridge Bards, and by pretending to forbid
laughter, he actually amplifies it threefold.

Hegley worked as a D S S clerk and as a bus conductor before
studying philosophy at Bradford University. He then acted with a
children's theatre troupe, busked around Covent Garden with his
own band, The Popticians, and was one half of a double-act, The
Brown Paper Bag Brothers, with Otiz Canneloni. He's written three
slim volumes of verse (*Glad to Wear Glasses*, *Can I Come Down
Now, Dad?*, *Five Sugars Please*) and cut an L P (*Saint and Blurry*).
His poems are ostensibly preoccupied with wordplay, but their
brittle wit conceals a powerful sense of pathos. Hegley's solitary
upbringing is echoed in his childlike perception of the world around
him, and his curiously mannered muse repays poetic influences as
diverse as Victorian nonsense poets such as Lewis Carroll and

Edward Lear, and Merseybeat bards like Brian Patten and Roger McGough. He is accompanied onstage by his beleaguered sidekick Nigel, who doubles as accompanist, stooge and straight man.

Richard Herring and Stewart Lee

'Now the time has come to answer the unanswerable, to dance into the abyss – to finally know the mind of God.'

Richard Herring and Stewart Lee are two of the most imaginative young writers on the New Comedy circuit, and though you may not have heard about them yet, you certainly should do soon. They wrote for Radio 4's *On the Hour* and have since created two radio shows of their own – *Lionel Nimrod's Inexplicable World* on Radio 4 and *Lee and Herring's Fist of Fun* on Radio 1. The latter is particularly exciting, since it is surely aboard the mass entertainment flagship of Radio 1 that the future of post-alternative comedy lies, rather than in the cultivated yet stagnant backwater that is Radio 4.

In both shows, Lee and Herring marry intellectual precocity with disarming idiocy – and although their wit is occasionally too puerile for adult tastes, it never sinks into pretension and that's its continual saving grace. Like every decent double-act, they represent nothing so much as a personality clash personified. Herring is the upbeat optimist, Lee the downbeat pessimist, and their onstage and on-air antics are fired with the comedy that stems from fundamental disagreements of the most disastrously funny kind.

Lee won a best new comedian of the year award from *City Limits* magazine as long ago as 1990, but Herring's distinctive yet idiosyncratic talent has taken considerably longer to bear fruit. Herring's most recent stage show was *Ra-Ra Rasputin*, an exuberant if ramshackle costume spoof, which dovetailed the incongruously disparate histories of Gregorii Efimovich Rasputin, the mad monk who held sexual and political sway over Tsarist Russia, and trash aesthetic German disco divas, Boney M, who did much the same thing to the seventies pop scene. This hilarious, harmless romp was snubbed by the stuffier critics, who still stifle the Edinburgh Festival Fringe. A staged version of *Lionel Nimrod* fared little better, even though this anglicised *Wayne's World* precisely duplicated the childlike spirit of these post-modern times.

Lee and Herring have helped resurrect the sketch show from medical revue purgatory and if *Fist of Fun* takes off, they could become the next Newman and Baddiel. Now there's another pair of populist comics whose popularity far outstripped their critical recognition. Punters are the best pundits – Lee and Herring need only study box-office returns and viewing figures, rather than reviews.

Harry Hill

*'I had one of my testicles
brought down – from Derby.'*

Harry Hill lit up the 1992 Edinburgh Festival Fringe with an
innocent, childlike and utterly enchanting show, which won the
inaugural Perrier Most Promising Newcomer Award. *Flies* was a
midget masquerading as a showbiz giant, a miniature extravaganza
with ideas way above its station – and audiences of all ages were
charmed and ultimately seduced by the warmth and ingenuity of this
startlingly original fantasy. Appropriating 'Welcome to My World'
as his signature tune, Hill fashioned a fresh comedic landscape out of
old cardboard boxes and a miscellaneous hotchpotch of junk-shop
odds and ends, forming a wonderful antidote to the clinical stark-
ness of contemporary stand-up.

He shares this strange yet amiable universe with his adopted son,
Alan – played by the vertically challenged Mat Bradstock – whose
one ambition is to escape from Harry's cruel (and often wilfully
sadistic) clutches and relocate his real parents. The 1993 Edinburgh
spectacular, *Eggs*, was essentially a variation on this theme, but Hill
has also rapidly developed into one of the circuit's most solid stand-
ups with a bullet-proof, gag-rich twenty-minute set which belies the
tangential invention of his out-to-lunch solo shows.

A former junior doctor, Hill's life-affirming wit is a reaction to the
dehumanising effect of daily life on an NHS hospital ward. Heavily
bespectacled and prematurely bald, with a weakness for the sort of
secondhand suits you find in charity shops, his on- and offstage

demeanour is as ageless as his olde worlde wit. Indeed he bears a weird resemblance to the late great Eric Morecambe, who I suspect would have heartily approved of Harry Hill.

Dominic Holland

*'IKEA doesn't sell furniture – it
sells expensive puzzles.'*

Dominic Holland is twenty-seven but looks ten years younger – and
his comedy is rooted in that queasy transition from late adolescence
to early adulthood that for most middle-class folk now seems to last
the best part of a decade. His material is unashamedly bourgeois –
but stand-up shares fiction's first commandment: write about what
you know. Hence the resolutely affluent context of his stockbroker
belt observations is actually comparatively radical beside the
proletarian posturing of many other mockney stand-ups.

   Holland's upfront Catholicism lends his lite yarns an unusually
refreshing edge, for most left-footed comedy comes from a working-
class Irish rather than a middle-class English perspective. Nevertheless, inverted snobbery almost stole from him the prestigious Perrier
Most Promising Newcomer Award for 1993. Had Perrier turned
their noses up at Holland, however, all would not have been lost for
promoters had already spotted his considerable potential and before
bringing his first solo show to Edinburgh he'd been booked to
support Eddie Izzard on his national tour that autumn. His subsequent TV appearances revealed his relative inexperience but to
produce such a precise and perceptive solo show after such a short
apprenticeship is a comic achievement date-stamped for future
posterity. Watch that man.

Eddie Izzard

'Being white, male and middle-class is useless if you're a comedian – so thank God I'm a transvestite.'

The first time I saw Eddie Izzard, in 1989, the audience was so small that he met us all in the bar beforehand and bought us a round of drinks. Four years later, he filled the Ambassadors Theatre for six weeks solid, and in 1993 he won the British Comedy Award for best live comic in the country, an accolade which he followed with another West End run in a venue twice the size.

After Newman and Baddiel, Jack Dee and Julian Clary he's probably the most popular new comedian in Britain, even though he's only spent ten minutes on television. However Eddie hasn't been neglected by the telly moguls, more the other way round. From the beginning he was smart enough to realise that his humour was incompatible with the one-eyed god – not because the material was too spicy for suburbia (far from it), but because his rambling, freeform delivery is impossible to trim down into neat soundbite-sized morsels.

Izzard's stream of consciousness style is tangential, wallowing in cross-reference and re-incorporation. Occasionally this hit and miss format can deteriorate into a puerile string of random associations, but as a street performer, he perfected the art of befriending an audience and his unaffected affection keeps his act afloat even when his innovative delivery falters. At its best, his style comprises a pure comic improvisation far superior to the banal and repetitious rag-bag of parlour games commonly known as Impro. Izzard doesn't even tell jokes as such – let alone crack one-liners. Rather, like a jazz

musician, his routines are foundations upon which he builds
ramshackle anecdotes and observations, peppered with unlikely
detours and diversions. A life-long transvestite, he has recently
started performing in female clothing, although his act remains
remarkably unaltered when he does. Izzard is his real name.

Mark Lamarr

*'I recently won the Most
Reasonable Man In Britain
competition. Well, I didn't
actually win. I came second.
But I caused such a fuss that
eventually they gave me first
prize.'*

The first time I saw Mark Lamarr, he was compering an obscure stand-up bill at T&C2 (the Town & Country Club studio) in Highbury. It was midweek, it was mid-winter, it was dark and it was raining. There were about two dozen people in the audience, and almost all of them were pissed off. Lamarr introduced the first two acts, who both died on their respective arses, and that was when I realised Lamarr was special – because he didn't give a damn. Instead of trying to paper over the cracks by pretending nothing had happened, he admitted both acts were crap – and challenged us to leave. Nobody moved. For the rest of the show, he took the piss out of his audience, picking petty squabbles with anybody who took the bait. Against all odds, the evening began to pick up, and by closing time we were all pissing ourselves. Lamarr had been saddled with one of the grimmest gigs you could imagine, and by daring us to hate him, he'd turned it around.

A year later, I saw him steal a Sean Hughes show in Brighton with a similar 'couldn't give a damn' masterclass. I feared that without a gimmick he wouldn't win wider recognition. I was dramatically wrong and I'm damn glad. Within six months, he was co-presenting two top-rated TV shows, *The Big Breakfast* and *The Word* (both on Channel 4). Suddenly, he's a star.

Lamarr's uncompromising confrontational persona is custom-built for these freewheeling chat-shows, dubbed Zoo TV. 'Who were you shagging during the LA riots?' he asked Zsa-Zsa Gabor, and when Shabba Ranks advocated crucifying homosexuals, his silence was eloquent as he walked off the set.

His stand-up appearances remain as abrasive and unconventional as ever. At the 1992 Edinburgh Fringe he performed ten minutes entirely from the wings, and last year at the same gig – the notoriously rowdy Late and Live at Edinburgh's Gilded Balloon – he narrowly avoided being punched out by an enraged punter. He's forever looking for opportunities to drop his pre-prepared material in favour of comedy around the room, wherein his off-the-cuff instincts always find their sharpest focus.

His entrée into stand-up couldn't have been more oblique. He was born and bred in Swindon where his mum and dad worked in a cake factory. An adolescent poem was published in a Faber anthology, on the strength of which (and while he was on the dole) he blagged five consecutive nights at London's Royal Court Theatre, hallowed birthplace of *Look Back in Anger* and *Waiting for Godot*. After a comprehensive seven-year apprenticeship on London's comedy circuit, he is, at twenty-six, much younger and yet far more experienced than most other comics in his field.

Donna McPhail

'I don't have a bikini line – I have a bikini paragraph.'

Cometh the hour, cometh the woman. Donna McPhail finally broke away from the large pack of adept yet anonymous stand-up comics at the 1993 Edinburgh Festival with a precise and provocative one-woman show which located a middle-ground between Jo Brand's blunderbuss equality and Jenny Eclair's lipstick chic. The media focused on the fact (to the exclusion of virtually everything else about her) that she'd chosen comedy's most public forum to come out as a lesbian, shocking many punters and some fellow stand-ups, who seem to presume that any lesbian outside of a pornographic video must look like Brand (who isn't one). During subsequent performances she complained that such attention was inappropriate for a routine which lasted only seven minutes out of an entire hour. Certainly her scalpel-sharp tongue cuts large chunks out of a vast array of contrasting targets, but McPhail's post-Madonna lesbian-ism defines her perspective and informs every other aspect of her humour – even those which aren't directly connected with it. It's significant that her act suddenly acquired greater strength and focus (after a distinctly woolly double-bill with Jeff Green in Edinburgh the previous year) when she finally ventured out of the closet marked Ladies Only.

However, hers is no dry, didactic rant, designed to dismiss all men as potential or actual rapists, but a wry, and often delicate critique of contemporary sexual politics. 'If you offer to help a woman, you're patronising,' she argues. 'If you don't, you're a pig.' Her definition

of nineties feminism is equally enquiring: 'Letting a man open a door
for you, and then slamming it in his face.' Such acerbic witticisms are
balanced by frothier asides, in which a female condom is christened
a Rubber Jenny and solicitor is revealed to be an anagram of clitoris
(well, almost). With a soft exterior and an extremely hard centre,
McPhail has exactly the right mixture of sweet and sour attributes to
take her to the top of that greasy pole marked 'Britain's Best
Comedienne', currently occupied by Brand.

Bruce Morton

'There are some things that women can do that men can't. I mean I could no more give birth than my girlfriend could walk past a shoe shop.'

Bruce Morton was born and bred in the East End of Glasgow. After five years as a comedian, he starred in his own TV series, *Sin*, on Channel 4, but uniquely, he refused to move to London to get it. His success sets an important precedent: at long last, it seems, you can make it as a comic without migrating to the Big Smoke. Morton's compassionate comedy explores the miniature failures and humiliations of daily life, in sustained anecdotes that make a welcome break from English gag-bound stand-up. His Glaswegian roots give his humour a hard edge, but its central philosophy is actually more caring, rejecting the 'I'm all right, Jack' swagger of London comedians for a Celtic brand of humour which implores us all to give a damn.

While English comics were cultivating their alternative credentials at breeze-block universities, Morton worked as a clerical assistant in the superannuation section of the Strathclyde Regional Council Finance Department. After seven years the itch drove him into the arms of his local FE college, where his media communications tutors encouraged him to polish his writing skills. He left his wife and set up as a writer, encouraged and assisted by his new girlfriend. After submitting scripts to Kenny Everett and *The Two Ronnies* without success, he realised that the only way to get his jokes told was to tell them himself. In 1988 he won the inaugural So You Think You're Funny? stand-up talent contest, at Mayfest – Glasgow's annual arts festival – and founded The Funny Farm,

Scotland's first comedy collective, with two fellow contestants. In 1989, The Funny Farm won the Spirit of Mayfest Award (they now have their own series on STV) and Morton was named best new Scottish comic by the *Sunday Times*. He was shortlisted for the Perrier Award in 1992. He still lives in Glasgow.

Richard Morton

'Call that a riot? That's a stag night where I come from!'

New Comedy's most prolific agencies are Off the Kerb and Avalon, and Richard Morton enjoys the unique distinction of having been managed by both of them. After gigging with several rock bands in his native North East, he entered the comedy circuit as one half of the Panic Brothers. This musical double-act – with fellow guitarist Reg Meuros – was one of the first few acts to be signed up by fledgling agency Avalon.

The Panic Brothers split up after Meuros decided to concentrate on more serious music, and when Morton parted company with Avalon just as the agency was beginning to take off it looked as if his career had hit the buffers. Yet Morton reinvented himself as a solo stand-up, and worked his way back up from the bottom all over again. He's hardly a huge star today, but his face (if not his name) will be instantly recognisable to Jack Dee fans all around the country in his capacity as the most adept support act on the circuit.

Morton is blessed with stand-up's greatest gift, and one that can never be taught – the instinctive knack of befriending complete strangers. This delicate skill makes him the perfect foil for Dee, who owes him a significant debt for Morton's effervescent, life-affirming act complements Dee's caustic observations like a refreshing aperitif before a hearty meal.

Despite his relatively modest public profile, he's among Off the Kerb's most precious assets. It only remains for him to shed his supporting role for a full-length solo show in Edinburgh where his tendency to lean a little too heavily on his Geordie heritage would be mitigated by the resonance of his fundamental *joie de vivre*.

Rob Newman

'Picture the scene and pity me.'

More than any other comic, Rob Newman epitomises post-alternative comedy's claim to be the new pop. He's the only comedian to embrace and scrutinise the modern scene instead of flirting with stadium rock clichés. Moreover, his dressing room smashing antics seem reminiscent of tortured sixties superstars like Jim Morrison, and with his unruly long hair and dishevelled designer outfits, he talks, looks and acts like the wild man of rock. He began his career with impressions of media darlings like Jonathan Ross and Philip Schofield, but was brave enough to ditch this knee-jerk talent to create a string of iconoclastic characters, such as Ray – a man afflicted with a sarcastic tone of voice – and latterly an amoral lounge lizard called Jarvis, both of whom were first aired on the BBC's *The Mary Whitehouse Experience*.

Sour critics dwell on his intrinsic appeal to teenagers, especially girls, as if this were a fault and not an asset. There's no denying his dangerous good looks (Baddiel seems cute and cuddly by comparison), but Newman's material also displays a precocious, restless, even tortured, intellect. Yet the real reason he's so popular is because he communicates with older kids and younger adults about what's really going on in their lives: going out with girlfriends, watching *Top of the Pops* or tormenting ugly kids at school or college – the things that teenage and twentysomething life is really made of.

Alongside Baddiel, he confronts these topics instead of droning on about politics. His thirtieth birthday will be a watershed which should necessitate a dramatic sea-change in his material – but if Newman can continue to adapt his prolific talent to the shifting world around him, his best is yet to come.

Punt and Dennis

'The pound fell again today against the German Mark, the French Franc – and the Esso World Cup coin collection.' Steve Punt

'Don't go to Italy in a party of ten or more – you may be asked to form a government.' Hugh Dennis

In 1989 Steve Punt and Hugh Dennis teamed up with Rob Newman and David Baddiel to form *The Mary Whitehouse Experience*. It was a decision which was to prove both a blessing, and a curse. *The Mary Whitehouse Experience* took Radio 1 by storm and transferred successfully to B B C T V. Since this comedy foursome disbanded, Punt and Dennis have completed a sell-out national tour and released a neat little novelty record – and against any other yardstick, they'd currently be considered two of the most successful comedians in the country.

However, their career progression has been modest compared to their former partners, whose popularity since the split has reached stadium rock proportions. Beside Newman and Baddiel, Punt and Dennis are left looking like George and Ringo. It's an unfair comparison of like and unlike, since their Home Counties sense of humour occupies a completely different arena. Punt and Dennis aren't nearly as radical as Rob and David but their comedy is warmer and more proficient. Indeed their patter is so polished that their delivery alone is enough to marvel at.

Together they comprise that rare and precious unit: an instinctive, natural double-act. Steve doubles as principal writer and straight man (and a dead ringer for a youthful Eric Idle) while Hugh is a born stooge, clown and mimic. That their material is enjoyed by a pre-pubescent-cum-adolescent audience even younger than Newman and Baddiel's teenagers and twentysomethings is no insult. Kids are comedy connoisseurs and Punt and Dennis's thirst for fun is undiluted by pomposity. They stole the show when they guested for Jasper Carrott – give them a couple more years, and they could become his successors.

Reeves and Mortimer

'What's on the end of the stick, Vic?'

More broadsheet bullshit has been written about Reeves and Mortimer than almost any other double-act – but in this instance it's a case of 'believe the hype' because this bizarre duo truly are the most distinctive comedians in the country. Surreal is the most obvious (and overused) description of their comic style, but this vague approximation doesn't convey either their verbal precocity (with its flair for random word association and gymnastic conceptual leaps) or their primeval love of simple slapstick. Reeves and Mortimer specialise in inspired nonsense and Seamus Cassidy, Channel 4's Commissioning Editor for Comedy Programmes, took the biggest gamble of his career when he gave them their own television series. Cassidy hit the jackpot, and so did Reeves and Mortimer.

Before Cassidy granted them this enormous break, Vic and Bob were obscure, even by Alternative Comedy standards and their Big Night Out was conducted in a string of south east London pubs beyond the fringes of the London comedy circuit. That they have repaid Cassidy's investment is partly due to their prodigious capacity to turn over a huge amount of material in a very short space of time (back in their pre-TV days, they used to write a brand new two hour show virtually every week), but also because the British tradition of comic absurdism is actually remarkably broadly based. The linguistic games and grammatical pranks that delighted Victorian admirers of Edward Lear are echoed in the psychedelic psychobabble of John Lennon and latterly the rhymes of punk poets like John Cooper Clarke and John Hegley. Consequently, what appeared to be potentially one of the most esoteric and rarified comedy shows either live or on TV has actually attracted an extremely wide audience who empathise with a series of sketches that at times resembles nothing so much as *Sun* readers on acid. Much of their tighter material bears comparison with vintage Morecambe and Wise, but in its willingness to bend, break and remake comic rules, their humour most resembles Monty Python stripped of its public school pomposity. Vic and Bob would feel completely at home on a football terrace (as their tongue-in-cheek veneration of seventies bands like Slade attests), and their peculiar yet compulsive cabaret, with its faint yet enduring aftertaste of olde worlde music hall and vaudeville, has reintroduced classic tomfoolery to a truly popular audience.

Frank Skinner

'I was woken up by the postman this morning – that's the last time I'm sleeping with him. He could have slipped out quietly – he certainly slipped in quietly enough.'

Of all the comedians in this book, Frank Skinner may sum up post-alternative comedy best of all. He's not remotely racist, and he writes all his own material, but his humour is refreshingly free of that holier-than-thou political piety which distinguished the sushi-socialist comics of the early eighties. The rumour that he honed his act on the trad circuit is actually a myth, but Skinner's roots are working class, if not working men's club, and his proletarian heritage is the central plank of his amiable stage persona, and the secret of his broad appeal.

Reared in West Bromwich (like Lenny Henry, he's a West Bromwich Albion football fan), Skinner started his career by compering one of the few New Comedy clubs in Birmingham. It was a baptism of fire which few other comedians could have endured. The need to write reams of new material every week (unlike those London-based stand-ups who can quite easily tour the same twenty-minute set around the vast and constantly fluctuating circuit) sharpened his wits, as did having to cope with a far more varied (and often rougher) audience than a comic usually encounters in the capital. Hence he has acquired an unrivalled knack for befriending a crowd of strangers, and the bawdy banter that embroiders his gigs is distinguished by its warmth and lack of venom. (Skinner doesn't squash hecklers so much as actively encourage them, but there's no one on the circuit who can control a crowded room, and whip up a lather of laughter as effectively as he can.)

His humour is lewd, but there's an earthy egalitarianism to his end-of-the-pier punchlines, which only the most po-faced feminist would classify as sexist. Skinner himself is the most common butt of his bluer routines and there's a Chaucerian relish about his bedroom gags that's quite unlike the cold sexism of many mainstream comics. Malcolm Hay, *Time Out*'s comedy editor, once condemned Skinner for feeling the need to hit the laughter button at every possible opportunity. 'I don't ever want to take me finger off it,' he countered. 'There's no message. There's nothing else I want to do other than make people laugh.' He has described himself as comedy's answer to Bob Latchford, that muscular yet efficient Everton striker of the late seventies: 'I might not be that skilful, but the goals are going in – and that's what counts.'

So is it true of gags – as it is of goals – that there's no such thing as a bad one? As with pornography, it's all a question of context. On one of the few occasions that Skinner actually played a working men's club, he was hauled over the coals for doing a routine about masturbation: 'The manager really got on his high horse: "Who the hell do you think you are to do that sort of material? It's disgusting! I'll make sure you never work again!" And then he went back onstage and said, "Sorry about that last act, ladies and gentlemen – bit of a mistake. Still, you can't have everything. I was in this pub the other day and two niggers walked in . . ."' Anybody who thinks that Skinner's act is in the same league is naive, but his proletarian sense of humour proves that New Comedy can embrace a far broader brief than agit-prop polemic.

Arthur Smith

'I wonder if there are enough traffic cones in the country for every student to own one?'

To describe Arthur Smith as the best compere in the country may sound like damning him with faint praise, but only for folk who remain in blissful ignorance of the delicate mechanics of this deceptively difficult task. Smith forged his reputation as Britain's best MC precisely because he looks like some bloke who's just stepped out of the audience. Like lots of other skills (including stand-up itself) the better it's done, the easier it looks, and the biggest compliment he's been paid is that on several occasions, he's actually been mistaken for a punter.

This talent probably prevented him from evolving into a first-class comic, and of all comedians, he's perhaps the last person you'd expect to become a successful playwright, partly because of his informal charm but mainly because of his notorious inability to shed old material (is there anyone on the circuit who hasn't heard his white dogshit gag?). Yet with Chris England he wrote the West End hit *An Evening With Gary Lineker* – an acutely funny (and perfectly constructed) comedy about a bunch of Brits on a package holiday watching England losing to West Germany in the 1990 World Cup semi-final. After winning a Fringe First award from the *Scotsman* newspaper at the 1991 Edinburgh Festival, it took Shaftesbury Avenue by storm, and subsequently toured as far afield as Australia. His first play, *Live Bed Show*, an innovative stand-up/sit-down hybrid dovetailing outfront monologues, co-performed by Smith alongside comic actress Caroline Quentin, was also a success – if on a slightly smaller scale.

Paradoxically, Smith probably owes these achievements to his decision to front BBC 2's ill-conceived *Paramount City* – a cackhanded attempt to recreate a comedy club on TV in which he was chronically miscast and misdirected. Series producer Janet Street-Porter dismissed him as 'a thoroughly irritating man, neither young, attractive nor witty', and subsequently replaced him with Curtis and Ishmael – a black double act who fared far worse.

He has since disproved the last part of Street-Porter's criticisms (if not the rest of them) in a variety of media, not least on Radio 4's *Loose Ends* with Ned Sherrin, and in two more predictably amusing but surprisingly poignant plays (the critically maligned yet sensitive *Sod* in 1993, and the uneven yet intriguing *Trench Kiss* in 1992). But his inspired party piece is 'Arthur Smith Sings Andy Williams'. This was Smith's absurdist tribute to Arthur Cravan – poet, pugilist and nephew of Oscar Wilde. Cravan declared that 'streetfighting is a better artform than sculpture', and lasted an entire twenty seconds against World Heavyweight Champion Jack Johnson. Smith married this ridiculous biography with the ritual slaughter of several standards immortalised by the crown prince of crooners, charged 50p admission and offered punters £5 to leave. It premiered at the Pleasance Theatre in August 1992 and encapsulated the carefree spirit of the Edinburgh Festival Fringe almost as emphatically as his small hours tours of Edinburgh's Royal Mile.

Mark Thomas

'I want a god with a beer gut.'

Mark Thomas is probably the only unreconstructed alternative stand-up still thriving on the British comedy circuit. Ben Elton devotes most of his live set to sexual rather than party politics, while Lenny Henry has dismissed Alternative Comedy as 'that bollocks' – but Mark Thomas still flies the red flag for left-wing humour, even though he's a comedic generation younger than most Alternative Comedy pioneers. Socialist stand-ups like Mark Steel and Bob Boyton still scratch a living on the circuit – but Thomas regularly appears on TV (with Jonathan Ross on *Saturday Zoo*), and Radio 1 (with Kevin Day on *Loose Talk*).

The reason that Thomas can rub shoulders with post-alternative apolitical comics and appeal to their youthful audience is that he exudes a street savvy that's conspicuous by its absence in PC comics like Arnold Brown and Jeremy Hardy, and his barrow-boy charm sweetens the pill of his often bitterly leftist dogma. His delivery is deliciously fleet-footed, and he relishes the cut and thrust of real debate – either on a formal platform or in the most spontaneous (and volatile) forum of stage versus stalls.

He has appeared at the Montreal Comedy Festival (broadcast in Britain as *Just for Laughs*) where he went down surprisingly well, proving that despite its specific British anchors, his hectoring wit isn't half as parochial as it first appears.

1. Childhood

'You are the product. Everything about you is your product.' –
Dominic Holland

Kids are comedy junkies. If it's good for a laugh they'll do it
regardless of the consequences. Laughter is the motivation for most
sadistic childhood games as anybody tortured by infant bullies will
confirm. That grown-up phrase 'a sense of fun' means something
profoundly different to a child. Amusement isn't cute when you're a
kid – any more than when you become an adult – but when you're
young, it's your lifeblood, your *raison d'être*, and you'll do almost
anything to get some. Before they become distracted by the
mundane worries that invade the world of mums and dads, children
live their lives for laughter unsullied by moral considerations. If it's
funny, they want it, regardless of whether it's good or bad.

Stand-up, like alcohol, represents a forlorn attempt to recapture
(albeit fleetingly) that childlike state of spontaneity, and it's no
coincidence that these two escapist leisure activities are so closely
intertwined. Kids are also the most joyous creatures, even if their
joy can easily derive from cruelty and Jack Dee is among the many
comics who've been inspired by the pure spontaneity of their
children's laughter. Childhood is the only time when an appetite for
laughter isn't subservient to what's right or proper. This accounts in
no small part for the potent 'yoof' appeal of those post-alternative
comedians who so fiercely resist the pious Eltonisms (short cuts to
the moral high ground) of their Alternative predecessors. As any
kid will demonstrate, laughter is its own reward.

Childhood dominates the material of many ostensibly mature
comedians, suggesting that kindergarten scars last long into adult
life, for indignant performers and empathetic audiences alike. This
bleak truism is echoed in Dee's sour one-liner: 'They say parents
should stop smacking their children – perhaps they should stop
fucking them first.'

DAVID BADDIEL

Comedy is about retaining the child within you. Most comedians have it in them more than other people. It's not just about finding it – you can't help it, it's just there, and for some reason it's stronger than it is in other people. You haven't grown up. Frank Skinner, who I live with, is thirty-six but really he's like a very lovable twelve-year-old. Being able to access that childish part of you is really important. I know people who are eighteen, and they're always at their most immature when they're trying to be adult. Practical jokery is a different state. Hitler was a practical joker – I've always felt that practical jokery has a psychotic side to it which leads to Jamie Bulger.

The reason that I do this job is because I've got a deep confessional drive – my comedy seems to be all about confession. It's probably something to do with the fact that when my younger brother was born he was very much my mum's favourite – and although I wasn't neglected, I feel that there was a time when I wasn't being noticed as me. I remember when I was growing up, I was desperate to tell people about myself and for them to notice me and know who I was – totally. And that seems to be what I'm still doing as a stand-up.

Of the two of us, Rob [Newman] is the one whose art is the total thing in his life. For me, my life is slightly more important – even though I'm always subjugating it to my art. I don't want to destroy all my relationships with other people, although if that was true, I suppose I wouldn't constantly put stuff in my act that could endanger my relationships. Sometimes I can get away with it. On the TV series I did a routine about why I'm sexually obsessed being to do with the fact that I had a bedroom next to my father's bedroom – he used to make a noise like a wounded walrus when he was having sex. I did an impression of my dad having sex on the television, but I phoned him up beforehand and he said it was fine.

LEE EVANS

My dad plays loads of musical instruments – he's a talented bloke. He's never seen my act, although I've seen his. We were living in

Avonmouth in a block of flats by the docks. He had all the gear in the back of the car, and me and my brother used to travel with him up and down the country. We used to work our way up the country through the accents, from Portsmouth through Birmingham, Manchester, Newcastle and up to Scotland – so I can pick up accents very easily.

When we were kids, we got pushed into boxing. My brother was very good. He was Essex champion at one point. We went training every day, right up until we were twenty-one. We've always been physical in our family anyway. My dad bought us boxing gloves for Christmas and stuff. A moving target is hard to hit – maybe that comes from the mainstream circuit, dying every night. Keep moving, and you might be all right. I wouldn't dare stand in front of people and do gags. I'd never get away with it.

My father worked with Tommy Cooper when I was a kid. He was the funniest man I'd ever seen – naturally funny in everything he did. We were doing Blazers, which is a big variety club in Windsor. My dad was playing there, and Tommy Cooper was on as well. He turned up three-quarters of an hour late. The compere was saying, 'Fucking hell! Where is he?' He was a massive bloke, big feet. He brought his son with him, who looked very similar, a smaller version. The compere said, 'You're late, Mr Cooper.' He said, 'It's all right, don't worry about it.' The compere said, 'Look, we've got five minutes – I'm going to start the band up, or the audience are going to go mad.' 'That's all right,' he said. 'Start it up, start it up.' He handed his son a stick and a radio mike and said, 'You know what to do.' And then he took out a big bottle of whisky, opened it up, and starting setting up his props. The compere went, 'Ladies and gentlemen – Tommy Cooper!' and walked off. Tommy Cooper started saying, into the radio mike, 'Where do I go? Is it through here? What do I do? I don't know where I am!' And his son started hitting the back of the curtain with a stick, while all the while, Tommy was drinking whisky and getting his props ready. And for quarter of an hour, the audience were creasing up with laughter. I've never seen an audience laugh so much without anyone being onstage. And then when he walked on, quarter of an hour later, they hit the roof. As soon as he walks onstage, he's funny. He doesn't have to say anything – he's a funny bloke.

HUGH DENNIS

Until I was ten, I lived on the Isle of Dogs, and then we moved to
Edgware. My father's a priest – he was the vicar of the Isle of Dogs
and then he became the vicar of Edgware. He's a bishop now. My
mother was a teacher – my father always worked at home. I'm
younger than my brother. There are only two of us. He works as a
diplomat for the Foreign Office. The age gap is two and a half years.
We didn't really get on when he became a teenager and I was still a
kid. We used to throw chairs at each other, but we get on very well
now. My parents are very liberal and nothing was forced down my
neck. I certainly didn't feel restrained in any way. We were never
forced to go to church.

I found almost everything terribly funny. I think being a bishop is
a very funny thing. It's all silly hats and costumes, and I suspect that
probably affected me. I suspect that I'm not really nervous about
standing onstage because I used to see my dad in the pulpit. I'm sure
there's a direct correlation there in terms of self-confidence. Clerics
are very, very funny – because they're so formal.

My dad used to come and watch me play rugby every weekend. I
was in the first fifteen at school and he used to come to every game.
Everybody knew that my father was a priest, all the other parents on
the touchline. On one occasion, someone was treading on my head,
and I shouted, 'Fuck off!', really loudly – because you get a bit
worked up. And I was aware of all the other parents turning towards
my father, but he was sort of going 'Yeah, quite right! Get off his
fucking head!'

GRAHAM FELLOWS

My father is a funny man, but he doesn't know it. He's like a lot of
middle-aged men. He's got an obsession with maps, and he's
extremely practical. When he comes to my flat, he won't say, 'How
are you?' He'll say things like, 'How's the door? Oh, it's catching a
bit – isn't it? I'll just plane a bit off the bottom.'

The first time he saw John Shuttleworth, he didn't like it at all. He
said, 'Do people really pay money to see this? It's not funny.' That's
fair enough. That's the reaction I expected really – although secretly
I was disappointed. But then he came to see me in Sheffield in a

packed house, full of young people laughing heartily – and he said, 'Well! Maybe it is funny then! Very good!' I didn't really respect him for that, because he wasn't thinking for himself – he was just being seduced by the mob reaction.

When I was a kid, I used to breed mice for exhibition purposes. As a thirteen-year-old boy, that involved spending a lot of time with middle-aged and elderly men in St John's Ambulance rooms in Halifax and places like that. I think it had a rather strange effect on me. I think the act is about me being nostalgic about my childhood and adolescence. John Shuttleworth is in his early fifties, and yet he has total amnesia about the years prior to 1973. That's why he appeals to my contemporaries.

The picture that I paint of John Shuttleworth's life isn't compromised. I make no concessions. It's completely self-indulgent, because what I'm doing is getting back to my childhood in Sheffield. All the place names remind me of the bike rides I used to go on when I was a kid. And I suspect that if I went to live in Sheffield, the incentive to do the character might actually wane.

EDDIE IZZARD

I was born in Yemen, but I only lived there for a year. It was part of my dad leapfrogging up the hierarchy of BP. He was out in the Gulf for a time, and that was when I first heard about the Goons. It was bizarre. I first heard them on Radio Dubai. Dad just said, 'You'd like this.' We tried to record it on a tape recorder we'd just bought. That Spike Milligan stuff was a revelation.

I had my black experience when I was six, when my mum died, and everything has been spent getting over that. Things were tough. My analysis is that the audience is a surrogate affection machine to replace my mother. There was a lot of affection coming from her – which immediately stopped. It was decided that we should go to boarding schools after that, so the family could survive. I only saw my dad for about a third of the year, so a lot of affection disappeared. If I work hard enough with the audience, they give rewards, and I'm happy with that 'drug' set-up. My dad's very positive about me being TV [transvestite]. He just said, 'Oh, OK.' He's a very groovy dad.

DONNA McPHAIL

My dad saw me on TV and thought I was a bit blue but he doesn't really know what I'm doing. I said I was going to Edinburgh, and he thought I was going on holiday. He's just one of those middle-aged dads who's lost it a bit. He was in the forces until I was about ten. My mum was a businesswoman in the seventies. She ran her own PR company, worked with Robert Maxwell, and did some work for George Best. She died last year. She only saw me once, about four years ago, when I'd just started. She wasn't much interested then, but I think she'd be much more interested now because I'm more successful. She was a bit of a snob like that, but I think she'd enjoy it now.

HARRY HILL

I come from quite a big family, and we were always ganging up on each other. My parents were divorced when I was five, and I lived with my mother and stepfather – but he died a couple of years ago. I've only recently got back in contact with my real father. The last thing he knew, I was a doctor. He's a real show-off and he's actually quite a funny bloke. When he came to the recording of my radio show, he was talking to my agent, and he said, 'Oh yes, I used to work for EMI' – but in fact, he used to work for Thorn EMI, selling light bulbs.

MARK LAMARR

Pre-school is the time for laughter. Not only have you got no cares or worries in the world, you've got no problems with what you laugh at, at all. You've had nothing beaten into you – no right-on political theories, you've had nothing. Now if you see a fat person fall over in the street you probably won't laugh – you'll probably think, 'That poor person! I must help them!' But as a kid, you'll die laughing – and there's no reason why you shouldn't. Sean Lock told me about these three- and four-year-old kids he saw when he was round at someone's house. One of them came in with her mum's hat on and they all wrapped themselves up in a sleeping bag and laughed for half an hour. Every time they looked up at each other they died laughing. You have much more fun then than you do at school.

I remember two or three occasions when I was about six or seven when my grandparents and aunties came down to our house in Swindon, on Sunday afternoons. I used to take over the room and start singing silly songs and doing stupid dances. It felt like such a buzz, and then I'd go too far and my mum would say, 'Stop showing off,' and I'd feel like the biggest piece of shit on earth. I can only remember a few definite occasions – but it seemed like every time they came round, because those few occasions were, up until then, the most proud moments of my entire life.

VIC REEVES

I can remember walking into a sweet shop when I was aged about twelve, and asking for a packet of penny chews in a stupid voice. And I remember very distinctly coming out of the shop and saying to my mate, 'It'll be great when we're forty, because we'll be able to do that and they won't be able to chuck us out of the shop. They'll think that we're doing it sincerely.' And then the sad truth dawned on me the other day that here we are, approaching forty, and we're still doing it – we will walk into shops and ask for polo mints in a high-pitched voice.

Kids are amenable to a variety of situations. They haven't got any hang-ups, but they have an understanding of a situation, no matter how ridiculous it is – adults tend to get guarded in their thinking.

JOHN HEGLEY

When I was a kid, there were lots of things I didn't do that other kids did. I didn't have any friends – we didn't go out to public places. We always ate at home. We lived in a nice bungalow, but it cost us every penny so we never went on holiday. Adolescence was a terrible time – I was useless with girls. I always hated the summer holidays. They used to stretch endlessly ahead of me. We were a very private family. Now I try to live a more public life. I eat in cafés, I perform onstage, and I go on buses and trains as much as I can.

I read Billy Bunter books. I enjoyed the camaraderie by proxy of lads sleeping together in dormitories. When me and Nige [*his accompanist and side-kick*] go away, I always prefer to have a twin room, because it's nice to have a chat before the lights go out. I didn't read great literature. My father was a clerk and my mother was a nurse, so there weren't a lot of books around.

I gave my sister a terrible time – a terrible time. I used to tease her, and pull her hair, and torture her – that was one of the reasons why my dad used to hit me, because I used to hit my sister. We used to play Monopoly, and I used to hit her because she wouldn't be competitive enough with me. She wasn't playing to win, and I thought, 'This is no fun! You're not playing to win!' This is what happens when you've got no friends. I had no friends, and so I used to play with my sister – and she wasn't able to beat me. It was like a desert island nightmare.

Quite often reviewers slag off childhood reminiscences. I get a bit bored with sexual things myself, but childhood memories, I love them! I can hear them all day!

DOMINIC HOLLAND

I've always loved comedy, I've always loved making people laugh. It's the only thing I've ever done well. I've done everything OK. I've been OK at school, OK at football. But comedy has always been my thing. People have always said, 'Dominic, you're funny – you should be a comedian.' I've been doing it since I was a kid.

My parents are very supportive of my stand-up, because they're very proud of it. They tell all their friends. When I was a kid I used to tell my mum, 'I'm going to be a comedian, I'm going to be a famous comedian!' She always thought that was enchanting – but now she thinks it's a bit weird, because I'm doing it.

I had quite a funny upbringing – very Catholic, very disciplinarian father. He was a lecturer in French at London University. Now he's retired. He was very strict and quite draconian. He didn't like me living with my girlfriend. We're a very traditional family. My two brothers are both lawyers, my sister has a Masters in Philosophy. Now she's a town planner. I've got an MBA, so we're all very education-orientated. I'm the only person who's taken a novel career path. I was really worried about telling them – I always thought they wanted me to be successful in business.

When I was a kid, I always knew I was going to do it. I used to tell my mum I'd have my own TV show when I was thirteen. So I always thought, 'It doesn't matter that I'm not doing it now, because I know that I'm going to do it.' That's what kept me going. I always knew I was going to do it, so it didn't matter when I did it – I knew I was going to be a comedian. I was definitely going to do it, because it was always my obsession ever since I was a kid.

I used to like *The Two Ronnies* and *Dick Emery*, and I liked *Benny Hill* because I used to enjoy looking at women in bikinis. I was into sex – big time. I remember once on *Bruce Forsyth's Generation Game*, there were these dancers with G-strings on – and every time they span round, you could see their arses. Every time they span round, my brother and me both cheered. Mum and dad came in, and realised why we were cheering. It was so embarrassing. They accused me of leading my brother astray.

When I was a kid, I used to look forward to my parents arguing, because when they did, I got a take-away. That's my favourite joke. I love that joke, because it's true.

FRANK SKINNER

Ever since I was at infant school, teachers and mates had said, 'You ought to be a comedian,' and I always thought that even if I never did anything about it, it'd still happen – because my natural inclination is not to do anything about anything. Twenty-odd years later, it still hadn't happened – but I wasn't really thinking about it. I wanted to be a footballer, I wanted to be Elvis, and then I was out of work. I'd be in a pub with mates and I'd suddenly go into performance mode. I'd be with people and feel myself click, and they'd say, 'You're showing off, now there's more than four people here!'

I've got two brothers and a sister. My next brother up is seven years older than me, and the next is five years older than him. My brothers and sister are all married. My sister was a hairdresser – now she's just a housewife. I'm the baby. My dad was very funny around the house. He pissed about a lot – he was a pub singer. Sometimes he'd come in pissed, and my mum would go mad at him. They'd have a big argument, and he'd say, 'Never mind that – what about this one?' And sing a couple of numbers before we went to bed.

JACK DEE

One of the themes that seems to keep re-emerging in what I'm writing is being conscious of growing – of going up one step on the ladder, suddenly having children, who think that you're a grown-up. Sometimes I get the feeling that the stuff I'm writing is too old for my age – but I've always been like that. Even at seventeen I was staid – I had such a cynical view that people regarded me as sensible, because I wouldn't get involved in stupid things. Wearing a suit onstage is partly wanting to associate myself with adulthood rather than childhood, and adolescence in particular, because I could always see straight through adolescence. Even when I was sixteen, I'd go to a party and I remember sitting there thinking, 'What the fuck is the point of smoking? When they walk into a room, the first thing they do is light up. Why do they light up? Because they're not confident. They look stupid. You can see they're not confident – that's why they're lighting up. Why are they drinking? Because they can't talk unless they're pissed. What is the point in drinking?' I just thought like that. It wasn't even as if I'd learnt through experience. It was just looking at it and seeing it and being depressed. In a way, I wish I could have relaxed a bit more and let it flow a bit, but when I was at an age when it was genuinely a laugh to hang out at Reading Festival and sit in mud for two days screaming at Hawkwind – I just genuinely could not see the point. But, at the same time, I was wishing I could be into it in the same way.

STEVE COOGAN

One of my warmest family memories was watching *Fawlty Towers*. It really was a family event, because we loved comedy. It was a Catholic family, and we didn't like crude comedy – we liked inventive, intelligent comedy. My dad used to play Hancock tapes to me, and the Goons. I remember the whole family being called down, all eight of us, and the whole family would congregate in the living room. There were eight people in the room, laughing, watching the TV. And afterwards, we'd turn the TV off and my mum would be exhausted. With tears of laughter in her eyes, she'd say, 'Put the kettle on! Let's sit down and have a cup of tea to recover from it!' It was a real event.

My father doesn't have a very good sense of humour. He's a
dignified man. He's not someone who I'd joke in front of a lot. He
understands comedy, but he's the sort of person who would come up
with a pun and feel very pleased with himself, and all my brothers
and sisters would be crying with laughter at how bad the joke was.
We'd try to get on with our meal in silence, but then you'd look up
and catch someone's eye, and they'd be going red in the face – and
the whole table would start laughing, and he'd say, 'Why are you all
laughing?' Even my mother would be laughing. A lot of mealtimes
were spent trading insults in a witty way, trying to top each other's
lines.

I remember one weird thing I used to do, which was quite morbid.
My sister brought me this wax skin and blood back from America,
and I remember doing really detailed wounds on myself. I once went
to get the family allowance from the post office with two really neat
vampire bites in my neck, with blood trickling down from them – just
to see the reaction on the postmistress's face. She said, 'Excuse me.
You've done something to your neck.' I said, 'Oh, that's OK.'

One thing I did has become part of our family folklore. I did a
bullet hole in my head. It took ages to do. I did a little crater with
tissue, and a fork of blood dribbling down my face – I was aged
twelve. I lay over the sofa in the living room with my eyes open. It
was very realistic. I even used eye-shadow to get a blue effect. My
dad walked into the lounge, and saw me lying there with a bullet hole
in my head. He said, 'Stephen?' I said, 'Yeah?' He looked at me and
said, 'You're warped,' and walked out of the room. He didn't
understand it.

It's definitely a case of having to get people's attention. I did do
that in my family, because my sister tells me. She says I'd constantly
be saying, 'Watch me! Look, watch me! Watch what I can do! Look,
I can do this! Watch me do this!' When you're in a big family, you
need to fight for attention.

JEFF GREEN

I've got a big family background. My mum's been married three
times, and I've got two half-brothers, two half-sisters and two step-
sisters in the family. So I've had quite a disjointed childhood, but I
never had to move schools. Our family is incredible. My mum can

meet up with my dad, and my stepfather can chat with my dad. People who aren't even blood relations treat each other like family – and I'm stuck in the middle. My mum's retired now, but she ran a mentally handicapped home. My dad is retired/unemployed. I've got a lot of affinity for my stepfather because he married my mum when I was fourteen – and he made sure I went to university by giving us the financial support for that. If she hadn't married him, I would have had to go and get a job to pay my keep, so I feel very close to him. He works in a chemical factory – nothing special, just as a fitter's mate.

My mum likes my act. She doesn't like the drugs stuff but she'll come up to me and say, 'That female orgasm stuff's very good, you know,' and I'll say, 'Oh, mum, you can't say that to me – I don't want you saying that kind of stuff to me!'

ARNOLD BROWN

My mother and father weren't at war with each other, but they used to bicker over everything. My father ran a fruit shop. We were upper working class. We weren't poor, but we didn't even have the cultural ambition to have hot water in the house. We used to go to the public baths every week. This was in the fifties. We could have got it but the expectation wasn't there. I was slightly ashamed of my background and I felt alienated by being Jewish in Scotland. It was very rare that a non-Jewish person would come into the house. It sounds like apartheid, but that was the way it was. It was almost a ghetto mentality.

I came from an uncultured background. There were no books in the house. I remember going to a Jewish student society. The speaker said, 'As I read in the *Observer* . . .' I'd never heard of the *Observer*. We used to get the *Sunday Post*, which was called the *Empire News* at the time. I'd go out for my father and buy ten Woodbines, a bottle of Irn Bru and a copy of the *Empire News*. There was no television, no telephone, no fridge. That was my culture.

STEVE PUNT

At that age, your tastes haven't been shaped by peer pressure. When I was in my early teens, I could quite happily watch *Monty Python* one night, *The Two Ronnies* the next night, and *Dad's Army* the night after. My parents had a record of *Not Only But Also*. I used to hear it when I was a child, and from the age of about eight, I knew it off by heart. I can still do lots of it off by heart, and I loved it – even though I didn't really understand large chunks of it. My sister had a friend whose mother forced me to recite it to her, because she couldn't believe that I knew it all. There I was, eight years old, saying, 'We said we'd meet in front of the Flemish Masters . . .' I had no idea what Flemish Masters were, but there was something extraordinary about it which fascinated me.

JULIAN CLARY

When the Jamie Bulger murder happened, I was on tour, and I had a bit in the show which was a true story. When I was a baby, in a pram, my mother went to the butcher's, parked the pram outside, made her purchase and went home and forgot that she'd ever given birth to me – she had a blank spell for three or four hours. That little boy was abducted from outside a butcher's shop, and when we were in Liverpool I just couldn't do it – so I changed it to a delicatessen in the story. It didn't work as well, somehow.

CHARLIE CHUCK

My dad brought me up with good morals – he never used to swear. When he used to lose his temper, he used to shout, 'Balls!' And then he'd always laugh afterwards – he'd always see the funny side of it. My mum was as daft as a brush. She used to teach me gibberish. Her dad, my grandad, used to have a bowler hat and briefcase and clog dance in the pub. He'd always had this silliness, and my mum used to teach me: 'I won't stand such diabolical insolence from an incompocerous piece of crumption such as you!' So her nuttiness and my dad's straightness is where I get it from. One minute I can be telling pearls of wisdom, or I can talk off the wall and talk absolute gibberish. That's what's funny – that has them in hysterics. But it's only that. There's nothing else. It's total vaudeville.

  My dad died about three years ago. The night before he died, he said, 'Make progress, lad. Make progress.' He was very independent, and he was sort of saying to me, 'I'm dying, but you get on with it.' The day before he died, funnily enough, he called me over and said, 'I've got some good news for you. That man in the next bed recognises you from the James Whale show.' He was chuffed, my dad. He died the following day. That stuck in my mind. I'd only been on James Whale a couple of times, and that made me all the more strong. I thought, 'Yeah, I'll go for this.'

On the last episode of Vic Reeves [The Smell of Reeves & Mortimer, *Vic and Bob's latest TV series*], I got to sing a song – it was the biggest bit I'd been given. They wrote it, it was out of my hands, but it went, 'Daddy, I miss you, and I feel blue.' I said, 'Can I cry after it?' Which I did – acting, like, which came easy. Also, in the very last scene of the Reeves and Mortimer series, Vic dies – they pull the plug, and his spirit comes out of his body. My dad says, 'Make progress,' and the best thing that ever happened in my career so far was the last episode of Reeves and Mortimer, because I got a nice big juicy bit. That was a bit strange.

STEWART LEE

I'm adopted, but I don't know whether that makes any difference to anything. Rhona Cameron [*Scottish comedienne*] is adopted as well, and she thinks that makes her want to be wanted by the audience, having been rejected at an early age. That might be true, but it sounds like cod psychology to me. It annoys me that people draw conclusions from it. I remember at school, when I was eight years old, if somebody else got into a fight, they'd just behaved badly – but if I got into a fight, you could see the teachers trying to imagine some half-arsed psychological idea why that might be, extrapolated from the fact that I was an adopted only child with divorced parents. They got divorced when I was about four.

I grew up in Solihull, south of Birmingham. I lived with my mum. My mum's more or less remarried now, and my dad remarried as well. I haven't caught up with my original parents, and I never used to have any desire to. The only desire I used to have was a vain one: 'I wonder if I look like someone else?' I remember going out with this girl when I was about fifteen. I went round to her house at Christmas. Her whole family was there and they all had the same nose. I thought, 'Christ! That's what a family is! You actually have shared genetic characteristics!' So I was interested to see whether I was nature or nurture. But lately, I've started to think that perhaps I owe it to them to get in touch with them, because next year, with a bit of luck, I'll be on telly, and it might be really freaky to turn on, having managed to put your son to the back of your mind for twenty-five years – they know what my name is. I wonder whether I ought to get in touch with them, just out of courtesy. But on the other hand, I read this book about it – and loads of people get in touch, and think it's going to be really great, and their mothers say, 'I had to go through the effort of getting rid of you in the first place, and now you've opened it all up again!' I don't know. I think I probably will, within the next couple of years. It's very easy for me, because I've got their names – but I wouldn't like to say that it's informed the act at all. I don't think so. I do feel I've had a different life and background to other people. When other comedians are doing stuff about family situations, and their relationships with their brothers and sisters, I can laugh about it – but I don't feel that I have the same experiences or opinions or emotional reactions as other people. I know that I don't, but whether that's the result of my family background, I don't know.

I had to look after my grandad when he was dying, about three years ago. I did a routine about that. It went really well, but I've only done it once, and a few weeks ago, Dominic Holland came up to me and said, 'I really liked that stuff you did about your grandad dying. When are you going to do that again?' I found that really upsetting. He said, 'Was it all true then?' I said, 'More or less.' He was hallucinating while he was dying, from the drugs that he was on, and I was actually able to help him a lot more than my gran. I was reading *The Doors of Perception* at the time. It was like having a trip from lack of oxygen, basically. I was calming down all the furniture and getting it to sit still. He died a couple of days after that. When I came off after doing that routine I had to put myself through it all again. It was only about six months afterwards at the time, so that was a bit weird. He was probably my favourite person in my family, because I lived with him when my parents split up, when I was a kid. But I will do that again, and I'll do it in such a way that if my mum hears it, I won't be ashamed of it.

I got my parents to come and see me about two years ago, because they kept giving me Jim Davidson books. When I was doing a gig in Birmingham, the bloke my mum lives with said, 'Are you on in

Moseley tonight?' I said, 'Yeah,' and he said, 'You'd better not do all your Pakistani jokes tonight then, had you?' They didn't know what I was doing at all. So I got them to come and see me at the T & C 2. It was a really good gig. It went really well. The audience were all laughing, but my parents were shocked into silence afterwards.

RICHARD MORTON

When I was being brought up, in the North East, it was a joy to me that Lindisfarne made it nationally. I felt so cut off from London and the exciting world of national and international affairs. By the time I came to London, that feeling of coming from a small place and trying to take a big place by storm was a very strong one. I've kept it as a part of me now, though I haven't lived there for fifteen years.

You go to places like Reading and Bournemouth, and there's lots of people from Scotland and the North who've gone down there for work. When I go out there and say, 'I'm from Newcastle,' it sums it up for a lot of people. It doesn't really matter that it's Newcastle, because a lot of those people know it could be Glasgow or Liverpool or Belfast. You're the voice of the little man away from home.

When I did some gigs in Galway, I got introduced as 'from Newcastle, England'. As I was walking on, people were shouting, 'Spender! Gazza! Jackie Charlton!' It was as if they were running through a little Geordie C V for me, as if to say, 'This is what we know about you.' Television has shrunk that world – everybody knows about the North East mythology. There are reference points that you can touch on, and people know so much more now.

All my jokes about the violent North East are absolutely true – I got beaten to a pulp in a half a dozen different incidents. I got beaten up by gangs. The first time I ever came to London, when I was fifteen years old, on a school trip, I was bruised all over, because I'd had the shit kicked out of me for looking like a poof. Not even for being one, just for looking like one. I remember standing in Piccadilly Circus, seeing all the lights for the first time, bruises all over me, and thinking, 'I'm coming here! This is where I'm coming!' I came from a lower middle-class upper working-class background. It was a nightmare world. I got beaten up for going to grammar school. I got beaten up at primary school for passing my eleven plus. You feel

your little world is nothing. You're from nowhere, you're uninter-
esting and you want to go somewhere that's exciting. You don't
realise that everybody else feels that way. I'm voicing that now. I'm
trying to articulate that ordinary, semi-scary upbringing.

I actually got three 'A' levels, but I didn't go to university. I went
straight into a band instead, and worked in the Northern clubs from
the age of eighteen, which was a baptism of fire. I went back up to the
North East and did a working men's club. It went OK, but I hated it.
It was in Consett, County Durham – one of those towns that's nearly
closed down. The steelworks closed down and the whole town went
with it. It's recession-hit – really hard up. There's a working men's
club there called the Irish Democratic Club. They booked me the
night before Christmas Eve, when I was due to play in a club in
Newcastle. They were very unsure about New Comedy. They said,
'You don't really do jokes, do you?' And I said, 'Well, they're kind
of jokes. Trust me. It'll be OK. I'm from here. My dad used to work
near Consett, so I know the area, and I know a few things to say.' For
the first couple of minutes they looked at me as if I'd stepped off
Jupiter, but as soon as I'd got them with one decent joke, that was it.
I did a gag about Geordies at Newcastle airport, trying to go to
Yugoslavia for their holidays. The travel agent says, 'I don't think
you understand. There's a civil war out there.' The Geordie says,
'But we've booked!' And the travel agent says, 'No! They're out in
the streets with guns and tanks and bombs and rockets!' And the
Geordie says, 'Well, if they don't bother us, we won't bother them.'
If I was a Cockney or a Scot doing that gag, they probably would
have lynched me – but because I was a Geordie, from then on, they
felt they could trust me. I was in, and they loved it – except for one
table of really hard looking guys, and I mean really hard looking
guys. Their table was next to the stage but they just sat and looked
across at each other, and wouldn't turn their heads to watch me on
the stage. It was like, 'It's our club and you're not funny.' There were
kids and old people laughing, but they sat there glaring at each
other. They weren't even glaring at me. If you go away from the
North East and make it in any sense, when you come back some
people won't have you. They think you've betrayed your cultural
identity by leaving and acquiring an otherworldliness. They find it
unforgivable if you live in London. They think you think you're

something special. Wherever you come from, you can always go back and get a slap from someone who'll never accept that.

I'm doing a routine at the moment about my parents – about how when you're a kid they do all those things to you that now you're an adult you can do back. There must be something quite cathartic about it, because I'm thinking up reams of stuff about it. And the instant I hit the subject, everybody knows. There's a universal understanding and it gets really big laughs. My mum came along to the show in Newcastle and afterwards she said, 'Well, I wasn't sure about that routine you did.' I said, 'Mum, it's comedy. It's comedy parents – it isn't you.' It's something I couldn't resist doing and I feel a bit guilty, but I've never done anything about breaking up with girlfriends. I leave all that out, because I can't bring myself to stand up in front of two thousand people, and say, 'This is what happened when she left me.' I can't do it. Some comics use everything. They think, 'It's all material.' Me, I can't – I have to have a line where I leave the stage at night and say, 'That's my life.' I couldn't do it if it broke somebody's heart. I couldn't do that to somebody. It's a question of integrity, and I despise comedians who wash their dirty laundry in front of a crowd. You've got to be honest when you're out there, but I couldn't hurt somebody's feelings night after night, just so I can get a laugh out of it – except for my mum and dad!

JENNY ECLAIR

I had an idyllic childhood. This is why I've had problems. When I've had therapy, people have always delved into my childhood and said, 'Well, there must have been something wrong?' And I've said, 'No. Actually, nothing has quite lived up to it since – that's been the problem.' I was very happy as a child. I had a mad time, I had a right laugh. I loved my teenage years as well – there were some miserable times, but I always had loads of boyfriends. I was a slag – I had a great time. Schoolwork was easy enough for me to get by. It's the responsibilities of being an adult – I don't actually like being an adult very much.

ARTHUR SMITH

I have a theory that you turn into your own punchlines. There was one joke I always liked as a child. It's not particularly funny, but for some reason I always remembered it: 'I don't swear, I don't smoke and I don't drink. Fuck it! I've left me fags in the pub!' And a couple of years ago I found myself saying, 'Fuck it! I've left my fags in the pub!' And I thought, 'Jesus! That's the punchline to my favourite joke as a child!'

2. Schooldays

'"What can we do for a laugh?" That's how I was at school. Fortunately, it's spilling over into my adulthood now.' – Bob Mortimer

'You'll never laugh like you did at school,' says Jack Dee – and indeed, a good comedy gig resembles nothing so much as a classroom full of kids run riot. The comedian's role alternates between troublemaker and teacher. When a stand-up storms a gig, they're everyone's favourite ringleader. When they die on their arses, they're like teachers who can't keep order. Few folk encounter the hilarity and cruelty of the classroom later in life with anything approaching the same ferocity (unless they become teachers or comedians), and for a stand-up audience, comedy indulges our nostalgia for this collective state of mind. Only a handful of sad unfortunates claim their schooldays were the happiest of their lives – but most of us would admit they were among our most intense.

Maybe this explains the persistence of the myth that all comedians were the class clowns at school. Rather, it seems, they were often the second funniest kids in their class – and even at the height of their careers, most comics claim to have several close friends who are funnier than them on a daily basis. Maybe that's because the purest comedy is ephemeral, of the moment, and cannot be captured either in print or even in rehearsed performance. Successful comics wed the rebellious flair of the back-row joker with the quiet discipline of the inventive scholar. So, for any teacher eager to talent-spot a teenage comedian of the future, ignore the inane antics of your class clowns. Instead, watch out for their bookish best friends who follow diligently in the wake of the comedic chaos they unwittingly create, making subconscious mental notes on how it can be distilled and reproduced onstage.

JACK DEE

I've always thought you'll never laugh again as you laughed in school, where it was prohibited. If I could create that atmosphere, where people are trying desperately not to laugh but are bursting with it all the time, then I'll have cracked something that no one else has reproduced. At that age you have a very carefree attitude, and your conscience hasn't been informed by experience and doesn't intervene. You can laugh at more or less anything at that age. You hear the word 'spastic' and you're in hysterics, and yet two or three years later you're thinking, 'Hang on – there are people whose whole lives are a constant struggle. I can't laugh at that word any more' – and rightly so, because that's part of the maturing process. But there are other aspects of life where it's as well to give your conscience a night off and laugh at a few things.

STEWART LEE

A lot of new wave comedy is resolutely anti-intellectual. It's a rediscovery of playground humour and the personas that people had at school. I remember these two guys at our school called Richard Bishop and Ed Saunders. They were the school bullies, but they used to be so funny. The way they used to bully people was absolutely hilarious – as long as it was you that wasn't getting bullied. People say they were funny at school to escape bullying, but I wasn't picked on. I was really popular. I don't ever remember using it as a defence mechanism. Through my teens I remember laughing until I cried.

FRANK SKINNER

The last three or four years of my school life were absolute heaven. We were the school bad lads, and we didn't do any work at all. We were all quite funny blokes, and we sat around all day taking the piss out of other people, and making each other laugh. I was in a select little group with its own in-jokes. I am one of these people who's got things on their reports like 'spends too much time playing to the gallery', and 'thinks he's a clown'.

Looking back, one of the things that makes me laugh the most is that I once got a severe bollocking off the deputy head dressed in a lion outfit. He was rehearsing for the staff play – it was *Wizard of Oz*. He came in, took his lion's head off and said, 'You're going to have to go if you don't pull your finger out!' He was swinging his tail as he talked, and I was supposed to stand there and take it all completely seriously!

ARTHUR SMITH

I ran a lines syndicate. People would pay me a penny a week and I would write their lines for them. It was an insurance company basically. And then this teacher gave everyone five hundred lines except me, which of course was ironic because half of them were signed up with this syndicate that I was running. I would have spent the rest of my life writing lines, so I had to abandon it. I went bankrupt overnight.

I was a bit of a clown. When I was eight, I was chairman of the anti-girls club. I was popular because I could make people laugh and I played on that a lot. When I was seven, the teacher said, 'We're going to do *Peter Pan* at Christmas,' so that night I went home and wrote *Peter Pan*. Fuck knows what I wrote, but I thought that it was what we were going to perform. The teacher said, 'This is unperformable, but what part do you want to play?' Of course I picked Captain Hook. Peter Pan? What a shit part that is! From Captain Hook I learnt the power of ad-libbing. I could make people laugh – and it was intoxicating.

JENNY ECLAIR

I was suspended from school several times, but that was mostly for irrational behaviour – having fits, slamming desks, pushing things over and breaking things. I was always the class clown and the class bully. It was a real shock when I read a friend's diary, and realised that I actually wasn't as popular as I always thought I was. She went out of the bedroom and I saw the diary, so obviously I read it. It had little sentences about each of her friends. It said, 'Jenny thinks she's more popular than she actually is – in fact, quite a lot of people don't like her.' I do want people to like me. I think that's a throwover from going to lots of different schools, and having to invade your way into people's affections within a term.

The laughter I like is what I call 'school assembly laughter', when you get hysterical. The headmistress gets onstage and says, 'A fountain pen has been stolen from Form 2B,' and you start laughing. You haven't stolen it – it's not your fault, but you get hot, you start to sweat and you're helpless with hysterical laughter and you need slapping. I like that kind of laughter. I've always had an allergy to boredom. When I was fifteen, I had to snog eight boys at the cricket club dance. I was always spinning slightly out of control. There were terrible hysterical moments of boredom at school, when I suddenly had to shout, and basically be a bit of a prat.

EDDIE IZZARD

I liked to laugh a lot at school. I did chemistry 'A' level – and I'd realised I could make people laugh by this stage. The teacher had a style of saying, 'We take . . . er . . . the test tube, and into it we put . . . er . . .,' and at that point he paused, and you could shout anything out, like, 'Banana!' I quite consciously used chemistry 'A' level as a way of improving my gag hit-rate. The only practical joke I did was to try and make nitroglycerine to blow up this woman at school who was rather crabby. If you look in chemistry text books, they've got nitroglycerine and how to prepare it. So we got all the stuff, and tried to make it. We made this liquid. We poured it into a bottle and carried it around. We thought, 'If it is nitroglycerine, how do we set the fucker off?' So we poured it on to the pavement. It didn't explode – I think we had water, essentially.

BOB MORTIMER

Me and my mate made a tape recording of a fly buzzing. At the beginning, it was very quiet – and then suddenly it went, 'Cunt! Fuck off! Get out, you cunt!' We put it in the ceiling of the classroom, up above those polystyrene tiles that you can lift up. The teacher couldn't find it. He said, 'Where is it?' We didn't dare tell him so he said, 'Right! I'm going to get the headmaster!' I thought it was a cracking joke.

VIC REEVES

In our biology class when the teacher was writing on the blackboard,
I used to get the rest of the class to sigh. She turned round and
shouted, 'Will you stop sighing!' That buckled everyone. There's
always oneupmanship. If someone makes a farting noise at the back
of the class, it always ends up with someone at the front doing a very
loud one.

LEE EVANS

Moving schools is horrible because you've made all those friends
and then they're not there any more, and then you've got to make
fresh friends. I had to move school five times. It was the worst thing
in the world. I hate it when you're a stranger and the whole class
know each other. And then the teacher says, 'Meet Lee – he's our
new pupil!' I wasn't really a good-looking bloke at the time. I had
spots and that, and they all went, 'Fucking hell! Who's going to talk
to him?' I hated that. I really hated that.

MARK LAMARR

I always really loved the teachers who made me laugh – for some
reason, you always think they're better people. I still remember a
teacher in my infant school called Mr Archer – whenever he took us
I'd really look forward to it. To me, it was such a delight to have this
bloke in because he was always funny. He was a bit of a hero in that
sense.

Male humour at school usually manifests itself in very unpleasant
ways – the old one is putting the girl's pigtail in the bottle of ink.
They're usually laughing at other people's misfortunes. Sadly, that's
the way the male mind works. I don't look back on anything I did at
school and think, 'God – that was really funny!' I'd probably look
back and think, 'Oh God – I can't believe I did that!'

JOHN HEGLEY

I wasn't happy at school. I was isolated and nobody used to speak to
me. I didn't have the vocabulary. That's so important, to get on with
other people and know the ways of the world. I didn't know how to

get on with girls – I felt completely embarrassed with them. I was a nauseating little person. I used to put bits of spitty paper on my ruler and flick them at the other kids, and they'd say, 'Why don't you grow up?' They were all growing up. I didn't want to grow up. I liked being a kid. They were all growing up, and that was something I didn't like. So I suppose by doing this I'm still being a kid. But it isn't to do with misery.

RICHARD HERRING

My dad was the headmaster at my school. It didn't really bother me at the time. It was quite a nice school – Kings of Wessex in Cheddar – but it was a bit weird my dad being the headmaster. I don't think I was immensely popular – it's a bit hard to be, if your dad is the headmaster. We were clever kids, but we used to mess around in lessons when we had weak teachers – and yet we went ahead to get the best results.

STEVE COOGAN

At school I wasn't class clown, entertaining everyone. I had a group of two or three friends, and we'd laugh at our own little comedy. It was more esoteric. At my school I had a very strong identity, because two of my brothers had already been there. I was very lazy and ill-disciplined – and to some extent, I still am. I don't mean I misbehaved, but I wasn't on time, and I always did the bare minimum – I did my homework on the bus in the morning. I was the kind of person who didn't make much effort. I used to get away with it because I was well brought up, I was likeable, and I knew how to charm.

I would never turn up for art classes, and the one time when I did, the art master would call me into his office to mark my work – and sit there chatting with me about what was on TV the night before, until the bell rang for the end of the lesson. All I'd done was to sit in his office for the whole lesson and chat to him, because we got on so well. All the other pupils would get really annoyed.

Mimicry got me attention quickly. I never worked on it. I never really practised. Occasionally, I'd look in the mirror, and try to do someone's voice, but I never really tried. I just found I had a good ear. I found that if I'd been in somebody's company for some time, and someone else said, 'Can you do that person?' I hadn't been watching them, but I could do them very well, including the gestures and everything.

There was a French teacher who'd come in and say, 'Right! Coogan! Get to the front of the class and do some impressions.' And he'd go and sit in the back row and say, 'Do Mr So-And-So . . . do Mrs So-And-So . . .' If I ever said, 'No, I don't want to do impressions,' he'd say, 'Everyone open your books!' And everyone would say, 'Do them! Go on! Please!' so they could avoid the work. I'd say, 'Ok,' and I'd do them and he'd sit at the back and laugh, until, after a while, he said, 'All right. I'm bored now. Open your books.'

I knew I had a skill, and it gave me an identity. People knew I could do something, and I enjoyed it. Sometimes I liked showing off – but I wasn't someone who liked to jump about and do crazy things in class. That was a bit unsophisticated for me. I liked doing witty things in books and passing them to people.

I didn't think, 'I'm going to be a comedian,' but I did love comedy. I never watched *Monty Python*, but I used to listen to the records at my brother's house over and over again. I memorised them. I knew them verbatim. I didn't learn them – I'd just heard them so many times that I knew them. Even now I can recite the sketches word for word. People would come up to me at school and say, 'Do that *Monty Python* sketch!' And I'd recite the whole thing, with all the voices. I was very pedantic. I'd correct people if they got one word wrong.

People would say, 'Did you see *Not the Nine O'Clock News* last night? And if someone hadn't, they'd say to me, 'What was on it?' And I'd do the highlights from the show. I knew I could recreate them accurately enough to make them laugh.

JEFF GREEN

I went to a comprehensive school in Chester. Basically, I was the cleverest boy in the school – I was the only boy from the school to go to university. I was always top of the class and I used to get fairly bored. I was looking back through a few of my old school reports, and my English teacher said, 'Jeffrey has the gift of wit, which helps to disarm.' They used to think I was really bumptious, because I did better than everyone else – but as a kid, there's no other way of doing better than anybody else – you can't do it gracefully. I was never picked on, I was never battered. I got on with most other people – they just thought I was a bit of a smartarse. Out of fourteen hundred children, six would go on to do 'A' levels. It was one of those schools where everyone left. They all wanted to be plumbers, or their dad knew someone who was an electrician. It was the crappest school in Chester, and also the hardest.

HUGH DENNIS

At school I played a lot of sport. I was captain of sport, and I was head boy. All my school reports described me as jovial, but I never set fire to the gym. I used to piss around – but I did silly voices rather than stick fire-crackers up the history teacher's arse.

I never did any acting. I left it alone completely until my second year at Cambridge. I had a mate at university who wanted to get into Footlights. He's now an investment banker, so it didn't work out for him. We wrote some sketches together and took them down to Footlights, so I only started doing it at all at the end of the second year. I hadn't thought about doing it in the slightest. By the time I left, it occurred to me that possibly I could do it, but I remember a conversation with my parents in which I said, 'I think I might want to be an actor,' not daring to say, 'I think perhaps I want to be a comedian,' and my mother said, 'Well, you know you'll never be Hamlet.' My mother gets very upset because she's always telling me to stand up straight and I say, 'Look, it's just not as funny.'

DOMINIC HOLLAND

For as long as I can remember, I was aware that I could make people laugh. I was always the funny person in the class. The teachers used to write to the parents, complaining that nobody was listening to them, because they were all listening to me. I loved that. It became obvious to me that wherever I went, I would quickly establish myself as the guy who did the jokes. People used to associate me with being funny. That was the only characteristic that people knew me by.

I wish I'd started doing it at university. At Leeds there was no infrastructure to do stand-up like there was at Oxbridge. But maybe

I wasn't ready. I was very immature when I was a kid, both physically and mentally. I was very small and frail, and it's only lately that I've caught up with my peers. Showertimes were horrendous for me. At fourteen or fifteen, everybody would be growing pubic hair, and I'd be thinking, 'Christ! I'm really small!' I underperformed at school. I screwed up my 'A' levels, but I always knew I was going to do it – I had a stupid belief that I was going to be successful.

BRUCE MORTON

I was extremely average. I was a kind of a Charlie Brown. I got Cs for a lots of things. I was quite good at football, but not good enough for the team. I was good at English, but I wasn't good at much else. I was never the class clown, and neither was I the kid who was always telling stories to get out of getting bullied. I came into it really late, having discovered that I can string a few sentences together and tell a decent tale.

It was only when I went to college that I got an inkling that there were opportunities out there other than the ones that I'd been used to, which were very limited and routine. I'm a mature comedy student, if you like. I've got a world view, because I was married and I had an office job. I had an ordinary life, and suddenly everything changed. The most immediate consequence of that is that I count my blessings. I think, 'I'm fucking glad I'm not doing that any more.' Of course, if it all stopped tomorrow, I could always go back and be a clerical assistant, not that I'd really want to countenance doing that because it's not as interesting. It's not as much fun.

JO BRAND

I was born in London, and brought up in a village in Kent. When I was at school I liked a laugh, but I was always well-behaved – I always did my homework. I suppose if you asked my teachers now, they'd vaguely remember me – but they wouldn't remember me causing any fuss, because I never did. However when I was about fifteen, we moved to the coast. I didn't want to go, but my parents had to move. I moved to a new school but I never liked it there, so I decided to muck about – I skived off all the time.

ARNOLD BROWN

I always had an impish sense of humour – a lot of my humour is to do with pricking pomposity and conformity. The first time I realised my sense of the ridiculous, I was fourteen. I went to see that film *The Incredible Shrinking Man*. The little guy had been put into the matchbox by his wife – all the other kids in the cinema were shrieking, and I was the only one laughing.

ROB NEWMAN

A very close friend of mine was a bit wiped out by drugs and we really grew away from each other. I said, 'Why d'you do it?' because I was very priggish as a young man. He said, 'It's trying to catch that thing we had when we were two little boys just giggling.' Heckling the teacher was the main thing – shouting stuff out and getting laughs, which is why I've always liked hecklers, because they're doing the same thing. I'm a terrible football dilettante. I go to about one game a season and I spend most of the time watching the crowd, feeling like some sociology professor. I went to the last Arsenal game before they knocked down the North Bank and I laughed pretty much solidly for ninety minutes. The stuff that's shouted out is really funny, ninety per cent intentionally, ten per cent unintentionally. At Arsenal, there's a very modern type of sarcasm.

HARRY HILL

The London comedy circuit is very much like a school. You've got first, second, third and fourth years, and there's an awful lot of gossip that goes on. Comics talks about other comics. You get the fat bloke who's such a prat, and the one who's always getting off with girls – just like at school. The new material nights at the Meccano [*comedy club in Islington, North London*] are a real social club. Everyone does five minutes' new material and afterwards, about fifteen of us all go for a pizza.

MARK THOMAS

A group of us were involved in Socialist League, the old International Marxist group. Three of us were from Bretton Hall [*college in Yorkshire*], and three of us were from Wakefield, which was the nearest town. One of them was a part-time dealer, one of them was a part-time cat burglar, and they'd both ended up in this political group. We used to write shows for all sorts of things: TUC Women's Day, British Cuban Resource Centre, Miners' Benefits. We wrote the history of Cuba in two days flat, and performed it in twenty minutes. We'd meet up in people's houses with books and read up all the information and work out how to perform it. We used to do masses of stuff at the local Labour club. It was all about nursery closures – real bread and butter stuff. We used to do shows in the street.

The bloke who ran the Labour club was a huge Greek man with a Yorkshire accent who fought against the Nazis in the war. He used to come up to us and corner us and say, 'I hear that you are Trotskyites! You have two more years before you are men and then you must make your choice and be good Stalinists!' He kept the Labour club alive. He kept two hundred families fed during the miners' strike. It was the first time in my life that I'd met all these people from all over the country who were into performing, and I thought it was brilliant.

DAVID BADDIEL

I come from a group of people who were all very very funny. A lot of them still are the funniest people I know, so a lot of my comic understanding comes from them. Some of the people I know are funnier than me, but there was no way they were going to become professional comics. You need a certain amount of discipline to absorb it.

Initially, I used to hate school. I was bullied, and used to pretend I was ill all the time. Eventually I went to hospital, because I had this fake illness. I used to shake the wrong end of the thermometer. If you do that, it makes the temperature go up. Whenever my parents went out of the room, I used to take out the thermometer, shake it, and put it back in again. I did that for six weeks until they sent me to hospital.

By about the sixth form, I liked it. That's when I did my first comedy gig, at the school revue. The pupils loved it and it got banned by the teachers – that's why it went down really well. Every year our sixth form revue got booed off by the boys. Then I wrote it, and one sketch after another was virulently unpleasant about specific teachers and it stormed it. That's all they wanted to hear.

Some comics are teachers, and others are the ringleaders in the pack of unruly children. Sometimes there are teachers who can't control the class, and so all the class start humming or moving the desks forward. That's very similar to watching a comic die. Suddenly there's a unified mass action against the person in front of you. It's amazing how a crowd will melt into one animal – not only when you're dying, but when you're storming it as well.

3. Don't Give up the Day Job

'It's just like a job. Five minutes before I go onstage, it's the furthest thing from my mind.' – Charlie Chuck

The comedians in this book can be divided down the middle into those who went into comedy more or less immediately after college – and those whose comic careers were preceded by long apprenticeships in 'proper' jobs. And while those comics who graduated from university straight on to the comedy circuit (Newman and Baddiel, Lee and Herring, Punt and Dennis) often demonstrate a precocious flair for identifying twentysomething trends, their elder comic colleagues from the world of 'real' work often turn out material that displays much more strength and depth and appeals to a broader age range.

Jack Dee worked as a waiter, Jo Brand as a psychiatric nurse and Harry Hill as a junior doctor. For all of them, tedium, misery and exhaustion played their part in driving them to stand-up, and provided the emotional fuel for their initial routines. Arnold Brown spent half a lifetime working as a chartered accountant, which goes a long way towards explaining why his philosophical observations command such automatic respect. Brown's previous career was bearable, if not terribly stimulating, but most comic biographies reveal that it takes a fairly dreadful working life to provide the necessary incentive for some poor sod to risk the additional humiliation that almost inevitably results from the first few forays on to the stand-up stage. More than this, monotonous work is the common currency of most audiences. The bad times that stem from anonymity and drudgery are the stuff of comedy – fame and glamour gone sour can be equally gripping, but these tragedies yield fewer laughs. Charlie Chaplin, Buster Keaton, Harold Lloyd, George Formby, Norman Wisdom, Woody Allen – all these comic greats act out the role of archetypal loser – and the stage persona of the contemporary stand-up is also that of a workaday nobody who's momentarily seized the upper hand. In an era when comedians are becoming increasingly lauded, it's becoming more and more difficult for stand-up to sustain this precarious conceit of the dogsbody who's become boss for a day – yet the comics who've actually got their hands dirty (albeit briefly) certainly have a head start.

JO BRAND

You get to a stage where you don't have that much of a normal life any more. You're supposed to be going out there to talk to people about what life's all about, and if you haven't got a life like they have, you end up doing what lots of American comics do. Half their set's about being on a plane because that's normal for them. It makes a difference what you did before. I left home when I was sixteen and had normal jobs right up until the age of thirty-one, so I had a big backlog to draw on, as opposed to people who went to college and then came straight into comedy, and never did what I call a proper job.

Being a psychiatric nurse brutalises you, to the extent that you treat the excesses of it in a very normalised way, which the average person wouldn't. You might have an incident when someone comes in with a machete, and you have to get them on the floor and hold them down for an hour until the police come, which isn't a particularly normal thing to do. However, you have a laugh about it afterwards, so you find yourself doing strange and dangerous things and treating them as a normal part of your job. We had four or five incidents in a couple of years where people came in with guns, and we had to get them off them.

Most people get hurt at one time or another. I've been held against a wall with a carving fork against my throat. I got kicked against a wall by a six-foot-six karate expert who was hyper manic. He ran right across the room, gave me a flying kick, and I did one of those comedy splats against the wall. It was an exciting job.

One person on the ward where I worked nearly got killed – he got shut in a bathroom with a very dangerous patient who strangled him. A girl got her nose broken – she was completely over-aggressive with this bloke. When you've got someone with a severe personality disorder facing up to you, you don't look them in the eye as if you were Clint Eastwood, because it makes them more aggressive. You defer to them. If you stare at them, and look as if you're facing up to them, they'll hit you. That's rule number one for dealing with aggressive people.

Afterwards, we used to piss ourselves laughing about it – and I don't think there's anything wrong with that. Comedy is easier, because you're never in a situation that's that dangerous, or at least you never feel as if you are. I can assess in a split second what sort of person a heckler is, and change tack if I think I'm going to get hurt.

HARRY HILL

Most of the people at medical school are the sort who got three As at 'A' level, and so they stay in and work. I never used to see most of them, except at lectures and exams – they were very straight. The others are a bit mad – the rugby club crowd and the revue crowd. Robert [*his former double-act partner*] went to art school. You'd think that art school people would be much more creative and would want to express themselves, but they never had anything like amateur dramatics. They all went home and painted, whereas at medical school we did a revue every year. A lot of funny things go on and you think, 'This would make a great sketch.' That's certainly where the humour comes from – standing round the corpse.

Comics are very cynical – it's in their nature. You're cynical before you do it. Most comedy consists of taking the piss, and most comics have a frustration with life. Most jokes have a butt. Even in my jokes, someone's the fool – usually it's me . . . Working as a doctor certainly made me more cynical. It hardens you. You never cry. You can go in and tell somebody that their husband's died with a grin on your face.

I can remember telling this woman that her husband had died. It was Christmas, which is theoretically the worst time to go, and she said, 'And I just bought him a new Gibson guitar.' And I had this little devil in me, who was thinking, 'So that guitar, what were you thinking of doing with it? Because I play the guitar!' It's terrible – being a junior doctor is like being in a war. The worst thing I ever did, the most shameful thing I ever did, this chap came in. He'd had a heart attack and we tried to resuscitate him. We put this external pacemaker on. Normally, you put a pacemaker into the heart through the blood vessels, but this is a new thing – you put a pad on the front and a pad on the back and it gives you an electric shock, which stimulates the heartbeat. But when you've got it going, it stimulates the outside muscles as well as the heart [*giving the effect of a fit of silent laughter*]. We failed to get him going – basically, the man had died. And we were all standing around, saying, 'Oh well, we'd better go and tell the wife.' But I got the pacemaker and turned it back up and said, 'Oh no! Look!' Everyone laughed, but it was an awful thing to do.

I remember going in to see a woman who was dying. Her husband was with her, and she was basically gasping her last breaths. She was only about thirty-five. She had cancer, and was dying from some post-operative complication. I went in there, and thought, 'Oh my God!' I didn't know what to do, so I said to her husband, 'Can you excuse me for a minute?' So he went out, and just as the door shut, she died. It seemed like the right thing to do at the time. I had tears in my eyes, so I had to pull the cord and get the nurse – and I was supposed to be the doctor in charge. Since then, I'm really emotional. I'll cry during *Our Tune*. I wanted to be a doctor at one point, but it was a terrible life. Those two years were a complete blur – I was running everywhere.

LEE EVANS

I had nothing to go back to. After leaving school I went to art college, and after leaving art college I was unemployed for two years. There was a really bad recession on, and it was so hard to get work. I had a job in a rubber factory with all these old geezers who made linings for reservoirs. I had to go up to Barrow-in-Furness with this strapping great bloke called Stan. He liked to do keep fit exercises in the mornings, in the middle of winter – with all the fucking windows open. I had to do all the work. He told me what to do, and I went out and did it – in the pissing rain and sleet.

I wanted to get into the theatre so I got a job at the Futurist Theatre in Paignton. My job was cleaning the toilets – picking stuff out of the pan and all that sort of shit. I thought, 'I'll work my way up,' but it never led anywhere. I went out with a dancer from one of the shows who took a fancy to me but she was already going out with a bloke from Romford who suddenly turned up to visit her. He was a fucking big bloke, so I left.

My wife was our only source of income at times. She's a secretary. She used to work in the City – I hardly ever see her. I got a job in the Matchbox toy car factory. There was a machine that squirted water on to the toy tractors, so the wheels would fit on more easily, and I used to sit there in a bib, fitting on toy tractor wheels while it squirted water at me. It went straight up my nose. It was the middle of winter, and I got a cold. You didn't get paid by the hour, you got paid by the box. I was doing that all day. After a week, I couldn't stand it any more. My wife said, 'You've got to work! We need the money!' and I said, 'I can't do it, I can't! Please don't make me do it!'

I've done loads of jobs – a bit of building, a bit of painting and decorating. My dad used to say that was my advantage, because I've not had much of an education. He used to say, 'Experience of life! That's where it all comes from!' I used to think that was a load of old baloney, but I suppose he's right.

FRANK SKINNER

I got expelled from school at sixteen. I went into the sixth form, and lasted five weeks. I was expelled for lots of things, but on the letter it said, 'For embezzling the schools meals service'. Me and some mates found out where they threw the old meal tickets and resold them – we went into the recycling business. We more than halved the prices – we were Richard Branson figures and consequently we were oppressed by the establishment. I went home and the old man said to me, 'Well, you'd better get down the Burmid (which was the local foundry) with the darkies,' and threw a pair of his overalls at me. He'd worked there at some time – he'd worked at most factories in the West Midlands at some point. I thought, 'You are so narrow minded, Father!' So I went down the Youth Employment Office – as it was then. I thought I'd be a journalist. A girl in front of me went up to the counter and the woman behind it said, 'Well, what sort of job d'you want?' The girl said, 'I'd like to work with animals.' The woman said, 'Oh, we don't get many of them – here's Woolworths.' She gave her a card and off the girl went. That was the counselling. Consequently, I went up and said, 'I just want any job.' They gave me a job in a local foundry, and I worked there for two years – me head was caving in. I never did any work. I used to turn up late, and nobody ever knew. I never did a stroke, but I was dying of boredom.

So I started doing evening classes, got some 'O' and 'A' levels, did teacher training for a year and failed that – so by then it was looking bleak on the academic front. But one of the teachers said, 'You should be doing English – that's where your strength is. You're not very organised but you've got a way with words.' So I transferred to an English course, and got a degree in English. And then I went on the dole for three and a half years, as graduates do.

I met a bloke in a pub, and he said, 'They always want part-time people at the college of FE – you can teach the engineers how to write letters,' and so I went along – and that's where I met Malcolm Bailey [*his first manager*]. He said, 'You ought to be doing comedy,' and I said, 'Everybody says that.' But he said, 'I'd like to work on the managerial side of things,' so I had a manager before I had an act. It would have had to work that way for me, because unless someone had kicked me up the arse, I never would have got round to it.

ARNOLD BROWN

I'm against any form of deadness, and for me there's a deadness about figures on a page. It's only recording things, whereas comedy is about endless possibilities. When I came to London, I did the same job for fifteen years – I was an accountant for a group of employment agencies. The guy in charge was a maverick, so it wasn't like working in a normal office. He used to say to me, 'Mr Brown, if and when I die . . .' He was business-orientated, but very creative. I used to use him as a sounding board for my jokes. Once, he came back from a business lunch with a whiff of drink on him. He said, 'I looked at one of our employees from another branch today, and said, "You're half French" – and I was right!' I said, 'I've got the same facility! I can look at someone and say, "You're half pissed!" ' Jokes were very important as a release from the regularity and conformity of the system.

When I was an accountant, I used to go to the theatre a lot. I loved offbeat comedy and revues. I remember seeing John Cleese in a little church hall in 1963. I was a comedy voyeur. In the early seventies, there was an improvisation group at the Cochrane Theatre. I went along in my lunch hour. The guy in charge asked for volunteers. I wanted to outshine him, so when I went on, I tripped to try and be funny. When he saw what I'd done, he said, 'That'll be all.'

BRUCE MORTON

In a mundane tedious office job [*Morton worked as a clerical assistant in the Finance Department of Strathclyde Regional Council*], you're always looking for diversions. Whether there are two or three people who are the office wags, or whether it's the practical jokes that you play, those are the natural things that surface – the sort of things that break it up and bring a bit of life to things.

One of these things was that someone brought in that table football game, with those wee plastic men. You push their heads down and they kick the ball. So we got a league together. There were ten guys, and we had cup competitions and scoreboards and referees. It all became very professional. It was stupid but it was good fun – it took up the tea breaks and the lunchtimes. I thought, 'What we need here is a league magazine!' So in block capitals, I'd write out the latest transfer news and speculation. I'd do a society page about last week's office night out: 'Who was that wearing that horrible jersey?' I'd get it photocopied and sell it around the office at ten pence a time. The money would go in the kitty for the cash prize for the cup competition. In the end, it became insane.

One day, the East End Earthquakes FC star player was discovered missing. Someone had come into the office early, and kidnapped him. East End Earthquakes were up to play in the cup final about a week later. There was a lot of money on it – there was even a bookie in the office. Then someone sent in a ransom note, saying, 'Pull out of the cup competition or you'll never see your star player again.' There was a lot of tension in the office. The Earthquakes manager was really unhappy about it. In the end, he came into work one morning and found his star player hanging from a filing cabinet. It says a lot about the office environment and what it can do to people that we were almost coming to blows.

Billy Connolly will tell you that he worked with two dozen guys who are much funnier than him, and I know dozens of guys who are much funnier than me. It's like the Miss World competition. You can see women just as pretty in the street or even prettier and you may even know a few, but the women that you knew didn't go in for a competition. So they're not getting the prizes, the glamour and the attention – so you've got to get in a competition. If you enter the competition, the Comedy Miss World, there are events to be at, there are places to be seen, there are obligations – it's just that we're not as bitchy.

JENNY ECLAIR

I was brought up abroad: Malaya, Singapore, Berlin. As a child, I wanted to go to boarding school – I was a very Enid Blyton kind of child, and wanted to be one of the twins at St Clare's. Then I got into Noel Streatfield storybooks – *Swish of the Curtain* and *Ballet Shoes*. They were very girlish, the theatrical side of ponies. I was desperate. Me and my sister used to do little shows, but my parents were quite strict, and they wouldn't let me leave school at sixteen. They made me do 'A' levels, and after that I went to Manchester Polytechnic School of Theatre – which is actually in an old cinema. Graham Fellows was a couple of years older than me. John Thomson and Steve Coogan both went there as well. They bred crap actors, but good comics – my idea of acting is crying my eyes out and biting cushions.

Drama school wasn't very good for my psyche. They wanted to beat you down and rebuild you, and I lost a lot of confidence. I was told I was overweight and over the top, that I would have been fine if I'd been born fifty years earlier – because then I could have been a silent movie star, because I was always rolling my eyes. It's true – I was born a bit out of my time. I was never any good at any of the subtle Stanislavski stuff. Eventually, I became hideously anorexic. I had a boyfriend who formed a theatre company, and I played a lot of dying girls, because I looked very ill in bed – I weighed about six stone.

I was a Face. It's quite easy to be a Face in Manchester. There were some Manchester businessmen, who wanted to turn me into Manchester's answer to Toyah Wilcox. They decided that they would dress me up as a Pierrot doll, complete with a painted tear on my cheek. I was twenty at this point – stick thin with a lot of permed blond hair. They ran a newspaper called *The Flash*, and they were flash – they were on the fringes of everything. And so they dragged me into this recording studio, and I went along with it. At no point did I actually say, 'Listen! I can't sing!' This actually became evident. It was soul-destroyingly embarrassing. The song they wanted me to release was the Kinks' 'So Tired Of Waiting'. I was singing by numbers, and they were reverse tracking but I had a fit of conscience and I ran away from it. Money was going into it, and I knew there were girls my age who could actually sing.

After that, I was in a cabaret outfit called Cathy La Creme and the Rhumbabas. This was a comedy band, mostly a singing outfit, with me miming in the background and lots of buffooning around. The band split up as all bands do – because everyone sleeps with the wrong person and owes each other vast sums of money. I slept with the wrong person, who was the lead singer, and then found out that he'd been ripping us off – so I ran away to London, to seek my fortune.

I was so miserable for the first few weeks. I was the world's worst waitress: I was very anorexic, hated food – and hated people who ate. I used to look at people as if to say, 'You pig, you out of control pig, eating this! How can you? You make me ill!' It was in Covent Garden. I worked outside, in the Piazza. I did it for six months until I came to work one day in October and they'd closed it up, because it was cold, and I didn't have a job any more. If you've worked in these places, you never eat out again – you have to scrape mould off the clotted cream. After that, I sponged off my boyfriend for years.

JOHN HEGLEY

My first performances were in adventure playgrounds, parks and beaches. Sometimes, the kids were already there, but you had to draw an audience from the kids that were around. When we did an adventure playground, you were seen as an invader. The show we did was called *Explorers*, but sometimes we felt like invaders in that space. I didn't go into kids' theatre just as a stepping stone – but although we were doing comic shows for kids, adults would watch them and enjoy them, and I was very glad of that. Before I did kids' theatre, I worked with these kids who weren't at school. We used to have to keep them in this unit. There's a big difference between that and doing a show for people who've actually paid money to see you – in a place where they can have as much as they want to drink. These were kids who didn't want to be there. We had to keep them occupied, and there's not a lot of difference between keeping people occupied and keeping people entertained.

The first time I did a show with kids' theatre, we made our own costumes. I made some Elizabethan trousers and I was very proud of them. I sat down on the ground, and just as I was sitting down, one of the kids stuck some bubble gum on the hot tarmac – that ruined them. I had to put a patch in them.

Performing in the street with the Popticians was far harder than , doing stand-up. The Comedy Store was hard on your ego, but it wasn't physically threatening. You didn't generally feel as though you were physically endangered. One Saturday afternoon, some drunken yobs came up to us and intimidated us. There were about eight of them. They picked up the hat that we collected the money in, and walked off with it. We weren't going to go after them and ask for it back. They weren't kids, they were young men. They were frightening. There were other people standing around, but they didn't help. Russell, the drummer, said, 'Come on, let's pack up for the day.'

At other times when we were doing it, down-and-outs would come and watch us and dance to our music, and nobody else would come by. These winos would keep everybody else away. We had to stop for twenty minutes until they went – that was the only way to do it. One day, one of these guys walked up to us and gave us twenty quid. We couldn't believe it. He just put it in my pocket. He was very drunk, and very tatty, but I think he knew what he was doing. I said to the others, 'Shall I give it back to him?' But they said, 'No!'

JEFF GREEN

I did engineering at Birmingham University and then I did a sabbatical year as vice president of the Union. I had to do speeches, but I used to hate them, so to compensate I made them funny, to gloss over the fact that there was probably no substance to what I was saying. Then I made a nightmare move, which was actually quite crucial to my comedy. I joined a company called British Oxygen, BOC, as a commercial trainee. I had an overdraft when I left university, and I felt I had to get a proper job, so I rushed into this marketing job in Newport in South Wales while my girlfriend moved to London.

It was a complete and utter cock-up. I was in Newport on my own, and I was working as a salesman. I was out all day in a car, and then I'd come home. There'd be nobody at home, because I was living in a bedsit – and for nine months, I went out of my mind. I split up with this girl – she met someone else. At university, I had everything – a good degree and loads of friends – and suddenly I had nothing. I was completely on my own. I thought, 'She obviously thinks I'm a loser, because I had everything and now I've got nothing. She obviously thinks that's my lot. I'm not accepting that. I'm going to show her.' I wanted to prove to her that I was going to do something with my life – rather than eat expense account meals, and get a beer belly. I had no interest in any of that.

So I got a transfer to Guildford with BOC, and that's when I started going to the Comedy Store. I actually saw three comedians who I didn't think were very good. Some people say, 'I saw this great comic who inspired me.' I saw three OK comics and so I thought, 'This isn't hard. I can do this,' so I went to Jacksons Lane [*community arts centre in Highgate, North London*]. That was a complete fluke. A friend of mine saw an advert for comedy workshops in *Time Out*. I couldn't believe that somebody laid on something that I wanted to know about. I probably would have still gone into it, but it would have taken a lot longer.

I commuted from Guildford to Highgate every Tuesday. I used to leave work and get changed out of my suit and into my jeans and T-shirt. We used to use each other as a crutch. So we'd go and do a bad gig, and come back and swap these nightmare stories. And then there comes a time when you have to fly the nest. I was there for about three months. Eddie Izzard was there with me. Out of fifteen of us, four of us have stuck with it. For a lot of comedians, something traumatic happens in their life which makes them want to go and prove something, and that's what I felt myself. I'd split up with my girlfriend and made an absolutely appalling career choice. It was basically a big boot up the arse.

DOMINIC HOLLAND

I left university in 1988 and did three years as a sales rep – running round the country. For about six months before I finished sales repping, I was doing stand-up open spots. Then I did an MBA. That lasted for eighteen months, and when I finished my MBA, I went full time as a stand-up.

Getting appointments when you're a sales rep is like getting open spots. It's the hardest job I've ever done. People often say to me, 'How can you do stand-up?' And last night, it was the easiest thing I've ever done. I wasn't nervous, and I stormed it. It was a piece of piss. Being a sales rep was a bind. It was awful. I hated it – I hated every single day. In fact, I've hated every single day of my professional life, because I knew I didn't want to do it, and I used to loathe the shit I had to put up with, people treating you badly, with no respect. I used to hate people who were less able than me treating me like shit – it used to really piss me off. Meeting people who didn't want to see you, condescended to you and treated you very poorly. You'd drive somewhere to meet someone and they wouldn't be in, or they'd meet you in reception and say, 'Give us a sample,' and then they wouldn't entertain you. The mundanity of it – it was such a pressing-palms job. There was no actual mental requirement on my part. It was a case of pressing a palm, giving them a sample, entertaining them, making them laugh, phoning them up and saying, 'D'you want it?' It was a real low point in my life – it was terrible.

I went for this job at British Airways. There were twenty thousand applicants and ten taken on. I was the eleventh person. It killed me – it devastated me. My girlfriend now says it's probably better that I didn't get that job, because if I'd got it, I might not have done stand-up. Maybe it kick-started it for me. I thought, 'Dominic, you've got to do it . . .'

I used to procrastinate a lot about stand-up. I knew that was what I wanted to do but I couldn't actually visualise doing it. I always knew I was going to do it, but I couldn't actually visualise the idea of getting up on stage. In the end, my girlfriend Nicky said, 'Look, Dominic, I'm really getting bored with you talking about it. I know you can do it. All your friends know you can do it. Everyone encourages you to do it. Either do it, or shut up. All you ever do is talk about it.' And that was the best thing she ever said to me.

I used to trawl the circuit endlessly – going to gigs and watching people. Nicky would say, 'I don't want to go to the Store tonight.' And I'd say, 'No, you have to come to the Store! I want to see how good these people are!' And so in the end, she said, 'For Christ's

sake! You're not doing it, are you? I don't want to talk about it! Go
and do it!'

I was writing all the time. I've been writing since I was fifteen. And
I was writing furiously while I was watching stand-up. I was saying,
'That'd be really funny, wouldn't it, Nicky?' She'd say, 'That's
great! Do that!' And I'd say, 'Why do it now? I know I'm going to do
it. I'll be OK – I'll do it next month. I'm not even twenty-one yet – I'll
do it then.' I remember I went up to Jack Dee in the Comedy Store
and said, 'How old are you?' He said, 'I'm twenty-five,' and I
remember thinking, 'I'm only twenty-two! I've got loads of time!
He's twenty-five, that bloke.' And then he went on and killed, and I
thought, 'Shit! Maybe I should start.'

HUGH DENNIS

Steve was the major writer at Cambridge. He'd been commissioned
by *Weekending*, and he used to go down to Broadcasting House
every Friday. When we left, we were the only two who wanted to
carry on. There was another bloke called Nick Hancock [*stand-up
comic turned actor, recently starred in* An Evening With Gary
Lineker] but he was doing teacher training, so he stayed on for
another year. We'd never worked together as a double-act. We'd
only worked together in a group of six. I don't think we even knew
each other very well.

The summer before we left, Steve convinced me that a group of
five of us should go up to the Buxton Festival. None of us were going
to Edinburgh that year, so we decided to go to Buxton instead. We
did a show called *Nuts & Reasons* – crap title – in the Paxton Suite at
the Buxton Festival. That's the only occasion when we've run away
from a gig. We turned up at the Paxton Suite on a wet Thursday
afternoon. We had to do a matinee. There were three old ladies in
the audience, and we ran and put up a sign, 'Due to illness, there will
be no performance this afternoon.' It was grossly unprofessional,
but you can get into a downward spiral of depression when you
think, 'I can't do this any more.'

Steve and I shared a flat together. I got a job at Unilever, and took
a year off – and while I was working, operating the goods lift at
Harrods, we wrote a show which we then took back to Cambridge.
Then I went off to China for two months, and when I got back, I

started doing the job at Unilever, and we started doing the cabaret circuit. It's really difficult making a living just writing for radio, which is what Steve was doing – and I was on a normal graduate starting salary. I was quite well paid, and Steve was being paid absolutely nothing – and we did cabaret at weekends. Steve was doing what he wanted to do, and I was treating it as a bonus. There was a point when Steve almost gave up, and went and got a proper job. He thought about becoming an advertising copywriter for a bit. I was involved in advertising, and wasn't discouraging him.

To be honest I never realised the gravity of the situation. The night that Jasper Carrott came to see us, Steve didn't tell me he was in the audience. And even when we were asked to go on *Carrott Confidential* – twelve million viewers on a Saturday night – I didn't really take it that seriously, because I was still thinking, 'I am a marketing man.' I was in charge of a shampoo at that point. I was thinking, 'Wonder what I'm going to do with the cap colour for Timotei?' It used to get me over the nerves. I used to think, 'This really doesn't matter because I'm actually a businessman.' I used to take a bit of shit on Monday mornings. I don't think they'd ever been confronted with the situation before, but if they thought it was shit, they'd tell me. Everybody within the company had a view on it.

I was really upset when I left. I found it really difficult leaving. I actually quite liked having a desk and a phone. I used to love phoning up the factory and saying, 'Can you produce another eight thousand bottles next week?' It's that little bit of power, I suppose – you're completely powerless when you're a performer. I also love adverts. They weren't very exciting products – deodorant and Denim aftershave, rather embarrassingly – but I used to love it. I love all that stuff. The only reason I gave up my job was because it was taking up too much time. I only gave up work after the third series of *Carrott Confidential*. We were about halfway through the first *Mary Whitehouse Experience* radio series. I really enjoyed it – I had some very good mates there, and in itself it was quite a funny job. I'd go home in the evening and think, 'I can't get too stressed out about this because it's deodorant – I'm devoting my life to a deodorant!' I still know loads of people from there. I've got three or four really good friends who look after various comedy toiletry products.

When I was still at Unilever, I was at a company conference and this bloke of about forty-five who I'd never met came up to me and said, 'We've been watching *Carrott* on the telly, my wife and I. We saw your sketch on Saturday, and quite frankly, it was rubbish. Now my wife is a comedy writer – she's done scripts for *The Grumbleweeds* and she's a member of the British Guild of Comedy Writers – and we were wondering if you would like some material?' I was enormously courteous. I said, 'That's very interesting. I'm afraid we write all our own stuff, but thanks anyway,' instead of saying, 'Just fuck off and die, won't you?'

STEVE PUNT

I went to Cambridge University partly because I wanted to be a writer, and at the end of my first year I had four sketches in that year's Footlights show. To get stuff into the main show as a first year is quite unusual, so I was very proud of myself. In the show that year was Tony Slattery. He'd already been signed up by an agent, and so I accidentally wandered on to Fry and Laurie's coat-tails. Hugh Dennis and I were in the last year to benefit from that. Even then, that was purely because Stephen Fry, Hugh Laurie and Emma Thompson had all been signed up by an agent. Stephen had already written a play which won a [Scotsman] Fringe First. Tony had to go back and do another year, and he put me on to the writing team for the summer revue. The agent who'd signed him came up to see him in the show, and he said, 'I liked that Stephen Punt. Let's sign him up when he leaves.'

At the end of my first year, I went to Edinburgh in a student revue. One of the producers of *Weekending* said to me, as they say to everybody in Edinburgh, 'You should try sending stuff into *Weekending*.' I said, 'I already have,' but he was very encouraging, and in my third year I actually commuted down from Cambridge twice a week, to go to scriptwriting meetings – and as a result, I didn't get a very good degree. The first thing I was paid for was a one-liner on *Weekending*.

It was all a bit of a false start. It didn't make things any easier when I left. Hugh did have a proper job, and did it for three years after he came down, and was a part-time comedian. When I left Cambridge and came to London, I felt really small, because it's very easy to be a big fish in a small pond there. I think it's changed now – and a bloody good thing too – but our summer show went round the country and played the George Square in Edinburgh for two weeks and sold out. I'm proud of the show that we did, but it could have been the biggest pile of shite you've ever seen, and people still would have come to see it. That was the ludicrous thing about Cambridge Footlights. Because John Cleese and Peter Cook had been in it, twenty years earlier, people still came to see them in Edinburgh.

We'd all been aware of what was going on in London – we used to listen to the Comic Strip album – but we hadn't had time to accommodate ourselves to it. So we did a much more revue-based, sketch-based show, and it wasn't until David Baddiel's year that they fully adjusted to Alternative Comedy and promptly got massively slagged off for it.

I got to know Hugh in our third year. It was obvious that he hadn't been used properly in the Footlights show. He was doing one character throughout, which was the absolute opposite of what he should have been doing. I suggested that we worked together because we complemented each other – I like narrating, and talking to the audience, whereas Hugh is a very gifted physical comic, and is very good with accents and voices – and none of that had been used at all in our Edinburgh show.

We really had two separate apprenticeships. We wrote structured sketches for university revue, but then we totally reinvented ourselves when we saw what was going on in the cabaret circuit. Suddenly we could see ourselves in a different light. We understood why we were hated in Edinburgh, and why people thought it wasn't fair that we could sell five hundred tickets a night, because it wasn't – it really wasn't.

I saw Jeremy Hardy at Jongleurs, very shortly after I left Cambridge. It was like grown-up comedy instead of student comedy. So we went away and tried to work out how we could do a more upfront act. We had to design a show that we could do on stand microphones, because when you do revue, the audience don't heckle and you can do it without amplification, which is something that we've only just been able to go back to during the last two years. If you look at each other, you'll go off-mike – which makes it really difficult, because the whole point of a double-act is that you're supposed to inter-relate. Fourth wall comedy – an audience watching the two of us talking to each other – is a completely different thing from us talking to an audience.

Everything conspires against non-solo comedy in club environments. If you don't use a microphone, you're not loud enough, and people at the back get bored and restless. So if you've got to work straight into the microphone, and if there's two of you, you've got to work round this problem of how on earth you relate to each other. So we developed an act which was very fast-paced. I narrated and Hugh played all the characters within the narration, so we didn't have to look at each other – it was all seamless.

We wrote an hour-long show and went back and did it at the ABC Theatre in Cambridge for a week, to try it all out – just to make sure we hadn't made the worst mistake of our lives. We were very apprehensive indeed about starting on the circuit. We didn't want our revue background mentioned. Nobody knew for about two years, and it was a tremendous feeling of achievement to know that people weren't laughing at you because they were hoping that the next John Cleese was going to come on in a moment. It was actually a genuine audience.

STEVE COOGAN

I never wanted to do it. I tried to do Politics at university, but I didn't get the grades, so I joined a theatre company and travelled round the North, doing shows. I went into a Job Centre and saw an ad which said 'actor/actress required', so I applied for it. It was profit share. The director was director of his generation at Oxford, apparently. He was hotly tipped to be Mr Big. Patrick [*Marber, Coogan's writing partner*] knew him, and when he left university, all they heard was that he'd gone up North to form a theatre company with some real Northerners – I was one of those real Northerners. I went round adult education centres in really rough areas. The director was very highly disciplined. He did lots of psychological exercises with me – he got me into drama school.

I tried to get into the London drama schools, but I remember feeling very unsophisticated when I went down for the auditions. There were people there who seemed so at ease and so cosmopolitan, and I felt really suburban. Everyone was really confident. At every fucking drama school, a girl would come out in dungarees with her hair in a pony tail and say, 'Hi!' I wasn't used to that kind of over-politeness – I hadn't come across it before. I thought, 'I hardly know her! What's she talking to me like this for?' And that physical affection – hugging and kissing! I didn't do that with my parents! I'd give my dad a firm handshake, and my mum a kiss on the cheek, occasionally. I was very uncomfortable. I felt out of my depth. I got quite depressed. They were going in and saying, 'Hi! You know my father, Joshua? He works for the BBC World Service!' They had these well modulated RP accents, and I didn't open my mouth. I couldn't communicate with them.

At Manchester Poly I was a lot more confident about what I did. I went into the audition, and did a bad auditionee. It was virtually a clown act. I did the whole nervous thing – dropping things, picking them up, and apologising. I went up to the desk and spoke to each of them individually and shook their hands. It went really well, and they said, 'We'll offer you a place here and now!'

But even when I was at drama school, I didn't really like it. They frowned on what I was doing outside and I thought a lot of what they were talking about was crap. There were lots of talented people there, from all over the country, who had this middle-class cosmopolitan confidence about themselves. But I became more confident about my own talent and my own instincts. I thought, 'I know how to do some things that other people don't know. There are some things I've sussed out that these people haven't.'

During my first year at drama school, someone said, 'He can do impressions!' I did some, and a crowd gathered round me in the refectory. They were saying, 'That's amazing! You'll have no problem getting your Equity card. You should be on TV. How d'you do that?' It puzzled me, because I knew I could do it accurately – because I could hear the voice in my head. I would be irritated by the people I used to see doing impressions on TV that were just generalisations. I'd think, 'That's wrong! That's not how he speaks at all!' I wanted to get it dead right – and unless I could get it really close, I wouldn't do an impression.

BOB MORTIMER

I was a legal aid solicitor in Peckham. Crime and divorce, mainly. I did that right up until when we started filming the first series, and actually kept my job open. It was hard to believe that it could all really come to anything. But packing it in was the best thing I ever did. You put a lot into it to get your little certificate, and I never would have done it without something so ridiculous as, 'Would you like to do a television show?' It was hard to give it up, but the day after I gave it up, it was like a weight off my shoulders, even if the show had come to nothing. I had a bad job, but many people do.

VIC REEVES

I went to art school in Whitechapel. I did fine art, but I didn't really like it. I didn't think I was getting taught anything – I used to spend most of the time doing my own thing. I still paint now, and my drawings have always been an integral part of the shows. I spent seven years being an engineer. My last job was as an inspector in a factory in Croydon. I was getting up and doing long days and not having any night life at all. After a year, I thought, 'This is terrible! I don't want to spend my life doing this! It isn't any fun and there's probably a better way to make a living.' So I started running a night club.

CHARLIE CHUCK

When I was fifteen, I started playing the drums and then I took acting lessons. I met an old-time comedian called Bert Pearson. I did the clubs then – semi-professional. I turned professional at nineteen and went abroad – to Germany, Belgium and France. I did that for about five years and then I did the clubs as a comedian, first in a double-act and then on my own. I do a bit of everything, really: organ, drums, magic. I can actually play the organ and do a sing-a-long. I've always earned a good living out of it. I'm never low. I'm too happy. I enjoy life too much. Believe me, it's the truth –. I've had a barrel of laughs.

They call it surreal and alternative but I've been doing it for years. Tommy Cooper was alternative, but he was classed as mainstream – and that's how I've been. I should have come to London ten years ago. I missed my way. Perhaps I could have got on further ten years ago. But having said that, I don't regret owt, and if it all fell flat tomorrow, I could go back home and put my slippers on and call it a

LIVERPOOL JOHN MOORES UNIVERSITY
LEARNING SERVICES

day. I packed it in four years ago and opened a shop selling Volkswagen parts. I lost £18,000 at it. I realised I wasn't a businessman.

GRAHAM FELLOWS

My happiest years were when I left Sheffield to go to Manchester Youth Theatre, and then on to Manchester Poly Drama School – especially the year before 'Gordon is a Moron'. Having that hit as Jilted John aged me a lot, and made me rather world-weary. It was as if my innocence had gone after that. That was more or less the first thing I'd written. It was born out of naivety – even down to the chord structure and the way I played the guitar. I couldn't play the guitar, so I tuned it to an open chord. After that, I became very serious about being a songwriter, and I used to try dreadfully hard to write something that would top that song. I realise now that I probably won't, and I've grown to love that time. One of the good things about John Shuttleworth becoming more successful is that lots of people now don't even know about that. I'm known for this.

I was on a Christian Youth Camp when the record broke. I hasten to add that I wasn't a Christian. It was just a cheap holiday – and a way to meet nice girls from the Home Counties. My sister had run away from home a few times and then there was the obligatory religious phase after that. She started going to this camp in North Devon. She said, 'It's brilliant!' So I went the following year, and it was. The first year I won the table tennis competition, the poetry competition and the painting competition. And the second year, I was on *Top of the Pops*.

The record was already bubbling under when I went off on camp, and I used to phone in daily to my manager in Manchester – Tosh Ryan from Rabid Records, who also managed John Cooper Clarke and Slaughter and the Dogs, and eventually, he said, 'You're on!' I was very shy, so I didn't tell anyone. I just told the chaplain, and slipped away one night, and went to wait in a hotel. My manager was going to come down in a big car, and pick me up in the middle of the night and drive me to the studios in Wood Lane, so I went to this hotel but I didn't have any money. I said, 'Can I stay here for a while,

because my manager's going to come and pick me up to take me to
go on *Top of the Pops*?' The man said, 'Yes, all right.' So I bought a
pint of lager. But by the time I'd drunk it, he still hadn't come, so I
said, 'I'll have another pint of lager, please.' After a while, he
suddenly said, 'You're not going to the BBC, are you? You're
having me on, lad! You're having me on! What's your name? What's
your address?' And he started to get really heavy with me.
Fortunately, seconds later, the phone rang. It was my manager. He
confirmed my story, so this man went very red, gave me my drink
and a plate of sandwiches – and I got to sit upstairs in the TV room,
until he arrived.

I started out as an actor, and for several years I made quite a
decent living in TV and theatre – doing nothing remarkably good
and a lot of rubbish, but I was making a living – and then it all dried
up, so I had to have a rethink. I wasn't getting anywhere with my
music. I ended up trying to write hits for Five Star. That was very
dispiriting. I thought, 'This is completely wrong – I shouldn't be
doing this.' Because I couldn't.

I jacked it in for a while, and became a milkman – and did some
head searching. I'd been writing songs for years, and not getting
anywhere. I was very miserable. My dog and my mother had died. I
went to see a counsellor – I was very depressed. I wanted to do
something worthwhile, to help the community. It was good being a
milkman, because I learnt to whistle. For the first few days, I was
quite euphoric, and I remember saying hello to everybody in the
street. I got some slightly stand-offish reactions, but after a few days
they started to respond. But by this time, I was getting a bit fed up. I
only lasted three months.

I was doing relief – doing other people's rounds while they were
on holiday. I was getting utterly ripped off. It takes twice as long, the
people on the round don't know you, they just get to know you by
the end of the two weeks, and then the round is taken off you. I was
always fifty pounds short at the end of the round, and the manager of
the dairy used to say, 'Where's it gone, son? Where's it gone? I'll
have to dock your wages!' So I used to come home with about sixty
pounds a week – I realised that showbiz wasn't such a bad way to
make a living.

MARK THOMAS

I'd left college, I'd tried to get numerous jobs – and I'd gone back to work on a building site. I owed masses of money – I was hugely in debt. I used to work a ten-hour day, with a half-hour break which you didn't get paid for. That was deducted from the time that you were on the site. By the end of the day, I was completely knackered. I tried to get some jobs performing, which was what I really wanted to do, but nobody would employ me, in any capacity.

Working on a building site – day in, day out – is soul-destroying, I promise you. I really hated it. I actually earned my living as a labourer for three and a half years. I worked on the site during the day, and performed during the evening. I used to bunk off during my lunch break, and go and find a pay phone, and phone round all the people who organised gigs, and badger them. I used to spend my lunch break eating my lunch in a phone box – phoning up to get gigs.

You have to have an attitude of thinking, 'Fuck it! It can't get any worse! I'm going to try this – I'm going to give this a go. I've got nothing to lose!'

4. The First Gigs

'The first time I saw live comedy, I was on the bill.' – Mark Lamarr

An Actor Prepares is the title of Stanislavski's text about approaching a performance. It's no coincidence that no equivalent text exists for aspiring comedians. Since stand-up hinges on the interaction between an individual and an audience rather than other individuals on a stage, there's absolutely no proper preparation apart from the real thing (a stand-up script is the haziest of blueprints). Hence, at comedy clubs, apprentice comics rub shoulders with seasoned stand-ups. It's like RADA hopefuls auditioning alongside members of the RSC.

The starting point for any wannabee is to secure an open spot – i.e., an unpaid appearance, usually lasting five minutes, whereby a rookie comic hopes to secure future bookings. During Alternative Comedy's early days, open spots were filled with impromptu participants from the audience – but nowadays there's a waiting list of at least several months at all but the worst clubs, and phoning around for open spots (the most gruesome form of telephone sales) is generally acknowledged to be a far more fearful and potentially humiliating process than dying a death onstage. 'Make me laugh,' said one promoter, whom Jim Tavare phoned up for a try-out spot. Tavare was reduced to telling jokes down the phone.

Incredibly, some hopefuls survive this awful ordeal, and graduate via half slots (ten minutes), full slots (twenty minutes) and extended slots (forty minutes) to a sixty-minute solo show at the Edinburgh Festival. However, most comics never reach this stage – and even for the few who do, national tours and network broadcasts are a rare exception. Yet the initial trip to the mike is an experience which unites all comedians – eternal nobodies and future superstars alike. The first gig is almost sure to end in complete ignominy – but for a few this ritual slaughter will be the start of something special, and for some, one lone laugh amid a sea of silence is enough to hook a comedian for life.

ARNOLD BROWN

It was 1978. A friend of mine was doing some stand-up comedy in a coffee bar in Swiss Cottage. I'd been doing some improvised sketches with him and a few other people in my flat – merely for our own amusement. We used to play around with tape recorders. Someone heckled him, and suddenly everything came to a stop. I felt incensed that he was being interrupted, and I remember jumping up on this little podium. I didn't even say anything funny, just, 'You couldn't do any better! Give him a chance!' It wasn't anything comedic – but when I got up there, it was almost like entering a magic box. For some reason, I liked being there. I'd never performed before, but I felt a buzz, a frisson. Somehow, it connected.

By May 1979 I'd become involved with trying to write comedy for *Weekending*. There was a writing course run by a mainstream comedy writer called Brad Ashton, which gave you things like the telephone number of BBC Radio. To these seminars and work-shops, he invited people like Denis Norden. I was introduced to his world. Brad told me about a *Private Eye* advert for the Comedy Store starting. It said, 'What's more dangerous than sky diving? Doing stand-up comedy!' He sensed that I was interested in performing, because I'd told him about the sketches that I was doing in my house.

So I went along to the Comedy Store on the opening night, where I met the proprietor, Don Ward. There was certainly no audition. I was waiting in a side room. I didn't even bother checking out the room, or seeing any of the acts. For some reason, I thought I'd stay away from everyone. Alexei Sayle was the compere. He was billed as an intellectual yob. Emma Thompson was helping in the wings. It was in the old Gargoyle Club. In the thirties, aristocracy used to go there – but Don Ward owned strip clubs, and one floor of this strip club was turned into the Comedy Store. I'd never been in one of these clubs before.

I must have been clinically insane, because I thought that when I went on, I would have an act. I had one joke in my mind which was supposed to go: 'Good evening, my name's Arnold Brown – I'm an accountant, and I check things.' And the punchline was: 'Can you hear me at the back?' That was supposed to be a joke! But before I could say it, a guy shouted out, 'We can't hear you at the back!' It was a psychic heckle! How did he know what I was going to say? So immediately, someone else shouted, 'Put him out of his misery!'

For some reason, I thought that I could go on and talk to the audience about whatever I felt like. Obviously, I was a loony – I was out of my mind. Because I could talk in coffee bars, I thought I could speak to an audience. I took a long time getting the mike out of the stand, because I'd never handled a mike in my life. It wasn't so good to be gonged off so quickly – but for a second I enjoyed being there. There was that excitement of being in a buzzy place where things were happening, with luminaries like Larry Adler in the audience. I didn't see much of the show, but afterwards there were all sorts of funny people around, and all the media were there. Rowan Atkinson popped in. No one understood what it was all about.

On the opening night *Newsnight* came along. They came round to my flat in Hampstead and filmed me filling out a tax return, and did a story about the chartered accountant who wanted to be a stand-up comedian. It looked as if I was a mad person because I had no material. They said to me, 'How do you feel now, Arnold?' And I said to them, 'I know I was gonged off, but I think I'm funny. I'm going to come back tomorrow night.' And I did.

ARTHUR SMITH

When the Comedy Store opened in '79, I was still doing revue – jumping around in wigs and doing jokes about Batman. I went to see the Comic Strip and Alexei Sayle and I thought, 'Jesus! What I'm doing is so old-fashioned!' It was a revelation – that a bloke could get up and talk about social workers and politics. There was no model for it – they weren't wearing frilly shirts and bow ties. I went home and wrote a routine. I felt somewhere within me that I could do it – and it also held out the possibility of earning some money.

My first gig was at the Comedy Store. I'd been in a revue group so I was used to performing – but not as a stand-up. I'd plucked some rather low-grade bits from this revue that I did, which wasn't appropriate at all. I turned up at the Comedy Store when it was at Dean Street – the old strip joint. I was on with John Hegley. Tony Allen [*anarchic performance artist and one of the founding fathers of Alternative Comedy*] was compering. I got there at nine-thirty p.m.

to be told that I was going on at one-thirty a.m. – so I had four hours to wait and be very nervous, during which time I resolved not to drink more than two pints. I ended up drinking about seven pints, so by the time I went onstage I was completely pissed – and absolutely shitting my pants. I started off with some rather fey material, which wasn't at all appropriate – sweet little poems and that sort of thing. People started heckling – as well they might – and I made that old mistake of using pre-prepared put downs, which were far too fierce for the mild heckling I was experiencing. I came off traumatised, after five minutes, and didn't do it again for six months.

At my next gig, I came on and the microphone wasn't working, so I got flustered and some bloke shouted out, 'Why don't you turn it on?' I said, 'Oh, good idea,' but I couldn't do it. I had to get a member of the audience to come up and turn it on for me. I was hardly in command of the situation. I had three one-liners and I somehow thought that would fill up twenty minutes.

JEREMY HARDY

I always knew I wanted to do something, but I didn't know what it was. It went from being a poet to being an actor, to being a journalist to being a writer – and it was mainly because nobody was buying any of my scripts that I thought, 'I'd better go out and perform my own stuff,' which was nearly ten years ago now. In those days it was quite easy to get an open spot, because there weren't as many comedians. So you could phone up, do an open spot next week and then get a gig a month later.

My first gig was at the Banana Cabaret in Balham – which was my local, although I'd never been there before I went there onstage. You've probably got to have nothing else going for you – if you had a job that you were happy with, and a life that you were happy with, you probably wouldn't do it. I certainly didn't know what I was doing. I would turn up for gigs that started at nine at half past seven. I'd get there early, and wanted to see if I could work the room without a microphone, because I didn't know how to use one. I knew someone who had a band, so I'd go and practise standing behind a microphone in his cellar. I still don't take them out – I still can't get the thing out of the stand in one piece. I didn't know what I was doing, but I was quite single minded. I thought, 'I'll try this for a year, and see if I can do it.' There wasn't anything else going on so I thought, 'Well, I'll give it my best shot.'

MARK THOMAS

I sat down with a copy of *Time Out* and phoned up all the clubs. I thought I'd never get a gig if I said I'd never performed before. Actually, that didn't matter – but at the time I didn't know that. There was no hope of me ever getting a job working with any sort of performance group because I thought it'd be impossible to find people who would share the same interests and outlook on life, and because I simply wasn't good enough. The first gig I did was at the Fat Cats Club in Putney, at the White Lion. It was Sunday the nineteenth of November, 1985. It was a really awful gig. There's a pub in Thornton Heath where trad jazz bands play every Sunday, and all my family used to meet up there: my uncles, aunts, mum and dad and the people they worked with. They'd have a few drinks and then go off to Sunday lunch. My dad had bought me God knows how many drinks, and I was desperately wound up about it. I'd been drinking all afternoon, and by the time I got to the club I was actually pissed – my first time onstage, and I was pissed. I shambled on, did fifteen minutes and got one laugh. What kept me going was that I'd written all this stuff – of which there was one gag vaguely worth waiting for, and I was determined to get to the end of it all, that I would say what I had to say. I thought, 'I got one laugh. This is a start. At the next gig I won't be pissed and I'll try much harder.'

My next gig was only a week afterwards, at the Rosemary Branch [*fringe theatre in Hackney*]. I'd phoned up loads of places, and got bookings for open spots. I had about eighteen spots between mid-November and the end of December. I actually got quite a few laughs, and they gave me a booking. I was so thrilled that I was actually going to get paid for doing a gig.

Kit Hollerbach used to run improvisation workshops down at the Comedy Store. I went down there and met this bloke and got chatting to him. He came from a strong loyalist family in Ireland. He'd been in trouble with the police for nicking things. He used to shoplift to order. He left Ireland, spent his first three nights in England on a bench, and his first year and a half in a Salvation Army hostel. He was working at the Ford plant at Dagenham on the late shift. We only went to one of the workshops, because we didn't really like them. But we became mates, and went around doing open spots together.

The first gig was terrible, but after that I actually started getting better quite quickly, and getting laughs. Some of the stuff was still hung on the old ideas I had when I was in the Socialist League – that the most important thing was that you had something of worth to say, and that you somehow tripped people up. Sometimes I thought, 'Well, it doesn't matter if I don't get a laugh on this piece, because it's provocative,' which is a bit arse over tit, because it doesn't work like that. The laugh is the most important thing, because you actually get people to think by making them laugh. I did a series of about ten gigs when I got a good response – not hugely, but people were laughing, which was encouraging for an open spot. It was working.

I went through a period of about four months, of getting material together, but not knowing how the jokes worked – not knowing the mechanics of it. Those four months were really hard – you know you've got something, but you don't know what it is.

FRANK SKINNER

My first gig was a charity do on December ninth 1987. On the bill was the Midlands Jazz Youth Orchestra, me, Earl Okin [*a menopausal musical novelty turn who sings lewd songs dressed as an Edwardian gentleman*] some folk duo and a mainstream comic called Andy Feet – the centrepiece of whose act was an Anthony Newley impression. I thought, 'At last, I've found something I can do!' I imagined that next week I'd be on *Saturday Live* [*flagship stand-up TV show of the late eighties, which introduced Harry Enfield's Stravros to the nation*] – I sincerely believed it. So I went on and I was shit. I was absolutely stunned. I'd never experienced not being funny before, because at school, at work, and in the pub, I could always make people laugh. I was devastated.

I had another booking at that club – which I was actually getting paid for. Fifty quid for New Year's Eve – and I was booked for forty minutes. I think I did ten before Malcolm [*Bailey, his apprentice manager*], the disc jockey and the club manager were all standing in the wings going, 'Come off!' They put the house lights on, but I was still saying, 'No, you'll like this one . . .' I think a lot of people would have quit after that New Year's Eve gig, because it was terribly, terribly painful. There were these little trumpets which came free in the crackers, and the entire crowd were all blowing them. People of seventy years old were booing me off, and it was incredibly humiliating. Malcolm's approach was to take the piss out of me. I had no shoulder to cry on. I was very distressed, but I couldn't quit. I'd spent four hundred pounds on a room in Edinburgh. I had to carry on.

My first weekend in London, on the Friday night, I did a place in Notting Hill which was run by Tony Allen. That was a terrible club, really rough – not at all nice. On the Saturday night, I did a place called Drummonds. There were about nine people in the audience, and it slowly dawned on me as the night went on that about seven of them were acts. And on the Sunday night, I did the Tunnel. I think I lasted about eight minutes. I was only two or three months into my career and I was incredibly raw. I never had a set order – I wasn't aware of that. Every time I did a gig, I did different material. I didn't know you were supposed to do the same stuff and get it honed. I didn't know and I didn't have anyone to tell me because Malcolm didn't know either.

DONNA McPHAIL

My first ever gig was at Jongleurs, Battersea, which is thought to be the worst gig in town anyway in terms of having a horrible time. It was Arthur Smith who made me do it. I was with a theatre group called the Millies, and I had a little monologue that I'd written for a show we did called *Cover Girls* which was a spoof on women's magazines. It was a short story, and it could be done in a stand-up sense. I was down at Jongleurs, a bit pissed. Arthur was compering and he said, 'Come on, get up and do that thing you do in the show!' He was going out with one of the women in the group at the time. Having had a couple of pints, I thought that would be a good idea – I wasn't even dressed right or anything. I was drunk. That's the only reason I did it and I stormed it. I thought, 'This is a piece of piss – well, I'll do this then!' It'd never occurred to me to do stand-up. I remember seeing Jenny Eclair and Helen Lederer and thinking, 'Why are they doing this? I couldn't do it!' I never had ambitions to

do it, which I think is better than desperately wanting to do it. If you
don't care one way or the other, you don't have that awful need. Of
course, I thought it would be really easy – but the next couple of
times I went to Jongleurs, I died on my arse. It was an absolute fluke
that I stormed that first gig. I had three open spots there after that –
and each one was a nightmare.

JEFF GREEN

The first gig I ever did was at a club called Funny Business in Stoke
Newington. I was living in Guildford at the time, and I'd spent all
day pacing and pacing, and trying to remember every word in my
little five-minute routine. When you're starting out they don't put
you in a position where you're going to do well. When I started, they
used to put me on first, which is always the hardest spot. They saw it
as a baptism of fire. Since then they've realised that if the first act
bombs, it sets the tone for the gig, so now they put open spots on
somewhere in the middle. But they didn't realise that at the time,
and there are still a lot of clubs which use that format. I turned up
about half seven, for a nine o'clock start. The club was above a pub
and the pub was a shithole. It was really scary. Six people turned up,
and the manager said, 'Right, we're going on.' I knew no better, and
I couldn't work out why I wasn't getting laughs. I know now that if
there's only six people in, and you're in first, and the compere hasn't
got a laugh, and it's your first gig, the odds are pretty much stacked
against you. My second gig was in a club called Hackney Cabaret. I
did eight minutes, and I hit it just right. My material was dreadful,
but I was so full of enthusiasm that it carried me through. They gave
me an encore, but I didn't have any more material.

JENNY ECLAIR

There was an advert in the back of the *Stage* for novelty acts for a
comedy club in Wimbledon. I was on with a mime act called The
Great Smell of Brut and a woman who wore a lot of hats and sang
music hall songs, and was utterly ghastly. I wore a black cocktail
dress and fishnet tights and stilettos, and read some poems out of
my poetry book. John Cooper Clarke was big at this point in

Manchester, and there were a lot of John Cooper Clarke wanna-bees, including Cathy La Creme. Basically, I nicked her ideas and her act, and made up my own poems and copied her. There was a bloke at this gig who ran the Finborough Arms – which became a comedy club just after the Comedy Store opened – so I started performing poetry regularly at the Finborough Arms along with people like Jules [*punk poetess*] and Slade the Leveller from New Model Army.

I was getting away with it because I was only twenty-one and there weren't that many girls around. This was in the days of the GLC, and it was token-women time. You had to have girlies on the bill to get your grant: Helen Lederer was one, Jenny Lecoat was another, and I was the third. I don't think any of us were particularly good. And then suddenly Jo Brand came on to the scene, and seeing her was the biggest kick up the butt I've ever had. For the first time there was a woman coming onstage as if she had a right to be there, without apologising, without making excuses, without being girlish or coy.

HARRY HILL

The first gig I did was at the Aztec comedy club in Norwood. It's in a Mexican restaurant. You get a free Mexican meal – but not if you're doing an open spot. I've got a terrible sense of direction, so it took me ages to find the place. I was driving around for hours and hours. I had five minutes of stuff, which I'd been rehearsing for a month previously, but I still had all the words written on the back of my hand. I got carried away and forgot the lines – but it went well, I got a few laughs and I got a booking out of it. The gig was in September, and they booked me for May.

That was the first gig I did as me. Before that I was in a double-act. The first gig we did was at the Tunnel Club, because it was one of the few places you could phone up and get an open spot. It was terrible. We didn't use microphones, so we could barely be heard. We did a stupid Richard Attenborough sketch about an orange. My partner rolled it off the stage, and it came straight back. It hit him in the chest. We had these little bits of paper printed with our pictures on, and a phone number for bookings. Of course, these were screwed up and thrown at us and we were booed off. Malcolm Hardee faded the music up over the top of us while we were still doing it. We couldn't get out of the sketch, or react to what was going on. We just about got the last train home – the Tunnel Club was so difficult to get to. It was off some flyover by the Blackwall Tunnel with no houses for miles around.

We didn't do anything for six months after that. We were so shell-shocked. We used to go back occasionally and see other people die. I remember seeing Sean Hughes die one night. We did twelve gigs in two years. We never got any laughs and we never got any heckles – just silence. The only booking we got was at the Fruit and Nut Club, which ran for about three weeks. We went down very badly, and the bloke who booked us was almost too embarrassed to talk to us. If you die terribly, none of the acts talk to you, and the guy who runs the club avoids your gaze, so we had a policy that we'd always go up and ask, 'What did you think of it?' He refused to pay us – there were only about four people in. In the end, he gave us a pound each and we had to take the compere home.

I remember doing the Chuckle Club [*in Carnaby Street*]. Jo Brand and John Maloney [*angry young comedian cum accordionist*] were both there, but they couldn't be bothered to talk to me. I thought it was really odd. So I said to Jo, 'Have you got any advice for me on how to get gigs?' And she said, 'Do a bit of telly.' Thanks a lot. I always make a point of talking to open spots now, because you're feeling bad enough as it is. As an open spot, you've got the worst of the worst. You're announced as an open spot, and the intros that you get are, 'Now we've got someone who's just starting out – he's not being paid, he's just doing five minutes, but if we like him, we'll bring him back.' It gets worse and worse. Plus it's the first few times you've done it, so you're very nervous anyway, and everything's stacked against you. Those open spots are probably the hardest gigs you'll ever do.

BOB MORTIMER

Jim [*Moir, Vic Reeves' real name*] started doing it in Winston's Bar in Deptford, and then he went to a pub by Goldsmiths' College called the Goldsmiths' Tavern. The first time I went, there were about twelve or fifteen in the audience, and it went on until two a.m. I was hooked – I loved it. I thought it was fabulous, and so I went back every week. About eight or ten weeks later, we got talking, because there weren't that many people there at the beginning – and I eventually started doing little bits and pieces. The first thing I did was to present Jim with a cheque for millions of pounds, for helping children in Africa.

VIC REEVES

I got asked to put on a comedy club at Winston's Bar in Deptford. I couldn't find anyone who could put it on, so I did it myself. I didn't think I'd be doing it for long and I didn't want to be known as a comedian, so I didn't really care whether people liked it or not. I charged a quid to get in, and people liked it – so that was a bonus. I wasn't trying to be a comic, so it didn't matter if I failed.

For the first three years there was a little sign in a pub window, saying 'Vic Reeves' Big Night Out, Thursdays'. We used to write a new three-hour show every week. A lot of people came down for a late night booze-up. Occasionally, they'd start attacking each other towards the end of the night. Someone chucked a chair at me, so I chucked it back. Afterwards the sound man came up to me and said, 'Do you realise you could have injured someone throwing that chair?' I said, 'It could have injured me!' We'd get trouble that was borne of a late licence and young people being together. We had people appear with baseball bats, with their heads split open. We were doing a gig at Twickenham. I was eating a yoghurt, and Bob came up behind me with a spoon, trying to get some of the yoghurt off me and I wouldn't let him. People didn't like it. There was a rugby crowd at the back, and they immediately started hurling abuse – and bottles, so we went. We didn't get any further than Bob chasing me, trying to get the yoghurt – it was a bad crowd that night. There was another bloke there who'd done forty gigs and they gave him the same treatment – he had to get out of a back window. We met him in a pub round the corner – he was virtually in tears. He'd invited his family down, and he couldn't face them either.

ROB NEWMAN

I was writing for Newsrevue at the Canal Cafe Theatre [*in Little Venice*]. They did a Smoker and I told them that I'd done loads of comedy performance, although I hadn't. I'd done a party-piece

Tony Benn impression before, so I did this thing that was half stand-up, half-impression, plus a few stolen gags. It went really well, and I got a total rush off it – but before I went onstage I was bleeding from unusual places and thinking, 'Me and my big mouth! How the fuck did I get myself into this mess?' I was so full of fear.

The next gig I did was at Absolute Cabaret in the North Star pub in Finchley, run by a vile anarchist hippy – and that was deathly. To this day, I can still remember the audience being shocked by a joke I did, and not getting the irony. After that, the Earth Exchange [*the first comedy club to open in London after the Comedy Store, and for several years, the only other comedy club on the circuit*] went well, but the more I came off my script the better it was – the more intimate and warm.

The first few gigs I did, I remember thinking after the good gigs, 'This is what I'm going to do for the rest of my life,' and after the bad ones, 'I'm never ever going to do it again.'

JO BRAND

I'd been talking for ages about doing some comedy – and I'd always bottled out at the last minute. Then a friend of mine, who was helping to set up a benefit in a disco in Wardour Street, said, 'Look, I'm booking comics – why don't you go on at the end of the night, and do five minutes?' What I didn't know at the time is that benefits are normally completely shit. Nine out of ten are very hard to do. It's something to do with the attitude of the audience. They always seem to be a bit desperate and unfriendly, but of course I didn't know that, so I said, 'All right then, I'll do it.' I was a psychiatric nurse at the time, and I'd got these vague jokes together which were all about Freud. It was probably far too erudite for the average comedy audience – but I'd cobbled together this set, and so I went along.

There were a load of yuppies in who weren't interested in the comedy. I sat there and watched all the comedy die on its arse, and then I had to go on. By that time, I'd had about seven pints of lager, and I was completely pissed out of my head. I thought I was going on in the middle, and by the time I realised it was dying badly, and that I was going on at the end, I thought, 'Well, I might as well get drunk and then I'll enjoy it a bit more.' So although I was trying not to to start off with, after about ten o'clock I deliberately got drunk. I wasn't on the point of being sick – but the room was starting to revolve. There was a disco going on next door which was really loud, and nobody at the back could hear what I was saying. Also, there was a comic in called Tony Green who was infamous on the circuit for doing very odd gigs. He once did a gig when he got up onstage, and told the audience who was sleeping with who on the circuit – for twenty minutes. The audience didn't actually know who any of these people were, so they weren't interested at all.

As soon as I got up there and started my set, he started shouting, 'Fuck off, you fat cow!' Continuously – throughout the whole two-and-a-half-minute performance. I wasn't scared – I was just fed up. I was angry because I expected it to be better than that. I didn't get any laughs at all – he did. I slid off, humiliated, and packed it in for four months.

STEWART LEE

The first gig I ever did was on the way up to the Edinburgh Festival, where I was doing a student show in 1989. I did ten minutes at Newcastle Arts Centre, and that went really well. I did loads of open spots around Edinburgh that summer, and the *Festival Times* [*fringe student magazine*] said I was the funniest stand-up on the Fringe. At the same time, the student show I'd written was reviewed as the worst show on the Fringe.

All that proved to me was that context is all. Malcolm Bailey saw me doing an open spot while I was doing a student show in Edinburgh. He said, 'That was good but it was a bit studenty.' Then he saw me four months later at the Comedy Store, and said, 'I'd book you now – your act's really come on. The material's much better.' It was the same material exactly. It was just the context that was different.

There were some clubs which I rang up every day for two or three months, who never called me back. After a while, I really enjoyed it. I always get a perverse pleasure from being polite to people who probably aren't that interested in talking to me. I had a horrible temping job in an office on the North Circular. I thought, 'I've got to get out of this – here's a way out.' I had £2500 worth of debts to pay off, and I really wanted to be working. Plus, I knew I had an act which would work. Most open spots feel they still haven't really got the goods, so they're a bit embarrassed about ringing up, whereas I knew all I had to do was get a gig. Every open spot I did, I got a booking – until I did Jongleurs.

I was working everywhere by the time Jongleurs would give an open spot. My car broke down on the way. I had to run to get there. This was the summer of 1990. I didn't have a particularly good gig – nobody talked to me on the way in, nobody talked to me on the way out. I looked at all the faces of those people and thought, 'There isn't a single person here who I'd want to be my friend. I don't really care what a load of accountants from Battersea think of me. There's loads of blokes in suits with their dolly birds after work on a Friday night, it's midnight and they're all drunk, and you know that they're all the kind of people who play rugby and flush each other's heads down the toilet and talk about how big their cars are.'

JACK DEE

I first went down to the Comedy Store as an ordinary punter. I was working in restaurants at that time – which I'd been doing for a long time. I really enjoyed it – I liked what I was seeing. But at the same time, I had this feeling: 'Why aren't I doing that? I was always the funny one at school! I fucked up my entire education making people laugh, and yet I'm the one who's ended up waiting tables and I'm not up there! Why not?' I really and truly felt that I ought to be up there – that it was my birthright. I felt that sense of indignation as well as a strong feeling that I really wanted to try it.

I went back the next week, and they were doing open spots – one after the other and none of it worked. I asked the compere if I could give it a try, and he said, 'Sure, what's your name?' So I went on and I was crap as well, but I did get one laugh, and that feeling was enough to hook me. The rest didn't matter. The compere said, 'How long have you been doing it?' That really surprised me. I said, 'It's the first time I've tried it.' He said, 'I think you should keep writing and keep coming back.' It was as if all my Christmases had come at once. The missing link had been replaced. I'm not a superstitious person, but I felt it was timed exactly right. I was in the right place at the right time and I'd found something I'd been looking for to fill a huge hole in my life.

After that first gig, I went back to the Comedy Store – because I didn't know that any other clubs existed. In fact, I did the Comedy Store for weeks on end before someone said, 'What other clubs are you doing?' And I said, 'What other clubs are there?' I wasn't a *Time Out* reader. I was quite naive about the whole set up. I thought the Comedy Store was a one-off – but as soon as I realised there were other clubs, I started venturing out and getting open spots there as well – and I found it a lot easier there. I stayed away from the Comedy Store until I felt competent enough to tackle it again with the realistic hope of getting on the bill, which took about a year and a half.

After the adrenalin of the first one wore off, the following gigs were a process of realising how much I had to do in order to get past five minutes and survive up there. I realised that if I was going to do it, it was going to be very hard work. I started out thinking that I was there to deliver what was required, rather than thinking what I was able to deliver. A lot of people go about it that way, and the result is somewhat banal. When I discovered that there's something about me that's always been about making people laugh, and it's that which I need to find and enlarge, it became far more personal. My attitude was, 'If this doesn't work, nothing will – because this is what it's about.'

There was a certain amount of victory in surrendering to my real self, and owning up to the fact that I had a very odd vision. At that time I'd never seen *Saturday Live*. I was a complete virgin as far as the new comedy culture was concerned. I wasn't affected by anything I'd seen on television. I was thinking I need to be more like Bruce Forsyth, rather than one of these hip new jokesters. Looking back, it's been an advantage. I've done a lot of research since, and now I know a lot about it, but if I'd studied it before I tried it, I'd never have got started in the first place. At the time, the naivety of what I was doing was what drove me on.

I didn't start off deadpan. The first stuff I did was a lot more chirpy, but I never got anywhere with it – I don't think anyone quite believed it. The material was always there, but the delivery wasn't plausible and people picked up on that. I'd come into comedy at a time when it was beginning to get difficult to get gigs. I wasn't getting any, and I was about to give it up. I'd already stopped ringing round for gigs, but I decided I'd honour the last few in my book. I went along to those gigs with a take it or leave it attitude. I didn't care how they went, one way or another – and that was when it began to work. For the first time I was getting real laughs – not just for writing something amusing, but for being me.

EDDIE IZZARD

At the Comedy Store they used to do the open spots after the closing act, which is a nightmare. I went on three times after Gerry Sadowitz. I called it Death With Honour. I was hitting the punchlines and getting no reaction at all. I stayed on top of it, but there was still no fucking laughter. The Store had a narrow bus shelter of a dressing room. There's such a lot of fear endemic in that late night show. The intimidation of the dressing room is one of the biggest things, because there's a hierarchy there – there's an Oscar Wilde acid wit. People say, 'You were fucking crap the other night!' And you have to come back and say, 'Well I chose to be crap – and anyway, you're a crap human being!' Everyone's throwing insults around all the time and you have to be very fast. People won't talk to you until you hit it. When I killed, Bob Mills [*presenter of Carlton's Friday night post-pub blokefest* In Bed with Me Dinner] said, 'I suppose I can talk to you now.'

JULIAN CLARY

I'd been in a show with Covent Garden Community Theatre called *Winter Drawers On* and I had a spot in it as Gillian Pieface – which is what I called myself then. For about a year Kim Kinnie, who used to run the Earth Exchange, was the only one who used to book me – so I used to do Gillian Pieface once a month, with varying degrees of dreadfulness. I lived in Kidbrooke at the time and the gig was in Highgate, so it was several trains and a tube, and the last train back from Charing Cross was ten-thirty p.m., so I had to make sure I went on early in the evening – not that there was much danger of me going on last. I got changed on the stairs because there was no dressing room. There used to be a pattern – it would be all right for five minutes and then it would disintegrate, and I'd get off quick.

I never thought it would be something I could carry on doing – it was a result of failure at everything else I was trying to do, which was acting. I was too eccentric to be a pliable actor. I'd do an audition and they'd say, 'You flap your hands around too much,' and I'd think, 'Oh well, at least when I do a cabaret act, I can emphasise all these things that I'm supposed to be suppressing.'

I've got a very good friend who, for a couple of years, when it was all very dire, would come to every single gig, and often drive me home afterwards. It was the sort of thing which made me accept a booking rather than saying, 'I can't be bothered' – not that people were ringing me up for bookings. I had to ring round. It's very hard to sell yourself at the best of times, but when they said, 'So what sort of act is it?' And I said, 'I wear make-up and I've got a dog', it'd be very tricky. If I did a bad gig but I felt it wasn't my fault, I used to nick something, condiments or cutlery. I nicked a mirror from Jongleurs, which just fitted into my hold-all – I've still got it in my bathroom.

Fanny the Wonderdog started coming on with me at the Earth Exchange, because there was nowhere else for her to go. I thought she was just going to sit on a stool – but she got laughs, so I put her at the front. She was fine in a little room above a pub and for a couple of years she really enjoyed it. I could tell. She couldn't wait to come out, but then she got this look in her eye – she knew her routine, and she knew when she'd had her last choc drop, and then she couldn't wait to get off.

I was on tour, and I got out of a taxi with her in Newcastle – and she ran off into the road and got knocked over by a car. I thought she was dead. She wasn't, but she was very shaken and then she had to go onstage about an hour later – so that was a trauma for her. She somehow associated the two things together in her mind, and got very frightened. She started to shake as soon as I got the show bag out. After a gig, when we'd get back into the car, she used to think we were going home, but we weren't – we were going on to the next town. I don't think you can do the routine of touring with a dog.

Sometimes she used to leave prematurely. If someone at the back was eating crisps, she'd be off. We used to have trouble getting into venues. Night after night, doing a college tour, you'd get some jobsworth man saying, 'You can't bring that dog in here.' 'But she's in the cabaret!' 'Sorry.' 'But her name is on the poster!' She upset Paul Merton one night. He was on before me, and worked really hard and went down quite well. Then Fanny came on, and got a tumultuous welcome. He was outraged that she should get all that applause for doing absolutely nothing. For about a year, people were saying, 'Where's the dog?' But then I got Russell, who served the same purpose.

DOMINIC HOLLAND

Phoning round for gigs is hell. It wasn't until six months ago that I started to get some sort of interest – even though I'd nailed some of the gigs. To get promoters to pay me any attention was unbelievably hard. I didn't know anyone – I was a complete nonentity. Nobody had heard of me. I spent six months getting an open spot. At the Cartoon it took me eight months to get five minutes. I phoned the Meccano in January and I got a five-minute open spot – in June. I felt so indignant. I thought, 'I can do this!' I'd look at bills and see people who were stiffing. I knew they were going under, and they were getting gigs. I was determined to get on to the circuit, but there are so many comics, and to get through you have to be really resilient. I'd call the venues every day. They'd all be in – they just screen their calls. Getting gigs was a pain in the arse. The hardest part was getting the open spots in the book, and getting yourself mentally ready to go on and do the gig. It didn't matter how well the open spot had gone – it was all about getting the promoter on the phone the next week to give you something else.

I was very nervous. I used to spend a long time getting ready – I used to spend all day rehearsing material, rehearsing links. I used to write out little lists of where each routine followed on from. I'd be pretty much preoccupied with the show all day. I'd get to the show excessively early, and pace up and down – looking at the room. People couldn't believe how far I used to walk. I used to walk about three miles in a circle before a gig – I was like a coiled up elastic band ready to explode.

STEVE PUNT

The first club we went to was Jongleurs. In those days, you could ring up the day before. Tony Slattery and Richard Vranch were doing a main spot in the second half. At the time, that seemed like the height of achievement. We thought, 'Wouldn't it be fantastic to do twenty minutes?' We went on and did some monologues that we knew

backwards – very fast, with no gaps. In the audience was Malcolm
Hardee, who said, 'Come and do the Tunnel.' So a week later we did
an open spot at the Tunnel Club by the Blackwall Tunnel.

We made absolutely sure that there were some big jokes right at
the front. We had two or three years' worth of jokes to chose from,
so we were always at an advantage. We got an encore, and that was
the night that gave us the confidence to know that we could do it – we
knew we were on to a winner after that.

BRUCE MORTON

In March 1988, I went to audition for Karen Koren at the Gilded
Balloon with about a dozen people: jugglers, singers and comics. I
rehearsed and rehearsed and rehearsed until I'd got everything
parrot fashion. It went quite well and she offered me two gigs that
week. The first was on a Thursday night at the Gilded Balloon. That
went great, and I was so pleased.

The second gig was on the following night in a shopping mall in
Glasgow, which is now derelict. It was late at night, it was very
cavernous and cold – not really a good place to have a comedy gig.
But, fired up by the success of the previous evening, I went on and
did a bit – and it was terrible. I wasn't getting heckled – it just wasn't
the right room to do it in at all. Jokes were flying off into the middle
distance and nothing was working. Those were my first two
experiences, and I always thought it was useful to get the two of
them so close together, so as to get a perspective on the highs and
lows. From really early on, I knew how good it could be and how bad
it can be, and I wasn't under any illusions.

I've seen a few people who've gone out on a first gig and burned
the place down. And then they find it didn't happen the next night,
or the next night, or the night after that. They keep chasing it,
because they got that real big kick off the first one. It's a very
addictive buzz, and that's why people keep going back.

STEVE COOGAN

The very first time I went onstage was in 1986. It was at a Law Society
revue at Manchester Polytechnic. They'd done all these sketches
onstage, which were terrible. The hall was packed – there were

seven or eight hundred people in there, and it was going down really badly. They were asking anyone to go up, and some people went up and did some really crummy stuff and the audience were booing them. And then a friend of mine said, 'Why don't you go onstage and do some impressions?' And he literally pushed me on to the stage, and got someone to introduce me.

I did some really crude impressions with no structure: characters from *Rainbow*, and a few politicians. I wasn't saying anything at all, but they were quite accurate and that made up for any laxity in the material. The audience howled – there was all this applause and laughter. I can remember the amazing buzz I got from it. I came off thinking what an amazing feeling it was to have all these people listening to what I was saying. After a while, they all quietened down, and wanted to know what I was going to say. It was a tremendous high – I came offstage thinking, 'I want to do that again! I want more of that!'

DAVID BADDIEL

The first gig I ever did on the circuit was at the Comedy Store. I'd just come down from Cambridge. I went on at three o'clock in the morning. I was the fourth open spot. There was a fight just before I went on. Everyone in the room was either asleep or incredibly drunk, and I left the stage after about three minutes – having elicited almost no response whatsoever. Not a boo. Not a laugh. Nothing. It was like playing to dead people. That was terrible. I didn't do stand-up again for about a year.

CHARLIE CHUCK

The first gig I ever did was in a public house in Leeds. I was fifteen. That was in the early sixties. Now they were what I call rough. They were throwing glasses and stuff like that. I was paid three pounds a night. My job, working in upholstery, was nine pounds for the week so I doubled my money. That's when the Liverpool sound was hot. Rock bands were the thing then. My first solo comedy spot didn't work out. I thought I was a funny man, and I realised you need experience under your belt. You can't just go out there. It's all to do with timing, and you acquire that as you play year after year. I'd just come back from Germany, drumming, and I got a job as a bus driver. I was acting about all the time. I'm naturally half of Chuck. And so I thought, 'I must have got it wrong. I'll go for this again.' And that's what I did, and ever since then, it got better and better.

MARK LAMARR

I was very drunk – I'd had five or six pints. I thought, 'I can cope with this – I can do this drunk.' I don't think I was confident enough to do it, without having a drink to take the edge off it. It's a common complaint, early on in your career. You have a drink to take the edge off, and then you think, 'Right – I'm ready now.' But then you've got another five minutes so you think, 'I'll buy another pint, and have a sip of that,' and you knock that one back really quick, and then you've got another five minutes and you end up really drunk. There are a couple of occasions when I've been completely legless.

In the beginning, even if one gig in twenty is good, that keeps you going through the next ten deaths. I'm sure a lot of people give up because they don't get that one lucky night. There's hardly anyone who isn't absolute shit when they start off, and there are a lot of comics who've been going for years, who must have had some lucky gigs early on – and never had a good gig since. It's a common conversation between comedians: 'Why does that person continue?' But we all know why – we all know it's that thrill you get from doing a great gig.

JOHN HEGLEY

The first time I went down to the Comedy Store I went down all right. They thought I was a laugh. But for the following four weeks, I got gonged off – I didn't have the armoury. I didn't know how to deal with it – it's something that you learn. Now you can go to comedy classes and learn a bit about it before you go up there. But then there was a sudden change – I started doing a poem called 'Sport'. I played a school teacher, and I stayed in the persona, and I found that worked. It gave me complete control.

The Comedy Store and the Earth Exchange were two polar opposites. At the Earth Exchange, they were all lovely vegetarians, and at the Store, they were all pissed-up 'give me the meat and throw away the bread roll' people. So you'd go from the Comedy Store on Saturday night to the Earth Exchange on Sunday, and you'd bring over the Comedy Store attitude to the Earth Exchange. Arthur Smith tells a story about a Dutchman who shouted out, 'Hey, you are really nice!' He said, 'Go fuck yourself!'

When we went down the Comedy Store, it was a laugh. We used to have a good time down there – a really good time. A festival is more than the shows, and this was more than a gig. We used to get down there at midnight, and we'd be there till four o'clock in the morning in the kitchen, smoking joints and getting stoned out of our heads.

RICHARD MORTON

The first gig I did with the Panic Brothers was in a little pub in Fulham, called the King's Head. There were about fifteen people there, tops, including the staff. We were supporting a band. We were paid ten pounds, and at the end of the gig the guy who ran the PA came up and charged us a fiver each for the use of it, so we came out with nothing. The first gig I did as a solo stand-up was at the end of 1989. It was at the Old White Horse in Brixton – a Friday night bearpit with wall to wall heckling, but I got away with it. Musicians are so egotistical and unsupportive. After that, the world of comedy was a joy to me.

LEE EVANS

It was in a pub in Brighton – there was a talent show on down there. When I first started that was the sort of thing I went in for. They said, 'Will you please welcome, all the way from Southend, Lee Evans!' I ran on with a guitar round my neck, and all I remember is this red thing suddenly hitting me in the head. It was a fire extinguisher – I was out cold. An ambulance came, and that was it.

5. The Worst Gigs

'There must be at least two thousand people in London who can lay claim to having done an open spot, but there's only about a hundred who kept at it.' – Jeff Green

It's not the heckles that a comedian fears most – it's the silences. A heckle gives a comic something to get their teeth into – and a chance to turn a gig around. Silence gives a comic nothing – apart from a sickening sensation in the stomach. After the silence come the murmurs that build from a discreet hum into a boozy hubbub.

The worst stand-up death I ever witnessed began and ended without a single interruption – or a single laugh. As the girl began her set, the punters around the tables began to talk amongst themselves. They weren't talking at all loudly. Indeed, it was their sheer decorum which made them so devastating. It's not for nothing that comics describe a bad gig as 'dying'. What this whispering gallery most resembled was a crowd of nosy parkers, eavesdropping on a stranger's funeral. Their prurient comments were muttered in hushed tones – in an ostentatious show of etiquette. When the laughter dies, a comic can do two things – confront the problem or plough on through it. A good comic selects one option. This girl attempted both. At first she tried to ignore the growing tide, and then she acknowledged it with the worst possible retort. 'Do you want me to carry on?' she asked, in a tone that pleaded for dismissal. Silence. 'If you want to,' sighed one apathetic punter. Nobody else spoke. Her rash enquiry had robbed her of her only hope – an early exit. She was stranded. With misery in her eyes, she continued her muted set, and as soon as she did the murmurs began all over again.

A more dramatic disaster was Simon Fanshawe's swift and silent death at the reopening of the Comedy Store in its new premises off Coventry Street. The Store is famous for its ferocious punters, but this was a gala night to celebrate the opening (at a cost of half a million pounds) of the West End's flagship comedy club. Comedians were performing free at what was supposed to be an informal

christening, which is what made his fall from grace all the more
spectacular. Once a Store regular, he hadn't played it for five years,
and it showed. He fired out his opening one-liners, the ones that
comics call their 'bankers' – and back came nothing. Nothing at all.
Fanshawe blinked, stuttered, and ploughed on. Still nothing – then
worse than nothing. Suddenly the room grew colder – I couldn't bear
to look. Discomfort filled the Store like stale smoke. I felt sick – but
not half as sick as he did. Before he stumbled off, to the sound of his
own feet, he said something that was still ringing round the room
after all the punchlines had long since died away. 'It's very strange
being up here,' he said, with sudden, agonising honesty. 'It feels
very strange indeed.' Less than half an hour later, his canary yellow
jacket hidden beneath a sombre duffel-coat (hip stage clothes
suddenly look ridiculous after a comic has died a death), he slipped
out of the back door and off into the winter night.

Hardly anybody saw him go, and the few that did (including me)
looked the other way. I probably could have become his friend for
life merely by meeting his eye, but some primeval instinct for self-
preservation prevented me. After he'd gone I wondered, as the
laughter washed around me, what he'd do when he got home that
night, and how he'd feel the next time he went onstage, if there was a
next time. And it reminded me that however much applause and
laughter comedians are granted, they pay for every last titter – with
compound interest. Stand-up is a loan shark. As they say in B-
movies: 'You wanna play? You gotta pay.' Fanshawe played,
Fanshawe paid. And why did he fail, after so many years of fat
success? For the simplest reason of them all – and the only one that
requires no explanation. The punters decided they didn't like him
any more. And so it was time for him to go.

ROB NEWMAN

Everything goes black – everything's ashes, everything's meaningless. You're a disgrace, and you can't look at anyone who was there
in the eye again, and you hope you'll never run into those people
again, and how are you going to put the world back together again?
You're stopped – finished. You feel terrible. If it's total death, it's
much too total to learn from. I used to try too hard onstage – I
learned to stop trying.

I was once on a train with Alan Parker on the way back from a gig, and Frank Carson was on the train. He was in a locked compartment, but I told the guard we were comedians, and asked him if we could go in there as well. It was before I was well known – but for some reason he let us in. I was talking to Frank Carson and we had our pictures taken, and I was giving him lots of praise because I didn't want him to think I thought he was an old shit comic – and because a lot of those people look desperately unhappy. And he was saying, 'I've never died – I've never died!' 'You must have!' 'Never! Once they weren't listening, so I walked off – but I've never died!'

JEFF GREEN

My worst gig was at the Bearcat comedy club, on a Monday night in Twickenham. It was a nightmare – it was a feeling I'd never ever had before. I'd only done three gigs, I had a very bright green shirt on and so there was no chance of my escaping quietly from the gig. I thought, 'Black from now on.' The lights were so bright – I'd never been on a stage where I couldn't see the audience. I did my first line and it didn't get anything – and then I did another line, and that didn't get anything. And then I slowly started to work out that they weren't going to laugh. I also felt this wave of hatred – there was no heckling – and then people started to talk amongst themselves. The colour drained from my face and I dried up. I thought, 'Oh my God.' Then, slowly but surely one 'Get off' And then another 'Get off!' And then a slow hand clap. I started to go to pieces completely – I'd only been onstage eleven minutes in my life. And then this fear. I'd never ever felt it before. It was clammy and horrible. I came off and I was so depressed. No one wanted to talk to me in the dressing room. When you do a bad gig, people don't want to associate with you in case it's catching. No one will talk to you, and it's the one time you need someone to talk to you. It's as if you're shit, and until you prove yourself as not no one wants to know you. It's very cliquey. You very rarely get a crap comic who's got lots of friends within the circuit.

MARK THOMAS

The lowest point was probably at the Bearcat. That did a lot to destroy any boisterousness that I had. I went home and sulked really badly for quite a while. It's like a rejection of everything that you've done before – it's like having your confidence chucked back at you. I remember dying one night down at the Comedy Store. Paul Merton took me to one side and said, 'Your worst gig is yet to come.' And I thought, 'Yeah! Wise up! Dying is part of your life now.' Everyone dies. There are nights when you will die through no fault of your own. If it's your own fault, that's the one that hurts the most.

Me and James Macabre were booked to do the Oxford Polytechnic graduation ball. We'd both been going for about eighteen months and the gig was full of security guards, and people in dinner jackets. We both had our backs up just by being there. We were thinking, 'Why are we booked here? What's going on?' They'd all just finished their meal with the Chancellor and Vice Chancellor, and then James went on. He was introduced by a guy in jodhpurs. He did about two minutes, and then a group of lads who were completely pissed, and spraying champagne everywhere, got up, ran onstage, and carried him off. As he was carried off, he came past me, and he said, 'It's over to you now, Thomo!'

I jumped onstage and did about five minutes, and then the head of the students union appeared at my elbow and whispered, 'Could I have a word please?' I said, 'No! Say it on mike! Whatever you've got to say, say it here!' He put his hands over the mike, but I said, 'No! Say it here!' So he said, 'I really think you're most unsuitable! We've had complaints, and I really think it's time that you go. Just go! We'll pay you. There'll be no fuss.' It was really odd. I walked offstage with one of the security geezers, and one of the women doing the catering shouted, 'Get back out there!' It was horrible. We got the night train and you had to change. We got back about four o'clock in the morning.

I got booked to do Glasgow Tech. There was me, Ivor Dembina and Gerry Sadowitz. This was when Gerry was at his most provocative. We did Preston Poly and it was a great gig. They gave me a hard time but I did OK, and Gerry was being lauded at this point as the great comic that he actually is. We had to go up to Glasgow the next day, and one of the students said, 'We've got a house that you can stay in.' I said, 'That'd be great!' We got back there and immediately this bloke came up to Gerry and said, 'I really like your stuff. By the way, I've got some great pornography that you might want to look at.' Gerry said, 'Fucking great!' And started flicking through this pornography. I was feeling a bit out on a limb, and so I said, 'Look, where am I sleeping?' He said, 'You're sleeping in Wanker Rodger's room.' I thought, 'Oh no!' I went in there, and it was horrible. He said, 'You're sleeping in that bed.' He shut the door, and I pulled back the duvet cover and there were these horrible bright red sheets which were completely covered in stains. They hadn't been washed for ages. I slept fully clothed.

I got up the next day, and Gerry and I went to Glasgow. Gerry said, 'We can either go and get laid in this place I know, or we can go to the races.' I said, 'Let's go to the races,' so we went to the races, and Gerry lost loads of money – and then we went and did this gig. I was supposed to be onstage at nine o'clock, but they said, 'The person who's running it has gone away on holiday and we've had to put everything back.' I said, 'Well, I can't miss the sleeper train.' They said, 'You'll have to. We'll put you in a hotel.' So they put me on at midnight, after these two bands who were looking for record contracts and had all their mates there.

I'd only been onstage for a couple of seconds before 'Fuck off you English bastard' came up. I went mad. I said, 'You fucking idiots! D'you think this is a regional issue? D'you think you've got a monopoly on poverty and hardship? D'you think everyone in London is walking around wearing bowler hats with share issues under their arms? D'you think that you are the only people in the world who are poor? This isn't a regional issue! This is a class issue!' Of course, it all went up. Someone tried to clamber over the railings, and get onstage to have a go. Luckily, Security stopped him. Cans started coming up onstage, so I said, 'All right, all right. I'm not doing any material, because it's not working. I'll tell you a joke about anything you like.' And this bloke shouted out, 'Tell us a period joke!' I was really pleased. I said, 'All right – two Elizabethans walk into a pub . . .' It went straight over them. I thought, 'I've lost it!' So I said, 'Oh well, fuck you!' And I walked off. I'd done about five minutes.

As I came offstage, I heard a voice say, 'Can we have Security around Mark?' and about six blokes in yellow T-shirts engulfed me, walked me through the dance floor, into a lift, out of the lift, through the bar, behind the bar, down into the cellar, out by the cellar door, where there was a taxi waiting for me. They put me in the taxi and said, 'Take him to the hotel!' And the taxi drove off.

Everyone should have a good time, and if someone dies it doesn't help you. There was only one occasion when it has. John Lenehan [*American magician cum comedian*] was compering, and a comedian called Tony went onstage. He'd just got back from America and he was a little bit out of it. He was doing OK but then after two or three minutes, he hit some hecklers – and he blew it. He started saying, 'I'm not going to come back at you – I'm not going to say anything funny. Fuck it, why should I? You don't respect me, why should I respect you? I'm going to stay up here for my twenty minutes – and not be funny.' Everyone in the audience was going, 'What?' And older comics in the dressing room were saying, 'What the fuck is going on?' Tony was saying, 'I don't need you!' And he brought his wallet out, and started showing them his money. It was horrible. He died for fifteen minutes, the most horrific late night Comedy Store death that you can imagine. It was fucking brutal, and he did it himself. He dug himself in so deep that no matter what he could have pulled out of the bag, it wouldn't have been enough. He really did himself over, and I was on after him.

I jumped onstage, told the first gag and got a huge roar just because it was a gag that worked. As long as I had half a dozen good gags, I would have stormed that gig, just because I wasn't the person who'd been on before. That was the only time that someone died and it actually helped me. About two weeks later I was back at the Store again, and Tony was there as well. He was saying, 'I've learnt my lesson, it's all right – I know exactly what I'm doing. Sometimes you have to do that to them.' He wouldn't fully accept that he'd fucked up. He walked onstage and said, 'Good evening, everyone. I'd like to start with a bit of magic . . .' And someone at the back shouted out, 'Show us your fucking wallet!'

JEREMY HARDY

The first time I really came unstuck wasn't at a comedy gig as such. It was at Islington Town Hall. There'd been a demonstration – about cuts or something, probably – and then there was the entertainment. I was the comic before the disco. I had to use the DJ's mike. Rather than go out there and plough into it, and hope they'd gather round, I went out determined that I'd get them all to be quiet and listen before I started, which was never ever going to happen – so I never started, and after five minutes I went off. The worst thing about it was that there were about eight hundred people in this room, and there was no back door – so I had to walk all the way through all of these people in front of whom I'd just been ritually humiliated. Luckily, there was a friend of mine there who was very pretty, and I made her hold my hand and pretend to be my girlfriend as I walked through to salvage some sort of credibility. She was very good at pretending to be my girlfriend – I was very grateful to her. The first time something horrible happens, it's always the worst, and then you toughen up.

HARRY HILL

I did a gig in Norwich on the National Comedy Network [*a revamp of the college comedy circuit*]. When you do a student gig, you realise how old you are. There are all these young faces out there, and they all want to be dancing and drinking. Andre Vincent [*roly-poly comic and sometime street performer*] was compering. He had gastroenteritis, so he was puking up in the dressing room, going back on, doing his stuff, coming off, puking up, and going back on again. I went on and did about ten minutes to complete silence, so I stopped and said, 'Does anyone have any questions at all?' And someone shouted out, 'You're too abstract for us!' So I said, 'Oh, well,' and left.

I did the Greyhound pub in Streatham one Sunday night. That weekend I went home to see my mum in Kent, so I phoned up the guy who runs it, PJ, and said, 'I'll do the gig on the way home, so put me on about ten – and if it's cancelled (and quite often it is, because so few people turn up), that's fine.' When I arrived at the gig, there were twelve people in the audience – three open spots, all of whom had brought three friends. So I put my suit on over the top of my jeans, and I went on and started doing my stuff. PJ was standing there watching, but then he walked out. I said, 'That's brilliant! There's twelve people in the audience and even the compere walks out!' There's a stock gag if someone walks out. You say, 'Before they come back, we'll all hide.' So I said this, and then I said, 'That's what we *will* do.' There's an emergency exit at the back of the pub and I got the audience to all file out of it and shut the door. And then, as I was standing there, doing my act to no one, PJ came back in – so I said, 'Thanks very much – goodnight.'

JO BRAND

I've always found student gigs particularly difficult. A lot of it has got to do with my age. I'm thirty-six now, so it's quite a long time since I was a student – and I never went in for that student wildness. I used to do my own thing with my friends at college, but we never went to comedy or anything like that. It's to do with the contract you have with them. Because they either don't pay to get in or they pay very little, and they're quite young, and are more interested in drinking and getting off with each other, they don't feel they have any obligation to listen or to treat you with any respect.

Being that bit older, a lot of the stuff I do isn't suitable for their level of development. Jeff Green has lots of stuff that's much broader and appeals to students, because it's all about space-hoppers, and the sort of things they can identify with. But when I go in and say, 'The way to a man's heart is through his hanky pocket with a bread knife,' the male students haven't reached the stage when they've got enough of a developed ego to be able to withstand the irony of that joke, and just have a laugh about it. They're also far more right wing than they used to be, and if they're not more right wing then they're completely politically illiterate.

One of my worst gigs was at Loughborough University, which is mainly PE. It's full of these barrel-chested blokes with one neurone floating about in their brains. They were a very apathetic audience – they weren't that interested, even though there were seven or eight hundred of them. Added to that, there was a Geordie bouncer who got pissed and came in to see the gig and absolutely hated me with a vengeance. He was heckling me, but it wasn't in a lighthearted way in any sense. It was really serious, really vicious. He was going, 'You fucking filthy whore!' It was like being heckled by Peter Sutcliffe.

I was absolutely gobsmacked. I got the feeling that if he'd been near me, he would have attacked me. The worst thing about it was there was no support for me from the rest of the audience. It was either 'let him get on with it' or it was 'go on, mate – put her in her place!' I lost it completely, and I lost my temper. I'd had a few drinks, because I knew it was going to be a bad gig, so I was going, 'Come on then, mate – if you think you're hard enough.' He could have downed me with one punch and I knew it. In the end, I said to the rest of the audience, 'Do you want me to stay on or not? Well, fuck the lot of you then!' And I walked off.

As soon as I'd gone off, Mark Lamarr went back on and said, 'Well, that's the end of the show. She's gone. It's all finished now.' Then they all started shouting, 'Tell her to come back! Tell her to come back!' But I was too cross. If you appeal to an audience for support and you don't get it, you're in a very dodgy position. I've only done it on a few occasions, and it's gone horribly wrong.

The other occasion was a lunchtime gig at a poly in North London. People get drunk in a different way at lunchtime than they do in the evening. There was a load of rugby players in there. Also the performance area was below the spectators, so that you were down in a sort of pit, looking up at them. It gave you the weird sense of being in a bear pit. Mark Thomas had been on before me and done OK, although they heckled him all the way through. Then I went on, and these rugby lads started. I was giving back as good as I was getting, and then it all got a bit out of hand. One of them said to me, 'I'm going to ram a table leg up your cunt,' which was rather charming.

I had a pint of beer so I chucked it at him, but unfortunately he ducked and it went over this bloke behind who had a very expensive camera, so then that bloke was shouting, 'You've ruined my camera!' I said, 'Let's just forget the whole thing,' and walked off. I actually cried after that one – that's the only one I've ever cried after. I've had gigs that bad, and haven't cried after them, but I felt humiliated and I felt very cross that Mark Thomas had done all right and I hadn't.

Another time, I was in a pub in Ealing called the Queen Vic. The cabaret club was nice but the pub was really rough. Every time you walked past, a bottle would fly past your ear. It was a Friday night free-for-all down there. At the end of the cabaret one night, two lads walked in from the pub to see what was going on. They'd had a few drinks and they started heckling me. I put this bloke down. I took the piss out of him and made him look stupid in front of his mate and the audience all laughed at him.

When I came off, at the end of the gig, he came up to me and grabbed me by my shirt. I wasn't surprised. Having been a nurse, I could tell I was on dangerous ground with him. I worked in a place for ten years where we saw an awful lot of people with what I would call 'borderline personality disorders'. He was a classic case of someone who was always on the edge of losing their temper and becoming violent.

MARK LAMARR

Me and Jo Brand did a gig together in Loughborough. I went on and it was all right, though it certainly wasn't a particularly good gig. There was a bit of unpleasantness in the audience. But then Jo came on and there was a bloke in the audience who was so evil. He kept going, 'You fat ugly fucking cow! How dare you be on my fucking stage?' That was bad enough in itself, but the rest of the audience should react to that and they didn't – it was so unpleasant. I couldn't be that unpleasant to someone. I don't think there are that many people who've really got that much hate – but when you see it in a comedy club, it seems ten times worse. You think, 'Hold on – this person's come here to cheer you up, you fucking idiot, and you hate them!'

The first time I died was at Jongleurs, and quite rightly. I was surprised I hadn't died before, but when I did, I was astounded. I thought, 'How dare you?' Because by that point, everything had been offered to me and so I thought I must be boy genius. It sounds arrogant, but if everyone tells you you're brilliant, it's the only way you can think. I'd been there five or six times before – and every time I was there, Paul Merton was on. He was always very nice to me, but I didn't know who he was. We'd always have a chat in the dressing room – but because I always left before the end of the show, I didn't realise he was one of the acts. I thought, 'That bloke who works at Jongleurs is really nice – whenever I go in the dressing room, he'll have a chat with me, and he's obviously watched a few acts, because he knows a bit about comedy!' The night I died, I went on and got nothing but afterwards Paul said it was stunning to see somebody die who looked at the audience with complete contempt. He said he'd never seen it before. It wasn't like, 'I'm so sorry this is crap – I'd better be going.' It was, 'How fucking dare you not laugh at this?

This is genius! Don't try and sit there, and tell me this isn't funny. I *know* this is funny.'

RICHARD MORTON

Jongleurs is a hard club. It was the night that Chris Eubank half killed Michael Watson. There was a macho, heavy crowd in that night – tables full of what seemed like coachloads of football supporters. Somebody was going to go that night. Somebody was going to get it, and it was me. I'd never ever died in a London club. My act had always been bullet-proof. I've got the songs, I've got every heckle put-down under the sun, I've got the cheeky charm to get away with anything – usually. That night, I walked onstage and before I opened my mouth I knew I'd gone. They hated me – absolutely hated me. All the jokes I did, they just glared at me. There was one joke which had to get a laugh – I knew it was too good not to get a laugh, and they muffled their laughter. I had to do twelve minutes to get paid, and so I stayed out there. It was like riding a bucking bronco at a rodeo. I stayed on and I got my hundred pounds, but that was the worst gig I've ever had. It was awful.

I used to do a song about Margaret Thatcher, called 'My Name Is Denis Thatcher, I'm the Bride of Satan'. I did that in Cheltenham Town Hall, a week after she'd been there doing one of her big rallying speeches. It was back in 1990, before Major became leader. The gig was going brilliantly, until I did any politics whatsoever. I touched a nerve. That was it. I walked off to the sound of my own footsteps. It frightened the life out of me – I never realised you could offend that many people in one go. And it was very bland – just an observation, really.

Every comedian knows how hard it is to go out on your own, and take them on night after night – we all understand what a shit job it can be. I hope I've always been nice to the comics who've been on and died horribly before me, and made them feel better about it, because it can happen to anybody at any time, but you know that the comedian who goes on afterwards usually does brilliantly by definition. If someone has lost it through their own volition, and alienated an audience and made mistakes, then you know it and they know it. There's nothing you can tell a comedian. They did the wrong thing at the wrong time, they know it, and they'll learn from

...at. Everybody gets a kicking every now and again and you have to take it. It comes with the territory.

DONNA McPHAIL

Most comedy clubs are in pubs, but this one was actually in the bar itself – and it was free to get in. There was a tiny stage in the corner, which was in the short bit of an L-shaped bar. The pub was crowded with people, and then the barman said, 'After this next record, Donna McPhail.' I thought, 'This is fucking ridiculous!' I was standing in the corner of a pub, with the majority of them completing ignoring me, because they couldn't see me – and a few blokes standing around with their beer. I thought, 'I could just turn around and go away now, and never even say I was here,' but you can't, because you're letting down the promoter. But then you think, 'Well, they should have bloody told me this was going to be a nightmare!' Promoters set you up. They say, 'It's a lovely gig!' And then you get there, and then you think, 'I'm going to fucking kill them, when I get hold of them!'

You know that everybody knows you've died, and they're all creeping away from you in case it's catching. You say things like, 'That was bloody awful!' And they say, 'Oh, no!' And you think, 'Get real!' People who say, 'That was shit, wasn't it?' are far preferable. At the Comedy Store somebody will die at the late show and you just hope to hell it's not you. So if someone dies before you, you feel quite relieved – because they're the one, they're the sacrifice, and that probably means you're going to be all right. And unless you hold them in very high esteem, you think, 'I've got to do better than that.'

I love following someone who's crap, like an open spot, unless it's a female open spot – which is a very bad idea, because if she's crap and she dies, the whole of womankind is therefore unfunny. When the compere says, 'And now another woman . . .' you can hear people going, 'Oh God . . .' I've come on and said, 'Look, just because I'm a woman, that doesn't mean I'm shit, all right? Let's get that clear.' Otherwise, you'll die – because they'll tar you with the same brush. It's a very harsh thing to say, because it is referring to the fact that the woman who was on before was crap – but if you don't say it, you're going to struggle against completely closed minds. There are different psychological tricks for getting through to an audience.

If someone is crap on a regular basis, and carries on doing it, then they've got a thick enough skin to survive it, and it's up to them. If you've got a thin skin like me, you either get better quickly or you give up, because otherwise you'll be suicidal. Some people have got rhino skins, and even if you said to them, 'You're crap!' they'd go home thinking, 'She's jealous, because I go down better than her every night!' Either they don't hear the heckles, or they think they're getting more laughter. They have a different hearing system.

ARTHUR SMITH

Some bloke came into the Comedy Store and did a load of terrible impressions of people who were all dead: James Cagney, Sammy Davis Junior . . . I said to him afterwards, 'You really ought to do something more modern, maybe. For example, try to do someone who's still alive.' Then I happened to see him at the Earth Exchange on the Monday. He turned up and started doing impressions of all the comics on the circuit. He did John Hegley and Arnold Brown and stole all their material. I said to him, 'Listen, mate, just give up – you're hopeless!' Because the impressions weren't even that good anyway – you could see that he was a man whose desire clearly outstripped his ability.

JOHN HEGLEY

The last bad show I did was a benefit at the Wimbledon Theatre. Me and Nigel went on at the end, and we were crap. I was trying to get the audience to sing along – normally they join in quite happily. I said, 'This is the chorus! Join in!' But I couldn't hear them, so I said to Nigel, 'Take the guitar down, Nigel! I can't hear them doing it!' He said, 'It's normal level!' I said, 'Take it down!' So he took it down – and they weren't doing it! We were on last, after Lee Evans, who'd done absolutely brilliantly. I suppose I was a bit complacent, expecting people would just join in, thinking that we were great. For the curtain call, we thought everybody was going to come on singing one of the songs we do but we hadn't rehearsed it with them. It was a fucking shambles, and I was responsible for it. Nobody knew what they were doing but everybody had come back on, and they all knew it was a shambles – to fail in front of your peers is always humiliating.

Benefits can be so badly organised. Sometimes you don't know what you're letting yourself in for, so nowadays I ask a few questions – to see if it's going to be well organised. I once did a benefit gig for Ivor Dembina. He'd been asked to get a few people together, but he didn't know much about it either. When we got there, he said, 'It's not very well organised. You can have either sound or lights – they've only got one plug.' I chose lights.

I did a gig in a club in Soho, which was in some sort of strip joint. There was something about the way the people there were treating you. You were just fluff for their amusement. You were just a product. It's all to do with the context. I stopped performing at Jongleurs because I felt you were on par with the bar, really – part of a night out package. That's soul destroying. You become an alienated worker. I'm doing this because I don't want a proper job. I think it's worth more than that. I've done a few parties – they're basically pissed out of their heads. It was all right, though. I was young – sleeping on the floor afterwards. All for thirty quid. I was living on the Fulham Road. People would phone up and say, 'Will you do our party?' You'd go down there and have some beer. They were a bit over the top. It was a bit like Jongleurs, basically.

JULIAN CLARY

In a gay club in a Bristol disco, someone threw a full beer can. It hit Fanny the Wonderdog and she yelped, and about four people jumped on this bloke. I was furious, and so was everyone else, and the gig disintegrated. I got very cross and lost my temper, which has only happened three times.

The last time was at the State Theatre, in Sydney, Australia. Two gay boys kept changing their seats, which was slightly irritating. Then they started making high-pitched noises, over and over again. I made a joke about it and then I decided to ignore it, but in the end it was all I could hear. I said, 'Either you stop or I do.'

In Adelaide, there's a lot of aggression in the air, in the way the men walk down the street – I noticed it driving from the airport to the hotel. It's a very isolated city, so people are a bit stir crazy, and they can't escape very easily. Air travel is very expensive in Australia, so if you haven't got any money, you're pretty much stuck there – and it gets very hot. I was playing a late show on a Friday night. The interval seemed to go on and on, and then someone said, 'There's been a bit of trouble out there.' During the interval two big muscle-men types (who were English, actually) had picked on an obviously effeminate gay man – they'd punched him to the ground, and were kicking him. A woman of about fifty-five tried to stop them, and they punched her. Her whole eye was closed up. Then they carried on kicking this guy, who was also quite badly hurt, and then they came back in to watch the second half.

DAVID BADDIEL

I've been booed off twice, but only once after I was well established. I died terribly at the Comedy Store. My only excuse is that I hadn't slept the night before, and I went on at a time when the audience were completely gone. I remember people shouting and screaming, and then hearing through the general roar of abuse, somebody shout, 'The walls are closing in!' And it was true. I remember thinking, 'Is that a heckle or is it God commenting on the event?' And that was when I decided to leave. It was a late night show on Friday, and I was doing an entire weekend – but I came back the next night, and did one of the best nights I've ever done. When you've been booed off, the next gig you do you're really wired for it, and it can be a really great gig.

It's brilliant to go on next after someone dies. When I got booed off at the Store, Jack Dee went on next and absolutely stormed it. I was really friendly with Jack then and really pissed off with him for doing that. But I've done that as well. I've gone on after comics who have completely died, and thought, 'This is going to be an absolute stormer!' And it practically always is. Most audience's bloodlust is satiated by one comic dying – except at the Tunnel.

DOMINIC HOLLAND

I did a gig for Vic Reeves' club, which was called Rub-a-Dub. I was only about three months into it but I already had five minutes of stuff which worked. I went down to do this gig in New Cross. Vic Reeves was there and Sean Hughes. I was on after a band, and Tommy Cockles was compering. They were really offhand with me beforehand. They were saying, 'You'll die on your arse, mate. You won't last.' When you're an open spot, you're looking for a bit of warmth – a bit of encouragement. Tommy Cockles had a bit of a following there. He'd say anything and everyone would say, 'Yeah!' I went on with my observational stuff, and lasted about three minutes. I didn't get booed off, but it was obvious I should leave. My girlfriend was there, and she said, 'That was the most embarrassing thing I've ever seen.' That was my first real death.

I've had some shit gigs. Compering is tough. You can have some hellish compering gigs. You go on at the beginning, you don't get them and then you have to go back on four times after that. You can feel them thinking, 'Oh, fucking hell – the compere's back.' Doing a set's easier, because you're set up by someone – so when you go on, you're listened to. When you're a compere, you've got to make them listen, and when they are listening you've got to get off! It's very hard work. People don't appreciate how hard it is until they've done it, and the audience don't appreciate it either.

I took over from Eddie Izzard compering at his local venue, Screaming Blue Murder in Merton. It was like his own club – they were there to see him. I was ten months into stand-up, just doing open spots plus a few gigs here and there. Pete Harris [*Holland's manager, who also handles John Hegley*] said, 'I want you to be resident compere.' I was obviously so green. I must have looked so nervous. The audience could feel it. It didn't work, and there was nothing I could do. I didn't have anything else to go into. I just had to keep going with it. That would be my hell – resident compering.

EDDIE IZZARD

I've developed a thick skin to the humiliation of being crap. I started at the bottom on the street and that was really humiliating. I lost all my confidence. At drama school they break you down, and build you back up. I accidentally did that to myself, in 1985, on the street. I thought I could get it in a couple of weeks – that was my arrogant attitude. It took a year, and it really broke me.

I did about a year's worth of completely humiliating shows. That's what made me – staying in and coming out of the other end. You had to hold your audience. My partner and I used to do this trick of escaping from a woolly jumper. We'd start with it and hope it would hold their attention for the other stuff. It was stupid, but sometimes we did it really well. But then we found that if we did the woolly jumper escape too well, it'd create a climax . . . and then they'd fuck off because your build-up was so big. Half the audience would leave.

I started off writing sketches and verbally based stuff, but it didn't work on the street, so I ended up with all these bizarre knockabout bullshit tricks. I used to do the Amazing Disappearing Cornflakes trick. I'd get a bowl, and pour some cornflakes in to it, add some milk, and then say, 'I'm going to cover them with this magic cloth and make them disappear!' Then my partner would put the cloth over my head, and I'd start eating them. It was really messy – it was a really crap trick. Then he'd say, 'And now they're gone!' and pull the cloth away and I'd be left with a mouthful of cornflakes. Sometimes it worked really well, but often it was a nightmare. At the end of each trick we'd say, 'Go wild!' to encourage them to applaud.

All you've got to do is get the hang of doing the verbal stuff, and after that they're sitting there watching. You can be a lot more subtle. You have to be so aggressive and blatant out on the street. Indoors, you have ninety per cent control of the space – the heat of the room, how tired they are, hecklers, those things can throw you. In a theatre, you get up to ninety-five per cent – very little can go wrong. On the street, you're down to about sixty per cent – weather, cats, dogs, drunks, cars, dustbin lorries. Essentially, rain is the big fuck-up, and to a certain extent wind. If it was really cold, we still did shows – Christmas in the snow. You break your balls out there. After that, gigging indoors is like falling off a log.

VIC REEVES

We made an error on our last tour of having a huge white backdrop, which meant the lights splashed on to it and right back on to the audience so you could see everyone. People like to be in the dark to laugh. Doncaster was definitely the worst. It was a big, brightly lit basketball hall with a makeshift stage. The audience were all sat on horrible plastic chairs. It was devoid of any human touch. It was like a headmaster's speech.

BOB MORTIMER

There are some people who've basically been doing the same act word for word, week after week, for years. In the last four years, we've done fifty shows, but these people have probably done over a thousand, saying the same things that they've said for seven years. It's soul-destroying churning out the same thing. It's very sad to be getting paid forty pounds to go down to Up the Creek to say the same thing that the same audience has heard for three years running, to drag it off to Middlesbrough and Blackburn. There's no glamour in there.

JACK DEE

The actual process you go through when you die a death is horrible. Your mouth dries up. You lose all confidence in what you're doing and what you're saying. And then the audience pick that up – and so they realise that by now, even you don't think you're funny. And they're right – you don't – and they know it, so really you're just wasting everybody's time.

If you're dying a death, unless you really know you're going to get back up there and pull it together again, the best thing you can do is just get offstage. I've clawed my way back and stormed it in the end, but I still come off thinking, 'Was it really worth it – other than for the actual exercise of proving to myself that I can do it when I'm really up against it?'

My style is very much 'take it or leave it'. If something isn't working I feel frustrated. My way of dealing with that is to start ramming it home harder. Give it more throttle – not less. Frustration makes me turn in on myself. I begin to corpse. I start enjoying it on a private level, which is unprofessional – and then I start doing stuff which I know they'll hate.

I always feel for anyone who's died on their arse, even if I don't like them – or their act. I can't enjoy someone else's failure. When a person's died really badly, it's an appalling thing to follow.

Conversely, a very lively act can suck all the energy out of an audience, and exhaust them before you get on.

STEWART LEE

If a gig is going badly, I tend to try and make it as bad as I can, by being more and more obtuse and difficult. Ironically, that can often turn it around – which is really weird. I get further and further into the persona, and do all the most difficult material I've got. Maybe I do care, but I want it to look like it's 'take it or leave it'. I don't want them to think that I'm someone who's trying to please them. That's bigger than comedy. If you're in love with someone, you don't want them to be someone who has to ring you up every five minutes. You want them to have a bit of self-respect.

JENNY ECLAIR

At the Tunnel Club I've seen Harry Enfield throw up before he went onstage because he was so nervous. You used to walk onstage and your feet would be grinding over broken glass and the carpet was sticky with blood. It was a vicious place. They'd give you fifteen seconds and then they'd start booing you offstage – not heckling, the old-fashioned 'Boo! Get off!' When Malcolm Hardee tried to stop it, they started whistling and humming people off. There's nothing worse. I found it funny and I laughed and said, 'I don't care, because I'm irritating you by being here. In fact, I'm going to do three hours.' Sometimes I remembered my brownie guide law and smiled through it, which was equally irritating.

I remember doing a gig in Derry on Saint Patrick's Day. It was very bad news. I was actually issued with a death threat after that. At first I laughed at it, but then it made me quite upset. This guy came up to me afterwards and said, 'If you ever come back to Derry again, you'll go home in a box.' They found me blasphemous. It was a big family do, with kids running round – it was like a wedding in a social club. They hated me. At one point, I started to sing, and I don't know why because I can't. The reaction was absolute horror, but I was having a ball.

Where it really went wrong was when I mentioned that I was an unmarried mother, despite the fact that I live with my boyfriend. I said, 'The only point in getting married is to make your best friend look completely shit as a bridesmaid.' They were hissing because I referred to my child as a bastard. At the time, I thought it was very funny, but once I came offstage and the euphoria of being hated so much by so many people wore off – because you can get a bit of a kick out of that – and the reality set in, I felt very sorry for myself. I had a seven-hour coach journey down to Galway the next day and I was utterly miserable to be stuck in Ireland.

Sometimes I do feel sorry for myself. I'm stuck in some grotty bed and breakfast somewhere, and I'm having to pee in the sink because I'm too frightened to go down the corridor, and there's some pissed Glaswegian hammering on your door at three o'clock in the morning. I've been mugged twice going home after gigs, when I used to use public transport – once in Clapham and once down Camberwell New Road. It's a practical consideration that people don't take into account. You're a woman, you're working at night, and if you don't drive, it's actually quite a hazardous occupation.

HUGH DENNIS

The worst misjudgement of an audience that I've ever seen was a double-act called The Two Sloanes at the Tunnel Club. I thought we were struggling, because we were very obvious middle-class suburban boys, but they were awful. They got about thirty seconds into their set, and then one of them got hit by a can of styling mousse, thrown from the audience, and that was it – they're probably both very successful straight actors now. You used to be able to get your Equity card if you'd done eight paying gigs as a 'circus and variety artist', which is what both Steve and I are classified as. We had to go on straight afterwards, which was very scary.

We had a bit of trouble at the Dominion, because we had twenty completely pissed Spurs fans in, who hadn't really come to see us. They'd come for a night out after the Spurs game. They were out of their heads and having their own show up in the balcony – which was a bit difficult, because there was nothing coherent for us to latch on to. You don't quite know what's going on, because you can't see. It's completely dark, but usually that's a great security. We did the Birmingham Symphony Hall, which is vast, and designed for symphony orchestras. You can see everyone in the audience, and it's really disconcerting. You don't want to be able to see anyone at all.

BRUCE MORTON

A comic came up to Glasgow to do a few gigs and he stayed over at our place. He told us that he'd been hummed off at the Tunnel Club. He said, 'I just kept going. I said, "I don't know what's wrong with you people – they liked me in Rotherham last night." Eventually, the crowd got so enraged that the bouncers had to shepherd me offstage and help me out of the gig.' A few weeks later, Tony Allen happened to be up in Glasgow doing a gig. He kipped over at our place too, and I mentioned this. He said, 'I was there. It didn't actually happen quite like that – he was having such a poor gig that the bouncers threw him out.'

FRANK SKINNER

I did an open spot at Jongleurs in my very formative years. I thought I'd do it as a chimpanzee eating a banana. I completely died on my arse, and tried to get out of it by doing some other material. I thought, 'If I eat the banana, I can get on to other things.' I did sixteen minutes – I know it was sixteen, because John Davey [*Jongleurs' manager*] said to me afterwards, 'You did sixteen minutes – you're only supposed to do ten.' I think he was trying to get out of paying me. After two, I'd died – and I did another fourteen as a death rattle, to stomping and booing. I saw all the comedians' heads appear at the back. They'd all come out of the dressing room to watch.

I did an open spot at the Comedy Store very early on. If I'd known what I was doing, and if Malcolm [Bailey] had known more about it, we'd have known not to put me on. I went on at the Store in the days when they'd say, 'That's the end of the show, but now the open spots.' I went on at half two in the morning with another open spot. He went on first and absolutely stormed it – that was his first open spot. It was Lee Evans.

6. The Weird Gigs

'We ended up performing for a very weird vicar at his New Year's Eve party. It was in a church hall in the middle of Leicestershire – I don't know how we got that gig. He was alcoholic, outspokenly right wing, and, in retrospect, obviously homosexual.' – Richard Herring

The common consensus among stand-up comedians is that there are three things which can go wrong with a comedy gig: the act, the audience, or the room itself – and surprisingly, the most common scapegoat is not the audience but the room. Most awful gigs are staged in rooms where comedy should never have been on the menu in the first place, and the comic is nothing so much as an unwelcome distraction from whatever entertainment the punters had in store. Dances and trade conventions are the most common pitfalls and there isn't a first-rate comic alive who hasn't found himself in front of several hundred insurance salesmen anticipating a string of stag night gags, or a dance floor full of disco dollies interrupted in mid-rumba.

Most comics agree that the best option in such circumstances seems to be to do the bare minimum and get the hell out – but a weird gig isn't always a bad one, and some of the strangest locations can bring out the best in an audience, and a comic. Bizarre venues were particularly prevalent in the early eighties when the supply of clubs was far outstripped by demand for comedy. For several years the Comedy Store and the Earth Exchange were the only clubs in London – and beyond the Big Smoke the situation was even bleaker. Eddie Izzard and John Hegley honed their stage skills on the street, while Gerry Sadowitz hijacked the Glasgow pub-rock circuit. He'd find an unfamiliar bar where a band was playing, introduce himself to them as a friend of the landlord, and say he usually did a turn before the band. Then he'd introduce himself to the landlord as a friend of the band, and say he usually did a turn before the band. He was never paid a penny, but he certainly got plenty of stage time.

Outside London (particularly in Manchester, Liverpool and Glasgow) there are sadly still insufficient numbers of comedy clubs to sustain a self-perpetuating circuit and prevent aspiring indigenous wags from migrating to the English capital.

BRUCE MORTON

I was doing a weekend's worth of gigs around the press launch of *Sin* [*Morton's television series for Channel 4*]. I did the King's Head [*Crouch End comedy club*] and had a great time, and then I went to a club in Twickenham which I'd never been to before.

I got in touch with a friend called Susan who I'd known for a couple of years. She's twenty-one, she's from Dumbarton and she now works in the TSB bank down in London. I would say she's a fairly dynamic individual. I phoned her and said, 'I'm in town, I'm going to do this gig in Twickenham. D'you want to meet and go out to the gig together?' She said, 'That's a great idea!' So we met, and went on the train to Twickenham.

It's a very odd club there. It's called the Bearcat. There were six or seven comics, all doing twenty minutes. Harry Hill was the only one who did well. The rest of us had a tough time. I was on last, and it turned out I had the toughest time. I had Susan up at the back, next to Richard Bucknall [*Morton's manager – also represents Sean Hughes, Donna McPhail and Graham Fellows*] and Seamus Cassidy and his partner, so I had four people there, including one who I'd invited specifically, which I always think is bad news. You're really asking for trouble when you specifically invite friends along.

I come out and start rolling into what I'm doing, and I'm getting nothing. I think, 'No! Oh no!' I'm thinking ahead, and I think, 'In four minutes' time, I want to get to some material about waiting for buses. I have a strong suspicion that nobody in this room has ever been on a bus in their life. These people all own cars, possibly two cars, they drink their nice warm beer and they put their striped shirts on with their jerseys round the shoulders, and go down to the river and look at swans and play rugby. This is Penelope Keith territory!'

Three minutes later, it still isn't working, so I start trawling. I pull out all my twenty-four-carat gags. Short stuff, older stuff – stuff that always killed. I throw them in, but they all hit the ground in silence.

A guy up at the back starts in on me. 'Tell us a joke!' That sort of stuff. I think, 'Oh fuck!' I try to deal with it, but I'm feeling very alone, and very unhappy. I try to throw a couple of lines at him, but most comics will tell you that you can only get away with heckle put-downs if you can do them with conviction – and you can only do them with conviction if you know you've got the rest of the room on your side. Then you can throw out the daftest comments, because the room's with you – they want you to put them down. I don't even feel that I have the room with me, so the lines I throw at him don't work. Nothing works.

Then I make the mistake of asking for suggestions. I'm lost. I'm lost! I'm in the fucking tundra somewhere, wandering without clothes or shoes. Eventually, I think, 'Fuck this!' I start gathering myself. I think, 'I've got a TV series coming up. I don't need this shit!' So after six minutes, I say, 'OK, forget it.' And I walk off into the dressing room and put my head in my hands, feeling very humiliated.

About two minutes later, bedlam breaks out in the room proper. I'm not too sure what's going on so I think, 'I'll go out.' Generally I want to slink away and disappear after a gig like that. I don't wait to get paid, I just tunnel my way out of the gig and leave, by steamboat or something. And then I think 'Get a fucking grip! Everybody's up there – Richard, Susan and Seamus. Just go up there!' So I walk out of the dressing room, and as I'm going back up to the back of the room, by the bar, where all my friends are, Susan comes running towards me. And then she runs right past me. There are three young men running towards me. They're chasing her, and one of them is bleeding from below the jaw.

One of them shouts, 'Is that your girlfriend? Is that your girlfriend?' I say, 'No she's not, but she's a friend of mine,' and I start putting two and two together. I know Susan's history, and something of her personality, and subsequently I find out what's happened. He's been up at the back, giving me a hard time. He's killed the comic, the comic's left, almost in tears. Susan gets up out of the seat, walks over to where he and his cronies are standing at the bar. He doesn't know who she is, he has no idea there's a connection. All he knows is that an attractive young Scots lass starts flirting with him.

She says, 'I like your shorts – those are really nice.' He says, 'Oh
yeah?' She says, 'Those are skin tight, aren't they?' He says, 'Well,
maybe.' She says, 'You look like you were probably born into those
shorts.' He says, 'Maybe you want to find out,' and she smacks him.
He goes down, there's blood everywhere, and suddenly they're all
jumping about like a herd of fucking jessies. If it had been in London
proper, if it had been in Glasgow or any other big town, the guy
would have punched her back.

So they come charging after her, looking for retribution of some
sort, but I put myself in front of them and I realise quite quickly that
they're quite heavy, but they're not that heavy. I realise who they
are, I realise what's happened – and I realise that, very quickly, I
have to stop myself from smirking. I must admit I felt good. I confess
it. A friend of mine has just gone and punched out a heckler.
Excellent! I can hire this woman out to other comics! He was an
arsehole, and now his mates are going to slag him for the rest of the
year, because a young woman from Dumbarton punched his face in,
so that's all right.

It wasn't the most intelligent thing to do, and as one of our party
said to her afterwards, 'Now, Susan – you know that violence is no
solution to anything,' and she and Seamus said, simultaneously,
'No, but it is deeply satisfying!'

LEE EVANS

I played a bloke's living room once – he had some friends round for a
soirée. I thought it was going to be a big gig. I came on, they switched
the telly off and pushed the dining table up against the wall. There
were about seven people in there – it was crap. No mike, no nothing.

I used to do benefits just to get started, and I went down to Ipswich
to do one to raise awareness for blood donors. The compere was a
mainstream comedian by the name of Mickey Zaney. He had a very
deep tan. He said, 'I'm just breaking through – I'm making it! I'm
going to hit the big time next year!' I think he just had me there to
take the mickey out of me. He introduced me as 'alternative', I
walked on – and the place was packed full of old ladies. I used to do
this stunt where I walked over to the mike and fell under it. So I fell
under it and shut my eyes, and heard the audience go, 'Oooh!' I
opened my eyes briefly and saw the microphone stand falling

towards me. It hit me on the nose and my nose splashed across my face. I had a white shirt on and blood was pouring down it. At that stage, when you first start, you think, 'Carry on,' so I carried on, covered in blood, as if nothing had happened, while the audience were all saying, 'Somebody help him!' I was streaming blood – I was eating it. Mickey Zaney came back on and said, 'Ladies and gentlemen, what a great act! Very alternative. I've never seen that before, have you?'

I started compering at Newmarket cabaret club. They gave me a job there. I was actually thrown out because I didn't know Gene Pitney. I knew he was famous – but I'd never seen him live, and I'd never heard him sing. These guys backstage gave me a little note, saying he'd done this and that, and that he was over from Las Vegas. So I said, 'All the way from America, Gene Pitney!' He came on and started singing, and I fell to the floor laughing. I couldn't help it – it was so funny. There were all these women screaming. His bouncers said, 'Get rid of the jerk! Get him out of here!' Another time, I was appearing with the Three Degrees at the Pavilion Theatre in Bournemouth. It was a total fluke – I was the cheapest. I got a couple of quid – I was just the bloke who introduced them.

I thought they were all there, but unfortunately, one of them was still in the dressing room, doing her hair. So I said, 'Ladies and gentlemen . . .' And then I saw two of them waving in the wings, whispering, 'She's not ready!' But I was a bit short on material at the time, so I said '. . . the Three Degrees!' And then I said, 'No – only joking!' I thought I'd carry on, but I couldn't. I said, 'I can't carry on! I've got no stuff! The Three Degrees, for God's sake!' The other two said, 'We're not going on!' They were still waiting for the other girl to come on up. The curtain came down, she came up, and then they started rowing with me, saying, 'You introduced us when we weren't all here!' I said, 'I thought you were here! I'm sorry!' The crowd all starting singing, 'Why are we waiting?' And then they started to get up and walk out. They had to give back the money and then they tried to get that money off of me. I was only on two quid to compere it – it was a farce.

I was more or less living in my car. I was booked for conferences and stuff. How I got them, I don't know. There was a magazine called *Showcall*. I advertised in that, and got booked for a conference at a hotel in Rickmansworth. It was New Year's Eve and

I had three gigs to do – all across London. I went to the first gig, got slaughtered, went to the second one, died there. I thought, 'Maybe the third one will be OK.' On the way there, I picked up a hitch-hiker. He was going to Rickmansworth, but as we were approaching the gig he said, 'Can you drop me round the corner?' I said, 'Well I ain't got time now – you'll have to stick around.' We stopped outside this hotel and it was already five to twelve. I still had my jeans on and I was sweating profusely. I ran into the hotel, and through the foyer – which was full of people in bow ties. I still had my piano and guitar in the car – along with this bloke. The compere said, 'You're on! It's nearly twelve! You've got to go on before twelve!' I said, 'I've got to get my piano and guitar!' So I ran back out to the car and said to the hitch-hiker, 'Help me in with me stuff!' We ran in with my piano, and we'd just got it inside the door when the clock struck twelve and the bagpipes started.

HARRY HILL

I did a gig in the Falklands, in a little mountain station. I was only supposed to do twenty-five minutes, but I did about forty-five. They're the ones that people enjoy, where you mess about and don't stick to the lines. They went really crazy for it. I went up there by helicopter. I went with a crew – there was a band, a compere, dancers and a singer. We flew out there in an old Columbia Tristar. After we took off, a man came round in an RAF uniform, and handed out paper cups of orange squash. They issued us with camouflage jackets and trousers – but there weren't enough to go round, so I was standing there in my suit and mac. The weird thing about forces gigs is that those are the sort of people who I would naturally be afraid of. When I walk into a pub, I look a bit odd so people take the piss out of me, and they're the sort of people who do it. They're the opposite to me, so I was worried that I'd have a really hard time, but it went really well. They were coming up to me and saying, 'We've never seen anything like it before!' It was something completely new for them. They didn't know why it was funny – it was very odd.

After a forces gig, you're told to go and socialise with them, which is really hard work, because you haven't really got anything in common. The other thing is a lot of the soldiers don't really want to

talk to you – they want to talk to the dancers. The squaddies are
quite happy to laugh at anything, but the officers all sit there, like,
'The job that you're doing isn't a proper job. We're men, but you're
half a man.' I did a gig for the commandos in Belize. At the do
afterwards, I got shown into this big room. All the officers had their
wives with them, and we all got split up – so there was a dancer
on each table, and the unlucky table got the comedian. They
completely ignored me – it was really rude! Before the gig, the
sergeant-major came on and said, 'Right then! We've got some
entertainment for you, but no trouble, or you'll be in the
guardhouse!'

MARK THOMAS

There was a guy called Tony Green who worked at the Comedy
Store originally, with Tony Allen and Alexei Sayle. He was a
libertarian anarchist. He ran a gig at a pub called the Pearly King and
Queen, in East London. He used to work with the Kipper Brothers,
who were a pair of performance artists.

One guy called Ian – who was out of his tree – once came onstage,
and said, 'I'm now going to do an impersonation of Kirk Douglas.'
And he got a piece of glass and put it in a floorboard – this was in a
dirty old East End pub – and measured out the distance from the
glass and chalked it off. And then he said, 'Ladies and Gentlemen –
Kirk Douglas!' and fell, so that his chin nicked the glass – so there
was a little cut where the dimple would be. He stood up and said,
'Kirk Douglas!' People were horrified. They were saying, 'What the
fuck is going on?'

Him and Harry Kipper did this piece about how bad boxing was.
They were saying that boxing was a brutal, disgusting, bloody sport
and that it was inhumane for society to support it – and so what they
did was they actually beat each other up onstage. The audience were
going, 'God! What's happening?' Then they started hugging each
other, and saying, 'It's all right! It's just a game!' And then, 'Whack!'
You'd hear a crunch and see bits of blood coming out. They actually
hurt each other. I think the gig got shut down when the landlord of
the pub walked outside and there was a fishing rod hanging out of the
third-storey window into the street with a steel cable and a chair
attached to it which was on fire.

The Kipper Brothers used to do a sketch called Port Stanley Amateur Dramatic Society. They'd dress up as Argentinian soldiers, and pelt the audience with bully beef sandwiches. There used to be a gig called the Earth Exchange, which was a vegetarian restaurant. They'd give you your food, and then halfway through the night, they'd have a collection. They'd pass the plate around, divide up all the money, and whatever was there, you got a part of that. So you got vegetarian food, a divvy from the plate – and then you had to make your way home from Archway. The Kipper Brothers got banned for chucking bully beef sandwiches. It was a vegetarian collective – they went absolutely spare!

As part of the sketch, they used to bring out knives and threaten each other. One night a bloke in the front row said, 'Call that a knife? This is a fucking knife!' And pulled out a huge flick knife, and went up to them onstage, saying, 'Look at that! Look at that!' The Kipper Brothers grabbed him, put his arm in an armlock, and frogmarched him to the end of the room – where there was a landing, where the stairway went down to the pub. The had handcuffs as one of their props, so they handcuffed him to the banisters. He was still there at the end of the night. Everyone was packing up, and he was saying, 'All right, lads – very funny! It's a joke, it's a joke! Lads! Lads?' They finally came back, unlocked him and let him go at about a quarter to twelve. It was an extremely weird gig.

STEWART LEE

I got booked for the Lichfield Festival, which is a highbrow arts festival. The theatre was really dimly lit, so I couldn't see any of the audience, but I could hear that I wasn't getting any laughs at all. Then, when the lights went up, I could see they were all middle-aged, old people with blue-rinse hair, and little kids who'd been listening to my obscene ideas. I was doing a load of stuff about religious views of anal sex – I'd got all these leaflets from America from fundamentalist Christians. At the end there was silence.

DONNA McPHAIL

Any gig that isn't in a comedy club is impossible – like doing a gig in a cinema, or a conference centre where there are no lights and no stage, and the mike comes off the disco desk. I did a gig in Newcastle the other night, in a big night club. It was freezing, and there were about eighty people sitting there with their coats on. I didn't die, but there were no laughs to be had. It was one of those occasions when you go through the motions. Your mouth opens and closes and you smile, and all you're doing is waiting to get off and go home.

There's a cinema in Rayners Lane which has a comedy gig. It's been turned into a nightclub. There's a huge helicopter hanging from the ceiling, for no reason – the rest of the nightclub isn't the same theme at all – and they film you, and project your face on to a giant video screen. If you're a long way away, you can pretend to smile – but if they can see you in close-up on the screen, and you know they can, then that's a lot worse.

JEREMY HARDY

When I started, in 1984, there was a club called the Zenon Club which had Sunday night cabaret. It was a horrible night club in Piccadilly, full of foreign businessmen and hostesses and a few show business personalities. We got free drinks and snacks, but they had to stop feeding us, because we ate all the food. Before the audience had arrived, we'd cleaned out the whole kitchen. I was living in a squat in King's Cross. I used to get blind drunk, because they gave us wine, and I was performing to people who didn't have the slightest idea what I was talking about. My favourite moment was waiting in the wings with Bob Boyton [*bisexual building-site Marxist*], looking out into this audience of bemused foreign businessmen and peroxided women with long fingernails and high heels. Bob turned to me and said, 'I don't know whether to start with dog-ends or cock-sucking!' I thought, 'Either way, mate – you're lost!' It was so macabre that it was fun. It was beyond death – it was an out of body experience. That was a very odd gig indeed – it lasted for a few months, and then they gave up.

STEVE PUNT

In the first year, we'd do a gig for fifteen quid – and we'd be quite happy to perform to twenty people. But that means when someone comes up to you at the Comedy Store and says, 'Will you do our Christmas disco? We'll give you four hundred quid,' it seems like an awful lot of money, so you say, 'All right. We'll do it,' even though you know that it's almost invariably a miserable experience. The audience aren't there to see comedy, and you're there because 'this Alternative Comedy lark seems to be what the kids are into'. We did so many college events where some well-meaning entertainments secretary sees an act go well at the Comedy Store in front of two hundred people who'd queued up and paid six quid because they want to watch comedy. They've got two hundred people who've paid to dance and drink and get off with people. We did a charity benefit for the Jewish Blind Society – we even did a benefit for a housing association in Bow. It was pointless. We were completely ignored.

Guy's Hospital Christmas Disco was the biggest disaster. There were eight hundred medical students well advanced in the drinking stakes, standing up in a dark room. Cardinal rules of comedy: number one – do not put comedy on in a room where the audience is standing up. The stage was set up for a band, so we had to pick our way on over guitar stands and effects pedals and monitors, and there was no visual focus at all.

All we could see was a throbbing mass of medical students, oozing alcohol and sexual tension. All of a sudden, all the lights went on, and they could all see each other and the lager on the floor. We thought, 'This is going to be a disaster! They really do not want us.' And sure enough, they didn't.

JEFF GREEN

I drove all the way up to Teeside on the night before Christmas Eve for two hundred pounds – which is still a lot of money – but at the time, a couple of years ago, it was an incredible amount of money, and it was worth the six-hour drive. It was in a night club, and there was a mass of eighteen-year-old kids in flares, banging away to some Techno music. I thought, 'This is a shambles! Why am I here?' The DJ cut the music, the crowd all went, 'What?!' And the DJ just said, 'Comedian.' And on I went. I was thinking, 'I agree! I shouldn't be

here! But I've driven all this way, and so I've got to make an effort –
if only to haggle for half the money when I come off in ten minutes!'

FRANK SKINNER

I remember doing a gig for the Leicester University staff Christmas
dinner. They all went off at the end of the meal to do their Christmas
shopping, and there were only seven middle-aged women left. I said
to the bloke, 'Well obviously this is off,' and he said, 'D'you want
your money?' I said, 'Yes,' and he said, 'Well you'd better do the gig,
then.' So I did forty minutes to seven women sitting round one table
and got my money.

There are some gigs where there's no point in doing it. You get
there and you think, 'We shouldn't be doing this – these people don't
want to hear any comedy and I don't blame them.' Occasionally, you
find yourself in a place where comedy shouldn't be done, somewhere like a disco. If a room has got mirrored walls, you can safely
say you're going to die on your arse.

JULIAN CLARY

I can't think of one disco which went particularly well. Everyone's
dancing and having a good time – and then at one o'clock, they say,
'And now a spot of cabaret for you – clear the dancefloor!' But
people don't want cabaret – they want to dance. So they clear the
dancefloor, and plonk you on in the middle where you're not lit
properly. You haven't got a proper microphone or it feeds back, and
they're all drunk, and they're not expecting it. It's usually death.

I did an absolutely dreadful corporate gig about eighteen months
ago, which made me want to hang up my hat and never work again.
It was for a computer company in Scotland. They were paying me a
lot of money, and the theme of their three-day conference was the
Falklands War, if you please. Everyone had to wear combat gear and
the whole stage was done out in camouflage netting. It was eighty
per cent male, so it was all very aggressive. I did *Sticky Moments* and
picked the wrong people, who were too drunk to stand up – and then
tried to sing 'Leader of the Pack'. You know when it's dying and it's
beyond hope but I was contracted to do forty minutes – so I didn't
dare to do less than that, in case they wouldn't pay me.

ARNOLD BROWN

In 1990 I supported Frank Sinatra at Ibrox Stadium. It was an unreal situation. We weren't allowed to meet him – he was surrounded by people, although his manager wished me luck beforehand. My dressing room was in the boot room. There were ten thousand people out there waiting for him. There were wheelchairs at the front. It was like a Billy Graham concert. I was tempted to kneel down and heal a few of them. I did about fifteen minutes, and got a few laughs, but it was just a case of keeping it warm until he came on. I seem to earn more respect than money, but I earned two thousand pounds for that one.

The most inappropriate gig was at the Hacienda [*chic Manchester nightclub*]. I was supporting Yazoo. Vince Clark was into comedy, and he asked for someone from the Comic Strip. Nobody else would take it on, and I thought that since everyone was going their separate ways, it would be an apprenticeship. I thought, 'What a great challenge!' It was probably a typing error.

I couldn't do any jokes, because I was playing to fifteen hundred kids who were waiting for Only You. I had no function. Alison Moyet didn't have anything to say to me, and I didn't have anything to say to her. At the Hacienda the show had been delayed and people started throwing coins at me, so I went back to my hotel.

VIC REEVES

I was doing a half-hour stint in Blackpool with Ronnie Golden [*veteran alternative comedian, and lead vocalist with comic pub rock band, Ronnie & The Rex*] and Malcolm Hardee. Malcolm was compering. It was one of those gigs that he put on himself. Me and Malcolm kept going off to play on the fruit machine over the road in this pub – I missed my turn completely, and Malcolm missed his. Then we went and stayed in this bed and breakfast. There were three of us sleeping in one room – in three single beds. Malcolm took his pants off and got into bed with his shirt and tie on, turned out the light and lit up his pipe.

I did a talent contest at the Tunnel Club which Malcolm booked up. He used to put all these acts on, and then leave me to run it. All these people used to come up to me and say, 'What's the prize?'

There wasn't one. Malcolm had told them that there was, cleared off, and left me to sort it out.

CHARLIE CHUCK

Sizewell Nuclear Power Plant – that's definitely the weirdest one. They expected Roy Chubby Brown [*obscene traditional Northern stand-up*] and all that kind of stuff, but Charlie Chuck doesn't swear. He doesn't eff and blind it. If I had gone in there firing on all cylinders with gags, they would have appreciated me. But I gave them something different with Chuck, and they didn't understand it at all. I tried switching it to that kind of humour, but I'd left it too late. It was full of men, stuck there for weeks at a time, so they're ready to hurl abuse. I thought, 'This is a misbooking.'

The only accident I've ever had in twenty-seven years, a cymbal hit me on the nose and I had to have five stitches. That was because I kicked it. I usually kick it anyway but it's all under control. Normally, I kick a twenty-inch cymbal, but this time I put on a smaller cymbal, sixteen inches, which is lighter – and it bounced off my arm and slit my nose. I had to leave. I said to my drums, 'Now look what you've done, you one eyed dog!' I walked off and another act came on.

That was at quarter past eight. I had five stitches in my nose, got out of the hospital and got back onstage by ten o'clock. I walked back on to a round of applause. I laid into my drums and started cracking my gags – and it was more hilarious than ever. It was a disaster for me but I learned to be more careful in future, and that's the only accident I've ever had.

JACK DEE

Perth Prison was my most extraordinary gig: they just gawped at me. For the first ten minutes I wasn't getting any laughs. They were all looking at me with total bewilderment, like: 'What the fuck are you doing here? What is going on?' The problem was they couldn't relate to what I was doing. You say, 'I've had a shit day today,' and then suddenly you realise that by comparison, you haven't had a shit day at all. You mention something out on the street, and then you realise it's outside their experience. The only thing that actually got them going was low-level bottom humour. If you mentioned anus or policeman then they started to laugh.

It was a pity, but on the other hand I felt annoyed with myself for not realising before I got there. It was patronising to think that they were actually going to enjoy what I had to say. Really, I was reduced to the level of another plainclothes screw, trying to ingratiate myself with them. But I'd do it again because it brought me down to earth. It made me think very carefully about my material. Like any hard gig, it makes you look for laughs that you're used to getting on a plate.

The gig was in a chapel with strip lighting, and the microphone was on a tiny little lead so we did away with that. The prisoners had to sit there and there were guards standing around the sides. When you looked into their eyes there was death behind them – there was no life there. There was no soul to be made to laugh in the first place. These people had had their lives – it was like the undead. I spoke to the warden afterwards, and said, 'What are they in here for?' He said most of them were re-murderers – which is people who've done life for murder, been let out and killed again, and now they're there for good and that's that. Most of them won't get out, he said. So although Rob Newman and me made the best of it, and got what we could out of it for them, it was never a gig that would have worked.

It was almost impossible to bridge the fact that we were patronising them. You say, 'I was on the bus the other day,' and someone at the back shouts out, 'Lucky you!' And you think where do I go from here? This is an audience which has effectively had its sense of humour stripped away from it, because the soul is so darkened by their own experience. You hear your own jokes with new ears. You start thinking, 'How did I ever think that was funny?' But it's a mistake to punish yourself, because in a situation like that it really is unrealistic. You might as well go out in front of an audience who only speak Russian, and give yourself a hard time because your jokes don't work. At the time you don't think like that at all. You hunt out something that's going to make them laugh. I chanced upon a remark about one of the wardens and that got a big laugh. What they really liked was anal stuff – that's what made them laugh. Any reference to your arse. Arsehole and warden were the big buzzwords.

EDDIE IZZARD

There's an island in Holland where all these eighteen- to twenty-five-year-olds from Rotterdam and Amsterdam come to have a festival. It's like the island on *The Prisoner* – you can perform anywhere. It's a very positive attitude – there are all these people sitting around, and you can wander round and entertain them. We didn't know what to do, so we were doing anything. We were stripping off our clothes and ad-libbing around, and then the police turned up so we ran and hid. And then we said, 'Let's go and challenge the police!' The audience were still watching, and so we walked up to them as if we were the police. I motioned to one of them to wind down the window and he wound it down, so I thought, 'I've got to say something to him!' And I ad-libbed in Dutch, which blew me away! In Dutch, I said, 'What time is it?' And they turned on the siren, so we all ran behind this shed, and they followed us in their Landrover. They said, 'Get in the back! Get in the back!' So we all leapt into the back of the police car and they drove us back into the audience area – and we leapt out of the back! The police played with us in a show! They drove us around! It was beautiful! It wasn't in the script – we didn't know what the fuck was going on! There were no barriers – it was just happening.

RICHARD MORTON

Me and Lee Evans once had to play to twelve people. Twelve people in the audience, all sat in one row. They wouldn't give us the money unless we did the gig, and it was a big fee for us then – two hundred and fifty pounds – and we couldn't turn it down. So me and Lee did this gig for twelve people, and it was one of the best gigs we'd ever done. We said, 'Look – we're just as embarrassed as you are.' We made a joke of the whole thing, and they all joined in. Afterwards, we felt as if we'd really achieved something. But in career terms, if you spend every night playing to twelve people, it'll take you until you're sixty to get a following.

7. The Great Gigs

'It was the only gig I've ever done where I got a standing ovation at the end, and yet I was still thinking, "It was shit! It was rubbish!"' – Rob Newman

It's not about the number of punters in the audience – a comic can die a death in front of a full house, or storm a half-empty one (I've seen Mark Lamarr triumph before a single-figure audience, and Sean Lock teeter on the edge at Wembley Arena in front of almost 12,000 spectators). It's not even about the volume of laughter – an audience can roar with hollow mirth at an endless succession of knee-jerk one-liners, while glancing furtively at their watches, and secretly praying for the next act. Exactly what it consists of is impossible to define, but most comedians will tell you that although they cannot deduce its precise ingredients, it's got far less to do with big crowds and belly laughs than with something intangible in the air.

An electric shock shoots around the room when a comic is really cooking. People stop talking in mid-sentence, cigarettes burn unattended in overflowing ashtrays, drinks remain untouched. Laughter infects every nook and cranny, not just the front and centre stalls. At a great gig, punters play as big a part as the comic. A competent stand-up can warm up a cold hall, but it takes an audience full of newfound friends to make a routine really hum. Stand-up comedy is built on an illusion – that what is actually painstakingly prepared is inspired banter, and at a great gig this cerebral conjuring trick comes alive.

First appearances can be deceptive. A year ago, I saw Ben Elton begin his national tour at Southend. The gig was going well and the room was humming when Elton halted in mid-routine to apologise for accidentally spitting on a punter in the front row. The entire hall squirmed with collective embarrassment – and brittle nervous titters replaced the boozy belly laughs of a few moments before. 'Even such a superb technician isn't clever enough to wriggle his way out of this one,' I reckoned, and promptly watched him construct a five-minute ad-lib upon this hideous cock-up – and build the laughter back up again, to an even bigger pitch. I was so impressed that I went back to Southend six months later to watch him wind up the same tour, where I was gobsmacked to see him do precisely the same routine a second time – in exactly the same part of the show.

At a truly great gig, this deception becomes a reality – comics wander off their material and back on to it again without a clue as to how they got there. Running orders dissolve, rehearsed links are forgotten and new ones constructed out of the collective imagination of the room. The entire house is rocking, but the comic remains calm (yet never aloof) in the eye of a hilarious hurricane. Time stands still for each gag, and yet the entire evening flies by.

BRUCE MORTON

I would say that I've probably only done five or six gigs where I thought that everything clicked – where everything went properly. One of them was at East Kilbride only a few weeks ago. It was a surprise. I didn't know what would happen up there. It was full, we had about three hundred people in, the guy who was doing the support was hot. He killed, then I went out and killed, and then we did a bit together at the end.

The best a gig ever gets is when you can come offstage feeling as though you've made a whole bunch of friends – that there's a whole bunch of people out there who'd be quite happy to go and have a drink with you. I often feel intimidated before I go on. That's the ironic thing, since my intention is to get out there and make a bunch of friends. It's like being scared because you are going to be introduced to some new people.

So many people concentrate on the fear aspect of this job. They say, 'How could you do it? I could never do it! Isn't it really hard? What if people heckle you?' They forget that by and large, nine times out of ten, comedy gigs are generally great fun, and that's why most of us do it. It's not really all that scary. It's far more scary to be a miner or a soldier than it is to be a stand-up comic.

I once overheard a comic say, 'There's no such thing as a bad audience.' I'm not sure about that, because sometimes you can get an extremely good audience – and if you can get a good audience, you must, by definition, be able to get a bad one. Some kind of chemistry happens in the first five seconds – something happens in the room. This'll look fucking pompous in print but it's almost like a spiritual thing. I've felt like I'm actually half an inch off the stage. I'm not walking, I'm floating – and later, I can't remember how I got from one end of the stage to the other. That's as good as it gets. You come off feeling not so much, 'God, I was such a star there!' but just, 'What great fucking fun I had there! No wonder I do this for a living!' I'd say that's only happened a few times. I've had good gigs and I've had bad ones, but those ones are really special. You've told all the stories you want to tell, but then you find you can ad-lib about something for five minutes. When you find that you're saying anything and people are giggling, then you know there's something special going on.

There's a mystery to it, which is why people have a fascination with it, which is why I get nervous before a gig, which is why you're writing this book. It's a mystery. You can't say, 'I wish they were all like that.' You do, but if they were, then the mystery would be taken out of it. There'd be no sense of satisfaction or achievement if every gig was great.

ROB NEWMAN

A good gig is the biggest buzz I know – but it's always tinged with melancholy because you think, 'There were only a few hundred people there, and now it'll disappear.' You think of all the people who aren't there and of course when the journalists come that's when the headset doesn't work, and you have a tantrum onstage. There've been quite a few gigs on this tour when I've been so high I haven't been able to get to sleep afterwards, but it's always a case of 'you had to be there'. I remember compering the Punchline [*comedy club in West Hampstead*]. There was a running joke with several different people which all came together at the end. There was this bloke in the front row who was quite lippy. He was a market trader. I wanted a cigarette so he handed me one, and it tasted a bit funny, so off the top of my head I told a true story about someone I know who gets their E from a fruit market. You ask for a pound of cauliflowers and they put an E inside.

RICHARD MORTON

Some nights, when it goes fabulously well, I actually think something weird has happened, because it's too good to be true. Some
nights, I've gone out there and everything's been unbelievably
wonderful. You get laughs for the set-ups – let alone the punchlines.
One of those gigs was at the Empire Bar in Belfast. Maybe it's
because they don't get many comedians over there, but it was
unbelievable. They were a lovely crowd. I love all those cities –
Belfast, Liverpool, Glasgow, Cardiff . . . For me, coming from
Newcastle, there's something about them that makes me feel so at
home and I think, 'Right! It's going to go brilliantly tonight!' There's
a different feel about those places.

ARTHUR SMITH

To storm is to come off feeling fantastic – all the blokes want to slap
your back and all the women want to sleep with you. Dying is the
absolute opposite of that. No one wants to talk to you, no one wants
to buy you a drink. Everyone is embarrassed by your presence and
you are too because you've set yourself up as being able to do a job
that you can't do. The joy of stand-up is that when you've done
brilliantly, it's all you and no one else – but when you die it's your
fault. You can't blame anyone else – that's one of the great
attractions. Doing revue, we had six costume changes and a big van
full of props – when I became a stand-up, I had one matchbox. That
was my only prop.

JO BRAND

The gigs I like are the ones where it's incredibly difficult, the odds
are against you – and by working very hard, you gradually get them
on your side. I did one gig up in Bolton. I was on with Phil Cool
[*rubber-faced impressionist*] and John Maloney. Phil said to me,
'Will you go on last?' He was really famous then. He was on the telly.
So I said, 'Don't be ridiculous! You've got to go on last – you're the
one they've all come to see!' So I persuaded him to go on last, but it
was like a working men's club – there were about a hundred and

twenty people in, and three of them were women. All the rest of them were lads on a night out.

I came on and got this barrage of abuse from these blokes – a load of sexist rubbish about being fat and looking like the back of a bus, and, 'Is the stage going to hold up?' It was wall to wall, but I worked very hard and got them all on my side. The nice thing about it was that because they'd obviously not seen many female comics, and never seen what you'd call Alternative Comedy, they were gobsmacked that someone was having a go back at them – they couldn't believe it. Those gigs can go either way. It could've gone horribly wrong and they could have battered me but something about it changed. It's all to do with attitude.

When the circuit started off, it was all very comfortable – nice, middle-class intelligent people who were prepared to listen. I'm not saying I didn't enjoy those gigs, but if you can get your ideas out to a wider range of people, it's more satisfying. It makes you feel you're communicating with people who you wouldn't normally be able to talk to about what you think.

ARNOLD BROWN

It was October 1979, at the Comedy Store, and it was about one o'clock in the morning. It had been a rough night, but all the mad people and the drunks who'd been causing trouble had gone, and there were about sixty people left in the club. It was quite full, but it wasn't claustrophobic. I went on, and for some reason I started to connect with the audience. I talked about childhood memories, and I even tried some surrealistic *non sequiturs* – I was pretending to be Lenny Bruce. It was very esoteric, but part of it connected with reality.

My sister had a doll, which I actually brought onstage. It had two ends – at one end was a white face, at the other end, under the dress, was a black face, and you could turn the dress around. I said, 'It's only now that I realise the significance of this doll.' It didn't mean anything, but it got a laugh. Up until then, I'd been doing little soundbites, but comedy is about contrasts and juxtapositions – and that night, the contrast between my Glasgow upbringing and my Hampstead home both came together.

HUGH DENNIS

We did a gig for Jasper Carrott once, just after the first series of *Carrott Confidential*. It was an NSPCC benefit at the Birmingham Hippodrome. It was a very odd mixture of people: Rowan Atkinson, Lenny Henry, Dawn French, Bob Monkhouse, Max Boyce and Jasper himself. We were the least well known people on the bill. We were on because we were on Jasper's show, and people in Birmingham watch the show [*Carrott is a Brummie*], and so they knew who we were. We went on second. It was a full theatre. We'd never done anything like it. We were doing a set designed for the cabaret circuit, so we went at about a thousand miles an hour, but it was fine. Then we went up and sat in a box with all the other people. Bob Monkhouse came up to us, and quoted a joke back at us that we'd done on the radio, three years before. And then Rowan Atkinson went on. There was a tangible surge of air. We were sitting in a box that was right by the stage, and you could actually feel this air moving forward. It was extraordinary – absolutely extraordinary.

CHARLIE CHUCK

When I did the Pontins circuit, there were a lot of people in then. I took about six bows. They loved it. This man came up and gave me five pounds. He said, 'Get yourself a drink! Me mother's eighty-five, and she absolutely cried with laughter! You've made her night!' The best reception I've got recently, since Reeves and Mortimer, was Glasgow. In Leicester and Derby, they had to stop them coming in and the four dates I did in Edinburgh were packed. I hear people shouting things out all the time. It's nice. My feet are on the ground, though. I'm too old in the tooth to get too carried away. I've always been successful with my show. If I played in a pub tonight you'd see a different carry-on. It'd be 'Daisy, Daisy', 'Roll Out the Barrel' and 'Knees Up, Mother Brown'. I've played American bases, British bases, here and in Germany. I'm very visual. When I say, 'I walk into a bread shop,' I can say, '*pommes frites*' or '*schnitzel*'. It doesn't matter what I say.

JACK DEE

Comedy all comes back to the banana skin. We laugh because we're glad it hasn't happened to us. At last summer's Terrence Higgins Benefit there was an audience of three and a half thousand people united in a common cause, and thirty comedians and musicians, all doing five minutes each. At the end of the evening Roy Hutchins and Tom Robinson came on and stood on either side of the stage and read out the names of all the people who'd died of AIDS-related diseases in the last year.

As they were doing this, there was total silence – you could have heard a pin drop. Then, quite spontaneously, as the list of names came to an end, people in the audience started shouting out names as well. This went on for a full five minutes – just names, coming from all over the theatre.

It had been a fantastic evening, full of wonderful laughter, and I suddenly realised how many people there were in that audience who had brought their sadness with them. Through comedy, that sadness had been transformed into laughter. I was amazed that there had been so much laughter in the presence of such tragedy. I took it in very deeply. It really choked me up.

JENNY ECLAIR

I've had a few gigs at the Hackney Empire when I've come offstage feeling completely omnipotent. I'm ghastly to live with. I overdose on adrenalin sometimes. It's a downfall for a lot of comics. You get so hyped up that when you come down to reality, you can't actually deal with it. When I came back from Edinburgh, I took a couple of weeks off to be a mother again, and come eight o'clock at night on a normal night in, I thought, 'What do I do now? I've got to cook a meal, stay in?' I missed that winding up, the gearing up before a gig. I'm really only happy when I'm working. Otherwise, I get so depressed that I have to go back to bed. I don't actually like it. My daughter is a great substitute. She's the only other thing, but I couldn't be domestic and just do that.

LEE EVANS

I did a big ball at Trinity College at Cambridge University. It was seventy pounds a ticket, and I was performing to them. They had it all set up for me, and they treated me like a lord. I couldn't believe it. It was very classy. They had spotlights across the river, they were punting, the girls looked beautiful in their ballgowns, and the guys were very smart – and they were eating shit-hot food. I nearly cried. As I was walking out, with my bag over my shoulder, I thought, 'Fucking hell, man! This is it! This is brilliant! This is how it should be for everybody!'

STEWART LEE

The best gigs I've done were Glastonbury Festival last year and Reading Rock Festival the year before, because I was playing to the kind of people I spend my time with anyway – and to go down well with an audience composed largely of people who you'd like to be friends with is really good. I thought, 'I could easily be a member of this audience,' whereas at some clubs, you think, 'I don't think I'd want to be here.'

JEFF GREEN

I did an open spot at the Comedy Store, and I was on right at the end. I did an absolute corker of a show. It was a combination of nerves and enthusiasm. All the tired old comics didn't have that in them. I was twenty-four, and bursting with energy to do well. I was a mass of nerves onstage, but you can't help infecting a room with your energy. I went home, and I couldn't sleep all night. I was lying there with a big smile on my face. I was so pleased! You don't get that many of them any more. That's the sad thing. You get less highs now. Those first few months, the good gigs feel so good – and then slowly, they all start to get to that level.

Wimbledon Theatre last year – it was full, and I had a corker. When I came off, I was elated – but that mightn't even happen once a year now, unless you've overcome something. You start to overcome less and less within yourself, because you know what to do in every situation. The challenges become smaller and smaller because you've met them all. In the end, it's a case of making your own challenges.

Eddie Izzard makes his own challenges. He'll say, 'I'm going out there in a dress,' so he can buzz off that when he comes off. Or he might say, 'I'm going to go out there and not do any of my old material, and see how far I can get.' There aren't as many peaks any more, unless you put obstacles in your own way. A lot of comedians get a bit lazy – there's no fire in their eyes. When they're tired of their act, a lot of comedians tend to go on the offensive with their audience. They start to dig in – looking for heckles to deal with, so that something sparky can happen for them.

EDDIE IZZARD

I used to come home and say, 'In the bag!' Going round the circuit, I'd play a gig and say, 'Can I phone you back?' And they'd say, 'Well, it wasn't that good.' And then I'd do a gig that gets it in the bag – one of those ones that nails it to the fucking wall. And then you know that they're going to phone you up and say, 'Come and play again.' The person booking you has got to watch – that's the key thing. At the Comedy Store it was important to get Kim Kinnie to watch you nail it to the wall. If someone's delivering the goods, the performers all start bottlenecking out of the bars to watch. That's great. One night, all the mikes went down at the Comedy Store so I did an acoustic gig. I went into my street stuff, and did an entire set shouting. That was really electric.

JEREMY HARDY

Some of the best gigs I've ever done have been in titchy little places like Bunjies Folk Cellar off Charing Cross Road where you can't possibly have any pretence – you can't lord it over the audience. You can't have an aggressive stand-off with a heckler in which you defeat them. You've either got to win them over or fight them, because they're sitting opposite you. Probably the most pleasant experiences I've had have been in the smallest and least formal environments.

I went to Derry for the first time this year, and it was one of my favourite gigs I've ever done, because they hadn't got any expectations, and yet they really enjoyed it. Some of them were old people, dressed up to go to a show, and they were utterly baffled by this not-very-well-dressed young pervert coming on and moaning about things. But it was a really lovely gig. It reminded me of what it was like when I started and how fulfilled I was when it went really well. If I knew that any time I did a run in the West End, I'd pack it out, I think some of the thrill would be gone.

JOHN HEGLEY

My best gig was at the National Theatre, being accepted as a poet. There was a roster of proper poets there and I was one of them. I was a poet, and there were four hundred people in the National Theatre to see me. It wasn't in the comedy listings so I didn't have to be funny. It was something that I've always wanted. It was funny, actually. A few friends had come down but everybody went home, and after signing the books, I suddenly found myself on my own – but I felt happy. I went down the Bull and Gate, which is the pub near me, on my own, and sat and drank. I haven't often had that satisfaction of being accepted – I did poems and I was a poet. There were no heckles that night.

DOMINIC HOLLAND

Occasionally, you've no idea where it's going next. I was doing a gig at the Comedy Store which is always a bit of a pressure gig to do. It was a tough gig. It was really hard work. I was going well, but it was teetering on the brink. I was thinking, 'Shit! This isn't really in the bag. It could easily go either way.' And then I had a complete blank. I had no idea where I was going. I was making smalltalk with the front row – desperately trying to think where the next piece of material was coming from. It wouldn't come, and my smalltalk wasn't getting me any laughs at all – it was really inane. It was terrible – I was sweating, I was pouring with sweat. I had a silk shirt on, and I didn't realise until I got off that it was wet through. I scraped together eighteen minutes of the most disparate stuff. There were no links. It was Neil Armstrong to cream buns and cream buns to cycling in the park. I came off and Kim Kinnie was there. He said, 'Good gig!' I said, 'Wow! Did you think so?'

DONNA McPHAIL

The first time I stormed the late show at the Comedy Store was very important. It's traditionally harder for women there – so you get really worked up about it. You tend to think you're less good than the other acts, because you know the audience are going to give you a harder time, and you think that you deserve it. On my first weekend there, I was put on last, on the late show, on a Saturday. I was shitting myself. I stormed it, and was justifiably arrogant for a good three hours afterwards, just thinking, 'Yeah! You cracked it! You're the business!' And then of course a couple of days later, you do a shit gig in a really friendly place and it brings you back down to earth.

MARK THOMAS

The most memorable one was when Charles Fleischer – who was the voice of Roger Rabbit – was doing the Comedy Store. He did Roger Rabbit during the week – and at weekends he'd come and do the Store, and he killed. He was brilliant. None of the British comics could work the room at that stage and Charles would come on and work the room brilliantly. He used to insist he went on third, and he wouldn't do twenty minutes – he'd do forty. The audience would be knackered. He physically exhausted them. It was incredible trying to follow him – it was a real downer. I'd just begun to find a set that worked for me, that wasn't just a working set – but a good set that I was happy with. The first time I went there, they put me on fourth – opening the second half – and I just about held it together. It was falling away from me, but I just about made my twenty minutes and got off. Kim Kinnie said to me, 'Come back next week – I want you to close. You can do it.' Everyone on the circuit was saying, 'It's really hard following Fleischer. You're going to have a hard job there. He really takes the energy away.' I really hyped myself up, and went onstage and stormed it. I completely blew the place apart. I encored. That night, I didn't get a taxi home. I walked home – from the Comedy Store to Clapham. I was so happy. All the way home, I was replaying it in my mind, thinking, 'That was a great moment! You hit 'em just right! You hit exactly the right spot there!' I was lying there in bed, and I still couldn't switch off. I was playing the whole gig back in my head – all the moments when people interjected, and I just came back with something, and got straight back into it. To do that, that was brilliant. That was the one.

8. The Punters

'I hate being in an audience. I loathe it. I get hot and claustrophobic and bored. I want to stand up.' – Julian Clary

Some comedians never go near them (Jack Dee), others can't stay away from them (Frank Skinner) – but on one point all stand-ups are agreed: go into an audience at your own risk, because however many gigs you've done, you never know what you'll find. Every comic has a grotesque tale to tell about latching on to an anonymous (and innocuous) heckler – and ridiculing them for ten minutes or more before realising (long after every other person in the building) that the hapless target of their witty insults was either (at best) a cripple or (at worst) a mental defective.

Two of the sharpest stories in this field both belong to Boston comedian Denis Leary – best known for his sixty-second rants on MTV. The first is a classic of its kind. Leary was compering a gig in New York when he spotted a bloke in the front row with his leg in a plaster cast. 'How d'you break your leg?' enquired Leary, hoping the explanation would kick-start a few minutes of skiing/football ad-libbing. 'I didn't break it,' parried the punter. 'So what's wrong with it?' asked Denis, thinking only that he'd stumbled on a wise-guy in dire need of squashing, and deaf to the mental alarm bells that were already ringing around the room. 'I've got bone-marrow cancer,' Plaster Cast replied. For the first time, if not the last, Leary – whose solo show was entitled 'No Cure For Cancer' – was lost for words.

Yet this yarn pales into insignificance beside the story Leary tells about a compere's attempt to berate another punter for not clapping. The compere brought on a rookie comic for his first try-out spot. The rookie stormed it, and the compere requested a big round of applause. Only one punter kept his hands beneath the table. 'Why the hell aren't you clapping?' demanded the compere, or words to that effect. As the rest of the audience stopped applauding, the compere insisted that he start. In a hushed auditorium, the punter lifted his arms above the table to reveal two steel hooks, and – whether in a pathetic attempt to play the game, or as an inspired ploy to humiliate the compere – he began beating them together. The compere left the stage in silence, save for the clicking metronome of metal on metal.

Only two other professions – taxi-drivers and prostitutes – refer to their customers as punters, and for a stand-up and his/her audience, the relationship between employer and employee is almost as intimate, and every bit as fleeting.

JACK DEE

I never go into my audience, unless someone takes a swipe at me first. I leave them well alone – that's a strict policy I have. The reason I keep it like that is because as a member of the audience, I hate nothing more than audience participation. It's a betrayal of trust – it's a breach of contract. I've paid to come and see someone else being funny – I haven't paid for them to attack me. That wasn't the deal when I came in. I don't understand it, and I never find it funny, so I can't do it without thinking at the back of my mind, 'I'd hate it if someone was doing this to me.' If I'm sitting in the audience and some comic says, 'And you, sir! Where are you from?' I have to leave – I cannot take it. I absolutely loathe anything of that nature. That will ruin the night for me.

I like my audience, and I like them to have a nice time. I want them to enjoy my evening. I'm not embittered to the extent that I actually dislike my audience. Sometimes I get annoyed with a particular audience, because they're not playing ball – they're just sitting there like stuffed cabbages. You get a laugh, and then you tell the next joke and you have to start all over again. It's not as if they're entering into it and actually chucking the ball back. Some audiences are just thick – they're stupid, and they don't understand what you're talking about. I did a warm-up gig in Kings Lynn and someone came up to me and said, 'I loved the show, and my mum and dad came and they loved it too.' I thought, 'That's a lovely compliment.' There's no point being a comedian if you're going to deliberately appeal to your peer group. There's a certain amount that will always make your age group laugh and you have direct access to that. You can talk about taking drugs and being a student – to a certain extent, you've got a ready-made set. But when you actually appeal to people from a completely different background and age group to you, then you're being funny – you're doing it.

There's a certain kind of comic who is assigned by the audience to be their monster for them – to say those things which dare not be spoken which lurk in your deep subconscious. Sam Kinison [*American comedian – archetypal exponent of Comedy of Hate*] was that monster for many people. Some of the stuff I do is releasing thoughts and ideas that the audience wouldn't usually be able to get away with and the audience need you for that reason. That's why they don't want you to be ingratiating. They want you to have a 'fuck you' attitude, because a lot of people wish they could have that 'fuck you' attitude all the time.

If people like you, they'll be prepared to meet you half way – regardless of shared experience. I have a code of honour that whatever happens in my life, I'll try to reflect that in my act. I must be honest – being honest is very important. I'm not going to go onstage and disguise the fact that I live in a house that I own, rather than a small flat that I rent, which is how I started out. With some audiences on the circuit it would be more convenient for me to put it across that I don't have any money – but it isn't true, so why say it? I don't want to fool the audience into thinking something wrong or put across information that isn't true, so I'm relying on their goodwill that they'll like me, whatever I say.

It's also about trust – I've watched a comic, and thought, 'This is technically brilliant! Great lines, good ideas – but I don't trust him. He's not telling me the truth.' Whereas I can see another comedian and think, 'This is a bit rough around the edges, and he hasn't really thought about what he's writing, but I like what he's doing because I know it's coming from inside.' The audience want to know that they're not being had, and some comedians are very good at disguising the fact that they're not being honest – that they're putting across a different image from their real selves. If I watch a comic and I come away thinking, 'I don't know any more about that person than when I went in,' then I feel I've been conned – I don't feel I've seen stand-up comedy. I think I've literally seen an act, which you shouldn't think when you see stand-up.

ROB NEWMAN

I like audiences. I feel at home and happy there. Occasionally, I have a night when I'm not doing a gig – and I really miss it. That's why I do unpaid gigs – supposedly to work out new material, but often I'm not. I'm just doing it. The only time I didn't like it was the King's Head in Crouch End. It was a bit like *The Village of the Damned* or *The Midwich Cuckoos*: all these beautiful young people in the audience, and it felt horrible. I never felt I could relate to that audience – that was the only place where I felt I'd made no connection with people at all. When I started, the alternative comedians, for all their love of the proletariat, and their left-wing belief in democracy, were always denigrating audiences – especially the political comics. Ironically, their descriptions of audiences were like patricians' descriptions of the mob.

I used to tour a lot with Alan Parker Urban Warrior. He's one of the most innovative comics – he won't compromise. If it was up to me, I'd get those early laughs in and then I could expand and do the interesting stuff – if ever. Simon [*Munnery, creator of Alan Parker*] would be demanding the sort of attention a theatre audience would give. Once or twice he died, and I used to think, 'It's a shame that they didn't see it.' My need for them to like me has always been stronger than my disapproval.

VIC REEVES

We never really slagged anyone off to any degree. The worst we ever said was, 'You're a very confident young man.' We never did any of this heckling business. Stand-up comics will say, 'Have you ever noticed . . .?' We never did any of that. We never had any viewpoints for people to object to. We used to shout out, 'Very poor!' when we had a poor act on Novelty Hour, but that was the whole point of it.

There was one character we used to have on called The Toff, and as soon as he came on, the audience all shouted out, 'Fuck off, Toff!' It wasn't anything to do with us. Somebody in the audience shouted it one week, so every time he appeared, someone else shouted it – and by the time he'd been on for four weeks on the trot, the whole place was shouting it with no encouragement from us at all.

People get a bit excitable sometimes. I remember coming on once in Cardiff, amid a load of dry ice. I got an entire pint of lager on my head – a direct hit, hurled randomly into the smoke – but that wasn't really malicious, it was excitement.

We did the Wheel of Justice. Bob would be Judge Nutmeg. I'd get someone out of the audience and he'd say, from the other side of the stage, 'Look into his eyes – there's not a hint of human compassion there!' One time, the bloke I'd got out of the audience turned out to be blind, but Bob couldn't see. He was saying, 'Look into his eyes – there's nothing there!'

RICHARD MORTON

The night before the Jack Dee tour, I had to play Bournemouth University. It was the first day of term, and I got there really late. Five hundred clamouring, noisy, horrible students – it was a bear pit out there. Because I was so late, I had to go straight on. I raced onstage, and they were very noisy. I thought, 'I'll have to control them quickly – I'll have to show some authority here, and get in charge.' There's a little thing I do if anyone runs past the front of the stage, all hunched up and cowering, so they won't be seen. I say, 'Oh, look! I'm being heckled by *Planet of the Apes*!' It's an old Steve Martin line and it always gets a laugh. So as I went onstage, this girl ran across the front of the stage, so I said, 'Oh, look! I'm being heckled by *Planet of the Apes*!' She turned round and she was black! I absolutely died. I could see this big black bouncer by the door who obviously thought I'd come out with some horrible racist jibe. A table of skinheads were cheering. They thought they'd booked Roy Chubby Brown! The rest of them – the liberal consensus – were booing, and I thought, 'Oh my God! I've just made the most horrible racist joke in the world! I've never ever said a racist thing in my act, and honestly – in my heart of hearts – I've never thought it!' It was so awful.

I know comics who have made some horrible mistakes. I know a comedian who went out onstage and he was dying horribly. There was silence in this room. A guy got up to leave who had Parkinson's disease. Everyone else knew – except the comic. The comic said, 'That's right, mate, you start the dancing – get the atmosphere going!' Sometimes, when you're up against it, you say the worst

possible things in the worst possible scenarios. It's like being at a
dinner party and the hostess has put a bit of weight on and you say,
'What – are you pregnant, then?' Somebody else has lost their hair
and you say, 'Is that a crew cut?' They say, 'No. I've got cancer,
actually. I'm having chemotherapy.' It changes every night. I get a
tirade of homophobia, because I look gay. As soon as I mention that
I'm not and make a joke about it that a crowd can laugh at, there's a
palpable sense of relief in the audience that I find quite sad. If
they're worried by you, if they can't trust you, if they don't like you,
they're not going to laugh at you. You've got to get everyone
relaxed.

Last year I supported Bruce Morton at Mayfest. That was a hard
night because they were all there to see Bruce. It's his home town,
and he'd got his home fans in. It was absolutely awful. It was a
nightmare gig. I always start with, 'I'm from the North East. We're
rock hard up there. What's your hard area around here?' Nothing. I
couldn't get them on anything. There was no laughter whatsoever.
And I kept going back to it because that's where I start. It's a status
thing. You say, 'This is what I'm starting with, and I'm going to wait
until you laugh at this before I move on.' It's a parent–child
authority thing – you can't have your pudding till you've had your
dinner. So I said, 'What's the hardest place in Glasgow – apart from
here and now?' and it got a laugh. I said, 'I gave you that,' and it
established my authority. If you can't go out there and say, 'Let's be
friends – I'm going to be funny. Trust me – I know what I'm doing,'
then you have to take on this high status thing. When I do anything
contentious, that is going to be difficult for them to handle, I always
do it in a very forceful way. You've actually got to do it a way that
says, 'I don't care if you laugh at this or not.' The difference almost
comes down to keeping a straight face. Sometimes, if you do a gag
and glare at them, they'll laugh because they see that you're not
bothered about whether they laugh or not.

I'm fascinated by the psychology of a crowd, that psychokinetic
energy – the empathetic feeling that can transcend an audience.
Some comics have this idea that there's a power base in any crowd
who lead the rest – maybe it's the ten per cent who have the most
confidence – and if you can get them laughing, then the rest will
follow. The quicker ones will get the gag instantly, and there's
always a few people who lead a laugh or some applause – it's a group

mentality. I don't know how it works, but I know it happens. If they all move en masse, you lose them. Every night I go out there, I know they're the ones I'm targeting – and I don't even know who they are.

I was in Portsmouth. It was the twentieth night of the Jack Dee tour and we hadn't had a night off. I was in a bit of a blur halfway through my act, and I went and called two thousand of them Southampton. That's a cardinal sin. If you call a city the wrong name, they hate you – and rightly so. They didn't forgive me for several jokes. You offend two thousand people in one go, because you hurt all of them.

LEE EVANS

In South Wales I had my car and piano nicked by a bloke, because I had a go at his wife. This bloke in the audience said, 'You're not bloody funny – you're complete crap!' I said, 'Well, I am trying. I'm having a go – I've been travelling for days.' And he said, 'Well, it's no good – is it? We're paying you to do bloody comedy, and you're shite!' I said, 'Give us a break, mate.' And his wife was going, 'Well, he is shite, isn't he?' I said, 'You can fucking shut up!' I was a bit angry. I said, 'I've had a whole week of this shit! Fuck off!' And he said, 'Don't you bloody talk to my wife like that, mate!' And I said, 'Well, she had a go at me, didn't she?' And that was it – he went and got his mates, all these nutters from the factory down the road.

After the gig, they were all waiting outside, shouting, 'We'll fucking kill him!' The bloke's wife – a little woman with fuzzy hair – was there, shouting, 'Send him out!' I was shitting myself. The manager decided he'd help me out. He said, 'I'll keep them busy here – you nip out the back.' I said, 'All right, if you think that'll work.' So the manager kept them talking, while I crept through the kitchen – and out the back to my car. But there were a load of blokes out there as well, waiting by my car. They'd got my piano out of the car, and they were running down the road with it – then they decided to take the handbrake off and roll my car down the hill. I was chasing them down the hill shouting, 'You've got my car! You've got my life!' And they went, 'Your fucking life is shite!' And they pissed off with the car. I came home on the train – without my car or my piano.

The police found them both the next day, so I had to go all the way back two days later to collect them.

BRUCE MORTON

A couple of months ago, I did a freshers gig at Glasgow University. The bill was Fred MacAulay, Phil Kay, a guy called Ford Kiernon and me. Ford is a friend of mine, and he has been for a number of years. To my mind, he doesn't do enough stand-up. He should, because this man has the ability to make Connolly look ordinary – he's a star in the waiting, and that's why he's been supporting me on the Scottish dates on my tour. I know he can do it, but he's inexperienced, so I've been going out and doing fifteen minutes at the start to get things going a wee bit, to make a space for him to come on when they're settled, and he's rocked – he's killed. But that was not the case at Glasgow University.

For some reason, the organisers decided to cram eight hundred people into a room which should really only hold four hundred. Ford went on second last, after the interval – and you can imagine how long the interval was, with that many students wanting to get drinks. He came out, and there was a section of twenty young men who gave him a fucking hard time – I mean really bad. It could have happened to any of us that night, but with Ford being the most inexperienced of the four of us, the odds were stacked against him. He got really lost, and eventually he said, 'I'm out of depth, here. I'm sorry. I'm off,' and he left. I had to go on right after him, and I was fucking angry – not only because my friend had got hurt, but because I thought, 'These bastards have really wasted it for all the other people in this room, because this man can really tell some great stories.' Just as the compere was doing the intro to get me on, I realised I had this attitude. So I had to take a deep breath and think, 'Forget that. It doesn't matter. It's not relevant to them whether you're friends with that comic, whether you've slept with them, whether he's your uncle. It doesn't matter. That's got nothing to do with it. You've got to go and do a gig. You're working now.'

Having said that, when I went out, they started on me – and I dealt with them rather vigorously. I hit them hard, and got the whole room cheering on my side – against them. Ford didn't have the experience to know that if you treat them in a certain way, and get

the room on your side, you can win. You can make those people look
foolish – and they were fools.

JENNY ECLAIR

If I'm performing to an audience, and I've seen friends of mine have
a very hard time because they're doing subtle stuff that goes over
their heads, by the time I get on, I vaguely despise them. I
sometimes feel very cheap because I've been able to make that
audience laugh, despite the fact that I don't like them, by being rude
and loud. I feel then that I'm playing to a common denominator, and
they don't realise that there's some irony in it.

I'm one of those people who hates silences and awkward
moments, and will blabber on madly trying to make things all right.
Sometimes, it's a bit like throwing a shit party. I'm faffing round
going, 'Do have some more French bread! Dance with me!' Which
obviously, some people have an allergic reaction to, and so they
shrink back in their chairs.

I've used fake tan, so I take it one stage further and talk about fake
peeling – filo pastry stuck to my shoulders – and another stage
further and talk about faking a malignant melanoma – sticking a
chocolate raisin to my leg to freak myself out. And then I go to a real
story about having a mole removed: 'Well, not a real mole. Not one
of those sweet little furry creatures with a pink nose,' et cetera et
cetera . . . Afterwards, this girl came up to me and said, 'We
laughed and laughed and laughed – my friend had a moment when
he went off you, because he's actually suffering from malignant
melanomas and is basically dying. It was an awkward moment, but
he decided to get over it.'

The worst thing that can happen to me after a gig is that I'll be
dragged into a corner by a couple of very earnest women, who will
start telling me what I should and shouldn't do. I remember two
women giving me a hard time about the grossness of my childbirth
material. They said, 'Don't you realise that childbirth is a wonderful
female thing? Why have you turned it into this appalling litany of
disgustingness?' I said, 'Have you had a kid?' They said, 'No.' I said,
'Well come back and talk to me when you fucking have! Don't teach
your grandmother how to suck eggs!'

If I could have sung, then I'd have been a pop star. I want adulation, but unfortunately I have to get it through laughs. It's not the same. They're laughing at you, as well. I will sometimes pick up on a weird laugh in the audience, and think, 'That person is laughing at me.' Somebody who laughs slightly out of sync. You always go for the person who actually hates you when you're onstage. If you have three hundred people loving you, there'll be one person sitting there looking at you as if they want to kill you. And that's the person who you beseech with your eyes all the way through, saying, 'Please just go with me! Like me!'

FRANK SKINNER

A woman came up to me at the Red Rose [*comedy club in Finsbury Park, North London*]. I'd just come offstage, after doing an absolute belter. She said, 'I just had to say to you before I left . . .' That's the normal opening for somebody who's going to be very nice, so I went into 'Thank you, thank you, very kind of you' mode, and on my twelfth thank you I realised she was saying 'you are the most sexist . . .' But I was already too busy saying thank you, so I continued saying, 'Thanks for taking the trouble to come and say all that, it's very kind of you.' She was absolutely flummoxed.

There was a very big female glass collector in a pub I used to play in Birmingham. There was a woman in the audience that night who looked very much like Cagney from *Cagney and Lacey*. I was doing some gags about her being an American policewoman, and so, referring to Lacey, I said, 'So where's the big fat ugly one tonight?' At which point the glass collector walked across, and before I could stop myself I said, 'Oh, here she is!' She actually leapt on to the stage and started hitting me.

I used to do a joke which went: 'I'm a children's entertainer called Budum Budum the Clown because that's the noise that kids make. You don't agree? Well, you've obviously never run one over.' A woman came up to me once and said, 'I really like your act, and I think you're very funny – but my child was run over, and I wish you'd drop that joke.' I said to her, 'I'm very sorry but it's a joke – it's a different world, and I'm not going to drop it. It's nice of you to come over and I respect your opinion, but in my opinion, it's not making light of children being run over. It's something else.' I wasn't articulate enough to say exactly what I meant, and I'm probably not now, but I think you sense a comedian's point of view very early on. People need to recognise that attitude and listen through that filter – and usually they do.

Someone in an audience once hissed at me, and I said, 'How d'you think I feel? My parents were killed in a car crash swerving to avoid a chicken that was crossing the road – and my brother and sister were both electrocuted changing light bulbs.' And in the end, that's what it comes down to. There probably are people whose parents were killed swerving to avoid a chicken, but it doesn't put an end to those jokes.

JOHN HEGLEY

I did a show once in Forest Gate, where I used to do kids' theatre. That was when I was still doing my school teacher persona, to keep me on the rails. I came off, and this drunk bloke came up and said, 'You're a prat!' I wasn't thinking, and I replied to him as if I was still onstage. I said, 'Don't talk to me like that, mate, all right? Don't fuck with me!' The bloke said, 'Right! I'm going to smash your head in!' And he grabbed hold of me and started to drag me out. I called to my mate, 'Terry, can you get him off me? He's going to beat me up!' Terry talked to him, and quietened him down, and it ended up peaceably, but until he did, he was dragging me out of the room to beat me up.

Once at the Comedy Store they'd been really horrible to a woman who was on before. I thought they'd been really vile, and it was hard to go on and entertain them, after they'd been vile to someone else. That was quite difficult. It was definitely in my mind while I was doing it, but I thought, 'To show your anger and do badly yourself isn't the way round this.' I suppose you hope that, ultimately, if you're putting out something that's worthwhile, you make those people a little bit better.

It's up to them to deal with it. It looks horrible, but you can't interfere. You can try to rectify it afterwards and learn from it but you can't wade in at the time. If you do you become something other

than a performer – the human being takes over, and you go in there
and punch them out.

ARTHUR SMITH

There was a double-act called Clarence and Joy Pickles. They used
to be in the revue I was in, and they'd formed a little double-act.
They weren't bad – but at one gig at the Tunnel Club, they weren't
going very well. Someone threw a glass, and it hit Joy in the face. I
was on next and I was furious. She had blood streaming down her
face. When I went onstage, I was boiling mad (I was top of the bill,
but it'd been quite a short evening because everyone had been
booed off). I deliberately did the very best material that I could
possibly do, all distilled into three minutes, and I was slaying them –
I was going really well. And then I stopped and said, 'If you think I'm
going to do any more, you've made a big mistake, because what you
did to that act before was absolutely disgraceful – so fuck the lot of
you!' And I walked off. I tried to organise a boycott of the Tunnel.
Malcolm [*Hardee*] was very contrite. He wasn't there that night and
it might not have been so bad if he had been – but it contributed to
the Tunnel closing.

Another time there was a bloke sitting in the front row of the
Comedy Store, on a rather duff night, reading the *Sun*. I pulled it out
of his hands and tore it up in a frenzy of mock-origami. He came up
to me afterwards – he was really angry – and insisted I refund him
22p to cover the cost of his paper.

From my point of view, the special nights have often involved
someone from the audience somehow becoming involved in the
evening, and it taking an unpredictable turn. I was doing a gig at the
Duke of York's and I picked on some bloke who was sat on his own.
He was a right trainspotter. I said, 'What are you doing here? How
come you're on your own? Got no friends? Where d'you live?' He
said, 'Slough, and it's my birthday.' He never came back for the
second half.

Simon Fanshawe picked on some woman and she said to him,
quite clearly, 'Why don't you stop picking on me and say something
funny?' She sounded rather serious, and quite justified as well. You
could sense the audience thinking, 'Yeah – fucking right. Leave her
alone!' And he said 'Oooh!' and went for her again. You could

almost hear the audience's sympathy rushing towards this woman and away from Fanshawe, but he didn't clock it. With every line that he was doing against her he was alienating himself a little bit more.

MARK THOMAS

At Glastonbury someone invaded the stage in green Speedo trunks with grass hanging out of the front of them. He had an orange in one hand, and a stick in the other. He started saying how the earth was feminine and the sun was masculine, and that when the sun shone on the earth, it was interplanetary sex. He was tripping off of his face. I played around with him for a bit, having a bit of a banter with him, and the audience. Meanwhile, the stewards were creeping up on him – but the audience all shouted, 'No! Fascists! Leave him alone!' I was trying to deal with him by taking the piss out of him, and then he pulled out a butter knife, and made a lunge at me. I said, 'Oh, don't be such a silly old fucker! Put that away!' It was a big tent, and there were thousands of people there. The audience saw the flash of a knife, but they didn't know it was a butter knife. They didn't know that I was in no danger at all – and so immediately, they were on my side again. They thought I was really cool. Afterwards, they were all saying, 'You dealt with that really well!'

Ivor Dembina used to run these really ropy college gigs. At the time, there was only Addison [*Cresswell*] and him doing them, and Malcolm Hardee on occasions. He used to put himself out as the cheapest comedy around. You'd get sixty quid and a drive there and back. We did an agricultural college, and they're notorious for being complete and utter brainless bastards. Ivor went out and settled them down because he can be very schoolmasterly on occasions. Then Felix [*Dexter*] went on and did all right and then a comic called Steve Edgar went on. He was a wonderful performer. He painted brilliant pictures. He'd claim responsibility for all those weird things, like the road cone on top of the bus shelter – it was wonderful observation. He went up there and the audience booed and threw stuff. A can came up and Steve said, 'I don't need this, and I don't need you. Good night.' And he walked off. They called an interval and all the students were saying, 'What did we do wrong?' The bloke running the gig went round saying, 'You've really upset that guy. We've booked these people to entertain you. You can't behave like that.' And so when I went on, there was an atmosphere of forced joviality and I just didn't want to be there.

DOMINIC HOLLAND

If they don't like a friend of mine, then so be it. I still think it's my job to do a good show. I would never say to myself, 'I don't like this audience – I'm not going to bother.' I always go on thinking, 'I'm really going to kill this gig!' I've got some one-liners which I use at the beginning, which don't require any performance. I just recite them and they get laughs – so I front-load the set with those jokes, and then I go into stuff which is more performance-based.

You have to remember that they're always there to have a laugh. They're not there to see you go badly. I always remind myself that they all want it to go well. No one's thinking, 'I hope he stiffs.' I go on with the attitude of, 'This could be a really good gig, and they could really enjoy themselves.' I love doing stand-up, and I know that if I get the chance, I will do a good show. I love the idea that people will go home talking about my material. You can actually make people happy. They'll be pissed off and come to a gig, and you can really give them a good time. I've had people say to me in offices where I used to work, 'You know I've got friends who still talk about your line on that?' I think that's great – I love the idea of that.

DONNA McPHAIL

Men feel threatened by a woman assuming authority over them. Some men have an emotional problem with you getting that attention and praise. They say, 'I wouldn't fuck you,' when you hadn't even asked them. You hadn't even noticed them. They want to be noticed, and put you in your place. You learn to use an outrageous heckle like that to your advantage, If it's, 'You're crap!' then the audience can agree or disagree. Also, women don't like it. If they're out with their boyfriend, and their boyfriend's laughing at you, which translates to them that they fancy you, that's when they heckle. Everyone is very attractive onstage, even if offstage in normal life they're quite ugly. It's something about the light shining in the eyes of someone onstage that makes them look more appealing. Audiences either decide, 'This woman's not attractive and she knows it, so that's all right,' or women have to dress up and look good.

A couple of months ago, some guy poured beer over Jo Brand for no reason at all. She could have done him for assault – that is overstepping the mark. She was actually doing an encore at the time. She was at the Banana Cabaret, which doesn't have a raised stage. It was last orders at the bar – and instead of going round the back of the audience, he walked straight across the stage in front of her, about two feet away, an obvious challenge to her authority – which, as a woman, you have to stamp on straight away. And so as he walked on, she took the piss out of his clothes – which is the easiest thing to do, but it was very successful. He didn't like that at all, so when he came back with his drinks, he came back the same way, walked up to her really slowly, threw some of his beer over her, and walked on. Instead of going mad, the audience selfishly thought, 'I want to see how she deals with this,' even though she was on an encore and everyone was supposed to be on her side. It was a compliment in a way, because they must have thought, 'She's so good that whatever's coming is going to be really good,' but what he did was really insulting, and beyond a normal heckle, so they shouldn't really have sat there in secret enjoyment to see what she did. Of course, she managed to throttle him in the end, but it took about five minutes because she was shocked. It changed the whole atmosphere.

I've been storming a gig, and about five minutes in, some bloke shouts out, 'Get your tits out!' And the whole audience, as one, turn round and tell him to fuck off – about a hundred and fifty of them. It's great, but I say, 'Don't patronise me. I can deal with it myself.'

When I did material about being a lesbian, the audience were totally shocked, because they wouldn't have clocked me as one and they'd already made up their minds that they liked me. If they'd known beforehand, most of them wouldn't even have bought a ticket. Then they were scared, because they thought, 'Oh, no! She's going to say all men are bastards,' and when I didn't do that, and make jokes about it, that was a big relief to them – here was a lesbian who wasn't fat and ugly and didn't say, 'Men are tossers!' As long as you're not going to be political about it, that's all right. Everyone was thinking, 'I wouldn't have gone if I'd known,' so they have to go away thinking that their judgement about what lesbians are like is wrong. I tricked them by making them like me and laugh at me.

JEFF GREEN

You can dig, get laughs, dig, get laughs and then say one thing too many and you can lose them. I can remember watching another comedian completely lose it. He was compering, and he was doing all right. There were some Irish lads in, and he was banging away at them. They were having a go at him, and he was having a go at them, and then he said, 'Have you left any packages round here?' Someone shouted out, 'Not everyone from Ireland's a terrorist, you know,' and the whole crowd cheered. He was completely destroyed.

I've made mistakes. I've thought somebody's a twat and it turns out they're not all there. You hear someone shout out something and you think it's another pissed person in the gig, so you dig into him and then you see him being carried out by two friends. You feel terrible. They've taken him out for one day and you've had a go at him. One time in T&C2 this bloke was shouting stuff out, and I said, 'Stop shouting – you sound like Quasimodo!' I thought he was just being a prick. Sometimes people make stupid noises because then there's nothing you can grab hold of. But as I walked over to him, I could see he had a hearing aid, very thick glasses and a bobble hat on. He obviously wasn't particularly bright. I thought, 'Oh fucking hell!' The whole crowd could see him, and I'd just called him Quasimodo.

JEREMY HARDY

I've provoked people who I probably should have left alone. I had a drunk guy who was asleep in the front row, so I started doing some stuff about the fact that he was asleep. I wanted the audience to know that he was already asleep, so they didn't think I'd put him to sleep. And then I thought it'd be fun to try and get the audience to wake him up. So we all woke him up, but he was so drunk that he wouldn't shut up all night, and it became very irritating. I thought, 'Oh God, I should have left him alone.'

I had some weird old bloke come into the audience at the Bloomsbury Theatre. He was very drunk, and there was no way he was going to enjoy it. He started abusing other people in the audience for laughing, and going on about people being from North London, which seemed to be some sort of veiled anti-Semitism. Rather than deal with it from the stage, I decided to jump down off the stage and go and talk to him in the audience, which was a very strange thing to do, because obviously in a five hundred seat theatre, most people aren't going to hear you. I thought, 'It's too easy up here. I've got a microphone – I can shout him down.' And this idiotic streak of egalitarianism in me made me think, 'I will tackle him on his own ground! I will argue it out with him in the stalls!' Which of course was ridiculous. Though I was probably being quite funny, he was able to shout louder than me. In the end he was ejected – that's the only time somebody's actually been thrown out of one of my gigs. I suppose it is a failure. You've failed to silence this person and it makes people feel uncomfortable. I ad-libbed about it quite well, after it was over, but at the time I realised that I'd created a ludicrous situation.

Once I followed a singer who'd been given a really hard time by the audience. I was so angry, and I hated the audience so much, that I went on and attacked them. I maintained an attitude of antagonism throughout. I did my forty-five minutes with complete loathing for them. They were a bit baffled, because they felt they were justified in hating that singer, and they couldn't see why I was upset on her behalf.

JO BRAND

Occasionally, you do get sad people. In one of the first gigs I did some bloke got on a table and said something completely mad, like, 'The golden treasure is above the clouds of heaven.' I have to confess, I got a laugh out of him doing that – when I could tell that he was probably mentally ill, which I felt guilty about afterwards. Occasionally you do that because you're put on the spot with an audience, and you make a mistake.

JULIAN CLARY

I used to read out people's letters from their handbags, and at the Vauxhall Tavern I read out a woman's letters from her husband in

prison. She was understandably upset and I was told she was waiting
for me afterwards to have it out with me but I went out another way.
I remember having a go at a man who I thought was asleep – but
when he opened his eyes, there were no pupils, and then I saw the
white stick on the floor. He was blind – I absolutely died.
Fortunately he was right in the front row, so most of the people
behind him weren't aware of it, and I struggled on to the end.

DAVID BADDIEL

I saw Ben Elton about five years ago, at Leicester University. He
was halfway through the second half, and he said something about
being in Sheffield – and there was a sudden, terrible moment when
you realised that he does this every night. The whole illusion that he
was making it up spontaneously for us suddenly vanished. He
carried on for about five seconds and then he realised he'd got it
wrong, and he started apologising profusely – saying, 'It's a different
show every night,' but he lost it completely at that point.

Every night, particularly on tour, even though you do forget
where you are, you have to go on and treat each audience
individually, and not try to do it like you did it last night or the night
before that. Somewhere in there you've got to feel you're speaking
to a new bunch of people.

MARK LAMARR

Often when people die, there's no rhyme or reason to it. It's a weird
mass psychology where the whole crowd suddenly turn – and not one
person in the crowd can pinpoint why they did. There are a few key
hecklers who can say, 'We don't like this,' and the whole crowd –
who were pissing themselves to the last act – go, 'Yeah! We fucking
hate this!' Mild-mannered people, who come out for a nice night out
and a drink. I've been really storming it, come off, come back on and
they hate you. You say, 'Hold on! Remember me? I worked really
hard for you just now and you really liked it, and now you're telling
me you hate me!' It's that football fan psychology. Every night you
go out there are going to be lads who have a go, and then they always
come up to you afterwards and say, 'That was great fun, wasn't it?'
And you say, 'No – you just spoilt my whole night.'

It sometimes starts with blokes having a bit of a shout, without being at all malicious, but occasionally an act can't handle it, and everyone else goes, 'Hold on: there's a chink in the armour there. We don't want to see a chink in the armour.' And so suddenly, they say, 'We hate this!' Audiences have to sit through a right load of old shit – but when they're in a good mood they don't notice, because they don't want to notice. Generally, I think three-quarters of comedians are complete crap. I feel the audience are part of the show and I think that comes from compering. When you're a compere, you're not an act – you're a middle-man between the comedians and the audience. Often, you're more like the mouthy bloke in the crowd who thinks he's funny. You've got to do the initial bridging between what's happening onstage and what's happening in the audience, and that's why all comperes have to chat with the audience. It's an essential part of the job. There are often times when you have to go back on and say, 'Yes, that act was shit and I'm sorry.' I've had to do it about really good friends of mine, and they say, 'Yeah, I was shit and I nearly fucked up the night – you had all your work cut out, and it was my fault.'

I was doing a gig at the Bearcat. There was a bloke in the audience who was literally hysterical. He was crying with laughter at anything I said. I could have looked at him and said 'bookshelf' and he would have died laughing. And in the end, that's what I was doing. I didn't tear him apart – it was all quite good-natured, even though it does piss you off after a while because you can't concentrate on anything else. After the show he came up to me and said, 'Thanks a lot for that!' It transpired he had some really rare disease and he hadn't been out for five years. It was definite that he was going to die, and then he didn't. It was the first time he'd come out. He was over the moon, and I'd been saying, 'Look at this fucking wanker down the front! He won't shut his mouth!'

Sometimes the audience are so unpleasant that you think, 'What a horrible job this can be! I have to go out and entertain these people who I completely despise – people who are really full of hatred.' There used to be a gig down at the Albany Empire [*in South East London*]. I did it one night and didn't get a laugh, but didn't get any heckles either and then Mark Steel went on, and they tore him apart. They really hated him, but there's nothing in the world that'll make Mark get off. He carried on, and in the end, they were pissing themselves laughing, but then about ten minutes later on, they hated him again. He hadn't done anything. They'd just remembered that they hated him. It was like, 'The bastard tricked us into laughing.' It was one of the weirdest things I've ever seen. It was obviously a crowd who weren't out for a laugh. But because he was so good, he'd made them laugh, and they really hated him for that as well. I remember thinking that night, 'I really don't know if I like this job.'

Once I was compering and a comic did a joke that really disgusted me. It was to do with disabled people and I think that's something you shouldn't joke about at all – I found it very offensive. The audience liked it, but I went back on and said, 'How dare they do that, and how dare you laugh at them?' It was wrong of me to do it – but it was me being human, rather than being a comedian. Maybe that's something you should never do as a hundred per cent entertainer, but I think there's more to most good comedians than that.

STEWART LEE

When I used to do a joke about spastics, people would come up to me and say, 'I've got a mentally handicapped kid, and that's absolutely true to my experience. It's really nice being able to laugh at the discomfort that we feel.' And then someone came up to me and said, 'You should never use that word! I work with mentally handicapped kids, and you should never use the word spastic.' And just to see what would happen, I said, 'Well, I worked with them as well, for two years, and I think it's all right.' And then she started talking to me as if I was allowed to have an opinion about it.

Student audiences are really insecure. They're away from home, they don't know what they want, they're trying to define what they like. Someone might come up to you afterwards and say, 'I really liked it – I really understood what you were doing. I really appreciated that,' and although they're complimenting you, it's actually a way of defining themselves. They decide whether to like you or not depending on how it's going to make them seem. You become an accessory by which they're defined.

Lee Hurst [*cockney stand-up*] will go onstage in front of a completely placid audience, and whip them up into a frenzy. When they're ready to turn against him, he'll bring them back down again. And then he'll come off afterwards and say, 'They nearly turned on me there, but I got away with it!' And I think, 'Yes, they did nearly turn on you, but you made them like that! They were all right and you made them really angry!'

STEVE PUNT

It's almost unheard of for an entire audience to be hostile, and if a small group decides to, you can cope with that because at least it's a response. And you know damn well when you do TV that's probably millions. For every person who likes you, there is someone saying, 'Aren't they shit?' I find it far more upsetting when an audience ignores you. That's so depressing, because the whole illusion goes. Without that joke and response, there's nothing there at all.

There's an odd illusion that all comedians use, that they're not aware that what they're doing is funny, because it's obnoxious to an audience if you look as if you know. But of course, no one in their right mind would go onstage in front of an audience unless they had some inkling that what they were doing would work. Anybody who says, 'I perform comedy because I'm convinced I'm not funny,' is deranged.

So given that you hope that what you're doing is funny, once it's got the desired response a few times, it becomes very easy to shift the blame on to the audience. If a joke goes badly you can console yourself by thinking, 'Well, it's always worked before,' so any frustration about a gig that hasn't gone well tends to dissipate: 'It was the PA, it was the audience, they'd drunk too much, they hadn't drunk enough, my microphone was too quiet, they couldn't see properly . . .' There are a million and one excuses.

The audience need to know who you are, and where you come from. If you say 'Victoria Wood', you picture a whole world around her – of cups of tea and biscuits, and Marks and Spencer. That's what marks out really good comedy – it creates its own world. The Eldorado of comedy is to find something that hasn't been found yet, and get in there first. There's a slightly suburban Middle England-ness about our humour – it's the sort of humour that goes to Texas Home Care on a Sunday, because that's very much both our backgrounds. If you don't pursue that sort of thing, you end up being too anodyne. The only way to make headway is for the audience to come to know who you are.

JEFF GREEN

I never blame the audience. I always blame myself. A lot of the quitters blame the audience – you see them come off after a bad gig and say, 'Those bastards! They didn't give me a chance!' That's certainly true – they probably didn't, but I always say to myself, 'Would Billy Connolly have died in that situation? Would Robin Williams have bombed out?' The answer is no. Therefore it's your fault.

9. The Hecklers

'In the early days at the Comedy Store, the gimmick was the gong. It was dropped after a couple of months, because it got too mad – people used to come along just to heckle. If you did a minute, you were doing well. That's why Ben Elton's delivery is so fast. The whole atmosphere was one of not being listened to and having to break through the heckling – you had to be quick.' – Arnold Brown

A heckle is the final arbiter between theatre and comedy. If you can heckle it, it's comedy. If you can't, it's theatre. The implicit understanding that allows the audience to pitch in on equal terms with the person behind the mike – a comedic right to bear arms – is the first article of comedy's unwritten constitution. It simply isn't sporting to hurl abuse at an actor, however much you might hate them, but a comedian is fair game. Heckling is what makes stand-up special, and without the capacity for audience intervention, it would be reduced to a dull substitute for drama. Hecklers exercise quality control, but they can also kick-start a routine. Frank Skinner, Richard Morton and Mark Lamarr all cultivate interruptions as an integral element of their performances – and far from being a sign of strength, squashing a heckler with unwarranted ferocity is a signal of fundamental weakness.

The true test of a top-class comic is their ability to dream up spontaneous put-downs tailored to each specific situation. Only also-rans resort to off-the-peg insults, such as 'I remember my first pint too', and 'Isn't it a shame when cousins marry?' Probably the only exception to this rule is Mancunian punk poet John Cooper Clarke, whose off-the-peg and oft-repeated put-downs rarely fail to amuse: 'I can't hear you mate – your mouth's full of shit!' and 'Your bus leaves in ten minutes – be under it!' For apprentice stand-ups, one rudimentary device is simply to ape poor hearing and ask the heckler to repeat their quip. The rest of the audience will have heard it perfectly the first time – nothing sounds as funny second time around – and stripped of the spontaneity that defines it, even the wittiest heckle sounds trite and tired.

Audience participation is such a miserable experience because it's invariably conducted on the performer's terms. Heckling is the precise opposite: the punters set the agenda, and the comic must adapt or die. Skinner once teased a bouncer until he strode onstage and seized the Brummie comic in a bearhug. 'Now I know what Fay Wray felt like!' ad-libbed Frank, to his astonished audience.

However, comedians can turn nasty too. Malcolm Hardee is reputed to dip the most private part of his anatomy into the drinks of sleeping punters, while Rob Newman has asked hecklers to step outside, although he always did a runner. Gentle Glaswegian Arnold Brown once held a heckler in an armlock while finishing the final five minutes of his act.

Doublebass buffoon Jim Tavare has been the recipient of several classic heckles: 'Midget with a violin!' and 'It doesn't matter if you die – you've brought your own coffin!' 'I'm schizophrenic . . . ', he began. 'Then why don't you both fuck off?' came the reply. A dismal *Star Trek* routine was once met with the retort, 'It's comedy, Jim, but not as we know it,' but the world's best heckle was actually coined by another comic. 'What d'you do for a living?' asked US stand-up Larry Aramos of Tony Allen, working the audience at the Assembly Rooms in Edinburgh. 'I'm a comedian,' replied Allen, 'what do you do?'

At its worst, heckling can be banal, crude and boring, but it's an element that cannot be removed without ripping the guts out of live stand-up. With waitress service and air-conditioning, Jongleurs Camden Lock is the comedic equivalent of an all-seater football stadium, but 'No Heckling' notices point to the alienation that yuppification brings about in any artform. Stand-up comedy needs its terrace culture too.

DAVID BADDIEL

It's not the job of the heckler to be funny. The job of the heckler is to be a drunken idiot, and it's the comedian's job to make that drunken idiocy funny. It's a myth that there are so many funny hecklers out there. There have been about five funny heckles in the history of heckling.

Standard put-downs are never funny. I remember the first time I ever saw Frank Skinner at the Comedy Store. Someone, for some reason, shouted out, 'I remember you from medical school!' Which was wrong – he didn't go to medical school. It's a real left-field heckle, and you might think, 'I can't deal with that straight away.' But Frank said, straight off, 'Oh yeah! You were the one in the jar!' I remember thinking, 'That's brilliant!' because I would have been thrown by that. Maybe after chatting for a bit, I could have got something funny out of it, but he came straight back in with it – and that's a real art.

ROB NEWMAN

I've always loved heckles, I've always welcomed them – and I've always enjoyed playing around with them. At the Alley Club [*which Newman ran for a year*] it was hecklemania – not like at the Tunnel. There it was brutal – it was about trying to destroy the comic. Only twice have I asked hecklers for a fight, and that was because I wasn't really being me. Doing Comedy of Hate, you have to be larger than life. I did it a few years ago for a little while, and I had to do that before I could do the next thing. The comics who are good at that never interact with the audience. The thing I love most is coming off the script, and you can't do it if you're in a super-aggressive mode. I hate comics who take a heckle as an affront to their authority. You've got to work with the heckle, you've got to say yes to it.

I had a six-month period of doing Comedy of Hate when it was fun for me to ride rough-shod over heckles, but early on, when I was doing open spots, long before I could do material, the one thing I could do was deal with heckles. When I was doing open spots, I was like a total beginner – which I was – but when I was dealing with heckles, it was as if I'd been a comic for ages. I was totally myself when I was doing ad-libs. The whole struggle of comedy is to be yourself, to find what Sam Kinison calls your own colour of the rainbow. I always had that in ad-lib.

FRANK SKINNER

There was a time when I used to go on thinking, 'Oh God, I hope I don't get heckled tonight!' But now, if an audience is quiet, I'll encourage them to speak to me. I like to talk to them, and I like them to talk to me. I've tried to completely eradicate the idea of the set put-down. The last thing I want to do with a heckler is put them down. I don't want to shut them up – I want them to give me more. I'm quite happy to take the piss out of them, but I want to take it somewhere else. Sometimes, you can get five or ten minutes out of someone. When I was doing the Perrier show there was a bloke in who was about eighteen. He had a checked shirt, jeans and boots on – and there was another bloke of about seventy who was wearing something incredibly similar. One of the blokes was called Jim, so I started calling them Young Jim and Old Jim, like two generations of the same bloke. I used it all night. If I start having a go at someone and I can see that they really don't like it, I'll move off them. They're not going to say anything interesting and also it makes me feel unpleasant.

I got heckled by a blind bloke once. He shouted out, 'Get off, you bastard!' And then, 'Has he gone yet?' He was brilliant. I couldn't come back at him.

ARNOLD BROWN

I believe there's a dark, violent side to me – and this is why I do comedy. At the Tunnel Club, most of the audience were behind me, and this guy at the front started shouting, 'You're rubbish!' It wasn't the odd heckle – it was every other second. I was so angry that I grabbed him and got him in an arm lock. I actually got a laugh from it. I held him, and carried on doing my act, and the audience half-forgot him.

At the Comedy Store I got a heavy ashtray thrown at me by some drunk. I saw him out of the corner of my eye and, luckily, I ducked. I was very angry about that – he could have killed me.

I did a gig in a pub in Putney, I mentioned that I was Jewish, and some woman shouted out something about the gas ovens. I laughed it off because I thought it was so preposterous. My standard put-down is, 'Do I detect the long-term side effects of junior aspirin?'

LEE EVANS

I did this club in Liverpool, right by the docks. It would shit you up just driving there at night – it really would. I used to take a guitar, a piano and a few amps around with me. I knew I could get away with a bit of boogie woogie if everything else failed – which it usually did. I was onstage, going about my business, dying on my arse, and this bloke in the front row suddenly stood up in the middle of my act and said, 'Excuse me, mate.' I said, 'What? What's the matter?' And he said, 'You've got no punchlines, have you?' I said, 'Pardon?' He said, 'You've got no punchlines. You know, gag, punchline – and we laugh. And you haven't got any, have you?' I said, 'Well, I'm just sort of describing things, observing things.' And he said, 'Yeah, but when you observe something, you need a punchline at the end, so we can laugh. We gotta know when to laugh, you see.' And his wife went, 'That's right! You've got to have a bloody punchline, otherwise how can we laugh?' This was coming over the mike, and everyone was going, 'Aye.' The whole fucking club was going, 'That's right! You've gotta have a fucking punchline.' So I said, 'What can I do? I ain't got any punchlines.' They said, 'Well that's no good, is it? How will we know when to laugh?' It turned into a debate, and I left.

I used to do these fun pubs for this bloke in Manchester. He used to say, 'Fun pubs! That's it! Young people! That's what you want!' But they were packed full of old codgers. It was a working men's club atmosphere. I was doing the same old shit: 'Innit strange when you're walking down the street, and you trip over and people look at you?' And they were all saying, 'I don't know what he's fucking on about – I really don't.'

I was in the middle of my act, when this bloke came on behind me and said, 'Who's got a car, registration number UCU 1294?' I said, 'Fucking hell! I'm in the middle of a gag!' He said, 'I've got to find out some time – I've got to get the van out!' I said, 'Well, all right – but not when I'm onstage.' But he said, 'Whose car is it?' I said, 'It's my car!' He said, 'Well move it!' I said, 'But I'm onstage!' And he said, 'Aye, but you're shite. Come on, move it. It's in the way.' So I went outside and moved it.

I had a bloke once who actually drained me. I was at a country club and I was really trying, but everybody was saying, 'He's crap, this bloke. He's crap.' And this bloke came up onstage and said, through the mike, 'You're shit. Give up. Have a pint.' And I said, 'I'm going to have a fucking pint,' and went and had a pint. I thought, 'I ain't gonna do this any more.' He was dead right – I was crap. He hit the nail on the head, and everybody in the room went, 'Yeah.'

I've got no lines for put-downs at all – whatever comes at me, I'll go with. If somebody says, 'Fuck off,' I'll say, 'Well why?' They say, ''Cos you're shit!' and I'll say, 'Well why am I shit?' But it's only because I feel more at ease onstage that I can be more creative and fool around with them. I once said to a bloke, 'What are you going to do for a face when King Kong wants his arse back?', which was a heckle-stopper of my own, and he stood up and said, 'This!' and hit me in the face. And I thought, 'Maybe I'd better cool down a bit – take it easy.'

RICHARD MORTON

Every night doing Jack Dee's tour, it's like opening for a big rock act. They all want to see Jack. He's a big star – they adore him. The music comes on, Jack walks onstage, the spotlight hits him – it's rock and roll. But he walked out the other night in Leicester – at the De Montfort Hall, which is two and a half thousand – and this bloke just laid into him the moment he got out there: 'You're a fucking cunt! Tell us some jokes!' It was really horrible abuse. Obviously, he crushed him, but he was quite taken aback.

Sometimes, when I get horrible hecklers, it really upsets me. Normally, I'm so thick-skinned about all that abuse, that they can call me anything and it doesn't really hurt because I know a funny line to come back with. But sometimes you can't put a heckler down. They're the hecklers from hell. They interrupt you so much that you can't get your material out, and you just can't kill them. Sometimes I've got the whole crowd to tell a heckler to fuck off – and they still won't go away.

People look at me and think, 'This bloke's about eight and a half stone – he's no threat.' I don't weigh enough to hurt anybody. Somebody like Jack Dee could scare you. He looks a bit scary sometimes, so you don't want to take him on. Blokes will take me on, but women won't bother. A lot of my act is based on the aggressive world I live in and the violent world I was brought up in, but they just think it's funny.

I remember seeing Jo Brand compering at the Comedy Store. There was one table of blokes being really abusive and horrible to her, saying the most foul, vicious, nasty things. Jo is a really tough act. She's given so much shit to so many hecklers. She's demolished them! I've seen her nail them to the floor! But this one night, they were giving her so much grief – nasty stuff. She came back into the dressing room towards the end of the show and she was looking really tired, because she had to go out and fend for herself every time – let alone bring the next act on. I was so angry. She's done so many favours for me, and so I stormed out there and I laid into this bloke. Afterwards, Jo said, 'That was great, Richard, but he wasn't the one who was giving me the grief.'

MARK THOMAS

Me and Jo Brand used to do gigs together, and we did a couple of horrible ones. We did a lunchtime gig – it was a real rough-house. I'd gone on and survived and then I introduced Jo. But because she was a woman, they were heckling her – really nasty stuff, really vitriolic misogynistic stuff. It was really hurtful. There's nothing that you can actually do. I remember at one point Jo said, 'If you don't shut up, I'm going to get Mark Thomas to come and fuck you!' I jumped up and said, 'Come on! Which one is it?' I went over to this guy, and everybody was going, 'Yeah!' I didn't realise that I was actually creating more fuss. A whole hubbub broke out – and I was about five yards away from Jo. I was thinking, 'This is shit – this is completely shit!' She left the stage shortly afterwards, and we dived into Jo's car and drove off. She was really upset, and we had to do another gig in the evening.

I was booked to do a working men's club in Kensal Green. I thought, 'That sounds like a bit of fun!' It was a huge old room, really cavernous. They had a meal and we were supposed to go on in between the courses. I was compering, and it really got my back up – especially as I got heckled by the club treasurer. I said, 'What the fuck are you doing?' I was swearing at him and abusing him, and we started having a huge row. As the evening continued I was getting progressively more and more belligerent. I went on at one stage and said, 'Right! How many of you lot are in short-term housing? How many of you are in squats? How many of you are in council house flats? How many of you have moved into the area? I want to find the new money and the old money, and I want to find those who haven't got any money.' Half the audience were Ladbroke Grove squatters who'd bunked in with mates who were helping out with the catering. They started cheering, and the regulars started going mad. One of the waitresses started heckling. I grabbed the fire extinguisher and fired it at the front table. All these side salads went scooting off everywhere. The treasurer turned my mike off, and it turned into a running battle.

He got onstage and said that he would never book me again, I wasn't going to get paid for tonight, and that he had a vision of the inner cities working together with private enterprise to create a new culture that would benefit everyone, and all these hippies at the front started heckling him. I came on afterwards and said, 'Look, I'm going to introduce the last act – and then I'm just going to go away, because it's obvious that I'm not really wanted here.' And these hippies said, 'How much are you getting paid?' I said, 'I'm supposed to be getting paid fifty quid.' And they had a whip-round, and said, 'Here you are, mate – have that! That's for you! Do the gig – do the gig!'

JO BRAND

I still get plenty of heckling. It's good in that it does something to the atmosphere of a show, and on occasions it can lift it up on to another level and make the audience feel they're a lot more involved. Audiences like nothing better than a clever heckler or a comic who's good at putting the heckler down. Nine times out of ten you should be able to deal with it. In Leeds, someone shouted out, 'Why don't you put some jam on your shoes and invite your trousers to tea?' I thought that was a great heckle – it really made the audience laugh. The way to react in that circumstance is not to be petulant that a heckler's made the audience laugh, but just to acknowledge that it's a great heckle.

Lee Hurst gets lots of heckling because he's bald. Also, there seems to be a movement against ginger people at the moment. They're the new blacks of comedy. Owen O'Neill gets a lot of heckles because he's ginger. It tends to happen when groups of men are together – if a man's on his own and he heckles that's quite weird. They tend to do it to impress their mates.

There was a woman at the Comedy Store who didn't like me – I could tell as soon as I came on. I don't know why. She'd seen me before. I said, 'Oh, shut up, you stupid cow!' which isn't the cleverest put-down. It tipped the balance on to her side, and I was struggling to get it back to where I was before.

ARTHUR SMITH

I did a big miners' benefit in '84 or '85. It was a big bill, Ben Elton and Benjamin Zephaniah [*black performance poet*] – and someone shouted out, 'Racist!' I crumbled at that. The gag was 'A Rastafarian recites Wordsworth – "I an' I wander lonely as a cloud/ Him float on high, him move and dance/ When all at once, we see a crowd/ A host of golden ganja plants." ' It was a silly little joke, but of course the dodgy bit was that I was putting on a Rastafarian accent. I wouldn't do it now – but at the time the thought that I'd said something offensive to a right-on audience was scary. I could deal with it now, because I've got more confidence in myself, but it was the first time I'd compered a really big gig and I blew it. I said something like, 'Well, I don't think it is. Is it?' Something really fucking feeble like that – instead of saying, 'Bollocks! Of course it isn't! It's just a little joke!' That's the line you tread. It's acceptable for a black comic to do gags about white people – impressions of them dancing – but the other way round, you get yourself in trouble. After that heckle, everything else I attempted went horribly wrong.

I've had hecklers who've gone a bit weird on me – I remember at Jongleurs, this bloke really looked like he was going to hit someone – probably me. It was like talking someone down off a ledge. I could have humiliated him easily but that would have sent him wild. It was a very exciting occasion.

JENNY ECLAIR

I haven't had any heckling hard times for several years because I go on as if I'm the boss. I'm loud and raucous and it's basically all bluff. Underneath, I'm just a simpering girlie. I'm enjoying a renaissance as rock-chick comic from hell, snob-woman and all-round baddie in fake animal skins. I'm basically reliving my youth – strutting around and showing off madly. Someone's going to smack my bottom soon, and put me to bed early without any supper – it will all end in tears. The hard times I get now are not so much heckling as reserved disapproval.

I had a very horrible time at the Elephant Fayre [*hippy summer festival in Cornwall*]. I was twenty-one when I started doing this. I knew nothing – at that point, I was doing poetry. The Vicious Boys [*early eighties alternative double-act*] were supposed to be onstage, and they hadn't turned up. I was having a quick pee round the back of the tent, and Malcolm Hardee, who was compering, saw me through the flap, just as I was pulling up my pants, and announced me on stage to about eight hundred leatherclad motor-cyclists. This was in my twee girlie days when I just simpered around, and I started my act with the immortal lines: 'You know what it's like when you're having a dinner party . . .' And they all shouted, 'Fuck off!' I realise now that it's not my fault all of the time. Sometimes there are circumstances beyond your control which make for a duff gig.

STEWART LEE

I suppose I've done a thousand gigs, and I've only been heckled about ten times. It used to always absolutely destroy me, but when it happens now, I can usually go with it, because I can stay in character and deal with it in a way that seems appropriate to the act. I got heckled off two years ago in Southend, for being gay. I hadn't done any material about being gay, but compared to everyone else in Southend, I obviously looked a bit gay – and that was reason enough to get someone offstage. There was nothing I could say about it. It wasn't even as if I'd made a point about it – it came out of nowhere. The whole audience was chanting at me. It was a weird sort of hatred. I don't know where it came from. I was only on for about ten minutes. As soon as I went on, people started shouting at me. Somebody shouted out, 'Are you gay?' And I didn't know what to say. And then they all started chanting, 'Crucify him!' Which was really strange. I don't know what I did – I've never had anything like it. Afterwards, the bloke who ran the gig said, 'I can't pay you – you didn't do the set.'

You're in a vacuum on the circuit. Mark Thomas said to me that he didn't play army bases, because that was sanctioning their work. I said, 'Well, that's all very well – but if you're doing political stuff, and you're concerned about it, as you are, there's not really that much point in doing most of the gigs you do, because all the people there agree with you anyway. If you've really got something to say, you should take it out to the prostitutes and tax gatherers and see what they think of it, and see if you can use your comedy skills to win them round.' He said, 'The London clubs that we do aren't really that sound,' but they are compared to somewhere like Southend. Someone isn't going to get heckled off *en masse* by an audience at any London club just because they think they're gay.

Now, I quite enjoy it if people start to have a go, because I don't really care if I don't go so well at the Cartoon on a Friday night. It's not the end of the world – I can always do something else, whereas two years ago it would have been like, 'Oh no, I hope they book me again.' The less you worry about it, the better it goes.

EDDIE IZZARD

I first dealt with hecklers on the street. I'd developed what I called the Imposing Scenario technique. Someone would say, 'Fuck off!' and I'd say, 'This is Steve. He's going to be saying "Fuck off" at regular intervals. He's a beginner heckler from Kent – he's driven up here for the day.' You'd impose a whole identity on to him and although the audience knew it was all bullshit, he became your assistant. Every time 'Steve' said, 'Fuck off – you're crap,' I'd say, 'Good! Keeps me on my toes. Thank you, Steve!' And that deflected all the heckles.

When you hear a heckle that's garbled, you analyse and check if it's from someone who has a disability or not before you lay in – that's something I learnt from the street. I learnt so many techniques from street performing.

There are so many nutters on the street. They wander past and say, 'Hey! There's a show here!' And then they actually come into the show. If you ever got angry, you lost it. One time, seven guys started heckling – they do it in groups in the street. They attacked me really early, so the audience weren't with me. They were doing mindbogglingly crap heckles and they ruined the show. I had to cancel, and at the end they came over and said, 'That was great, mate! Well done! We loved it! Great fun! Did we help you? We were trying to help you!' I wanted to kill them. It's some sort of spillover from the vaudeville of yesteryear.

RICHARD HERRING

I get quite a lot of heckles, and I think I encourage it. I try to open up, and I quite like the audience to comment, because usually I'm actually quite good at dealing with it. Sometimes, when it gets too much, I do get too angry. It's a question of keeping your cool. Stewart [*Lee*] never gets heckled, whereas I'm more upfront, and I encourage people to talk back to me. I remember doing a preview of 'Ra Ra Rasputin' at the Red Rose, which was a very bad place to do it. Quite a lot of people had come along to see it but a few people had turned up thinking it was stand-up comedy as usual. They were heckling and shouting out, and I was really angry. So I thought, 'What would Rasputin do? He'd go and hit them in the face.' So I ran into the audience and it all got a bit nasty. I can sometimes misjudge things – it's when I get angry that it goes wrong. I don't do it so much any more, but I used to do it quite a lot when I was a student, if I'd been drinking.

BOB MORTIMER

We did the Tunnel Club once and they booed us off. Then as soon as we went off, they started shouting, 'More! More! More!' But it was just as a con. We came back on and starting singing 'Meals on Wheels', and they started glassing us.

When I went on as The Man With a Stick, you couldn't get out of the way of anything. Some cans got thrown – full ones, not empty. One of them smacked me right in the head. You can't see 'em coming when you're up there.

STEVE PUNT

Solo acts can deal with hecklers much more easily because they are playing themselves. But I'm not quite playing myself – I'm half me and half narrator, and Hugh is never himself – he's always being some zany character or other. So it's slightly fourth wall, and if you come out of that, it changes the relationship between you and the audience. If you're a stand-up, and you turn round and put down a table of hecklers, that's fine because it's an extension of your act. It's inherently theatrical to be watching two people, because they're relating to each other internally, whereas a stand-up is talking straight at you. For that reason, if the audience all buy into our act straight away, we have a fantastic time, but if somebody breaks that spell, it's very difficult.

If I have to stop and talk to a heckler, what does Hugh do? He has to stand there – or if he talks to the heckler, I have to stand there and say, 'Yes, I agree with him!' If they're enjoying it, they don't want to interrupt, because there are any number of stand-ups who almost invite heckling, and it's a change not to be constantly called upon to be responsive.

You can't hear heckles a lot of the time. Generally, the acoustics are too bad – and often the audience can't hear them either.

CHARLIE CHUCK

If someone tries to heckle Charlie Chuck, it doesn't register – he doesn't even know they're there. At Up the Creek you've got to be strong. Otherwise you'll go under. You've got to be believable, but they can't get through to me with a heckle, because it appears to go over my head. They think, 'Bloody hell, I'd better not say nowt to him, otherwise he'll go for us with that lump of wood!' They're drawn in and that's the difference.

I'd never been to London before. I didn't know what day it was. I didn't know what to expect. I couldn't understand it. Comedians effing and blinding – I'd never known it! The first time I went there, I knocked them dead. The second time I was a bit looser and I heckled back. I realised that was a mistake, because then they were all firing back. It went well – I still won them over. They didn't heckle me off –

they heckled me back on, actually. They wanted me to stay on. But I shouldn't have come out of character, and I did.

JACK DEE

I've never experienced a witty heckle – they've always been of the 'fuck off' variety, or someone desperately trying to join in and misjudging the situation very badly. Occasionally, you hear about very funny heckles that have gone on at some gig when you weren't there. You wonder whether it really happened.

There's an awful lot of nonsense talked about heckling. All it is is dealing with interruptions. Sometimes the most contemptuous thing you can do with a heckle is to totally ignore it and let someone sit there wishing he hadn't opened his mouth.

The other day, I was in Belfast. I went on and before I could say anything, someone shouted something out. That's a situation you must deal with – otherwise you're never going to have any authority. However, if you do deal with it, you've won them for the night. That's exactly what happened – the guy got squished, and it made my job a lot easier. And it's a good feeling when they shut up – it can be a very good feeling indeed.

JEREMY HARDY

Doing impro, abuse comes in the form of suggestions that people write down and hand in with the suggestions for the sketches. You get some fairly foul stuff of all kinds. People write down, 'We think this show's shit.' Just after we'd adopted our daughter, we got one once saying, 'Meanwhile Kit and Jeremy's baby died.' That was horrible. Kit [*Hollerbach, American comedienne and Hardy's wife*] picked it out, and she was really shaken by it. If I'd known who'd written that, I'd have been off the stage and at them with a beer glass, without doubt. I remember a time at the Comedy Store. This guy was heckling Kit. He was giving her a lot of grief – the standard sort of stuff that gets thrown at women. She'd nailed him fairly conclusively, but then she decided to stop and make a speech. She said, 'Look, we're getting really pissed off with this. We come here to make you laugh. We're not asking for the world. We're just asking for a bit of humanity and compassion and respect from you.'

The audience all clapped, and all the performers were on their feet – and then she just carried on with her act. That's the most brilliant thing I've ever seen in terms of dealing with hecklers. She was able to be serious, and then be funny again.

DONNA McPHAIL

The second time I went back to Jongleurs I had the worst heckle I've ever had. It was, 'Fuck off, you cunt,' from a woman. This was seven years ago – and it wasn't on at all for anybody to use that word, onstage or off. And coming from a woman, that was much worse than if a man had said it. Jongleurs is a very laddish club. All the 'gals' think what the lads do for a laugh is frightfully funny, so they all join in with what the boys do and they like to be very boyish in their attitude to comics, as well. They're not at all supportive. Women are not your friends if you're onstage. They can be worse than men, because they really know how to destroy you. Men just say say, 'Show us your tits!'

I got heckled once about my hair. A female heckler said, 'Where did you get your hair cut?' This was when I'd just started, so I thought, 'What can I say to that? What's wrong with my hair? What do you mean?'

Tony Allen gave me the key to dealing with hecklers. He said, 'Never assume a heckler is cleverer than you. They might manage to come out with one fairly witty line – but if you can come out with one back, you've won. And if you don't try, you've lost anyway – so you've got nothing to lose.' The majority of hecklers are very stupid and drunk. Their heckles tend to be very facetious and silly. With men, it comes from being intimidated by a woman onstage and trying to humiliate her. If you can absorb that, and open your mouth and hope something funny comes out, you've won. Even if the gig isn't going well for you, it'll go well for you after that.

I don't play Jongleurs in Battersea because I can't stand them. I'd rather shoot those people than make them laugh. I think they're disgusting. Jongleurs Camden is a different audience, but Battersea is still that eighties, striped shirt 'just been skiing over the Easter holidays with Ma and Pa in Switzerland'. You don't get normal working-class people down there. They're all City types who've got their own flats in Battersea, and Mum and Dad paid the deposit.

They've all been to university, and having not been to university, I can't stand that. One hundred and fifty of them is a nightmare. If I had a machine gun . . . I was doing a joke about my bank manager, and I said something about an overdraft and some guy said, 'What's an overdraft?' And the whole audience laughed. That's so disgraceful. Those people don't give a shit. Luckily, they've all lost their jobs now, due to the recession, and had their homes taken off them – I sincerely hope – but this was during the boom, when everybody who worked in the City had ten Porsches hanging off their ears. I said, 'I have absolutely nothing to say to you people,' and walked off. Every comic reserves the right to walk off. I've only ever done it once. I thought, 'You people are a bunch of fucking bastards, and I hope you die very horribly.' I was only doing a half spot anyway, and I was dying. But I didn't want to struggle through and simper to these people. You get to the point where you think, 'Right! I'm going to get something out of this gig for myself!' I saw Paul Merton do that once. Everyone had done really well, and he was headlining, but they didn't like him. So he started ad-libbing about nothing. He did the whole gig with no material, really annoying them. He thought, 'Right! I'll wind them up!' You could tell. He had a smile on his face.

JEFF GREEN

You can turn gigs around. You do develop the skills to do that. The first time I ever turned a gig around was at the Town and Country Club. It was a pointless gig. It was fifty quid on a Friday night, and they were horrible people. I was on first – I was getting nothing and then the heckles started coming. When you're getting no laughs, you know it's going to happen, and if you're not funny, there's no sympathy – the whole crowd is with the heckler because there's no point in you being there. You're just getting in the way. So I had to accept his heckles, and my status was dropping all the time. But I just knew from the way he was heckling that at some point he was going to drop himself in it. Meanwhile, I was becoming more likeable to the audience, because I was being put upon – that's the English way. And then, bang! He said something over the top, something quite hurtful. I didn't give a fuck, but I could tell that the crowd thought he'd gone too far, so I seized the moment. Suddenly the sympathy was with me, so I could attack him. I used a couple of stock put-downs, which got laughs. He came back again, but by now they were with me and my status was rising back up again. I bantered off him a bit and everyone was a lot more relaxed, because I'd started to get laughs, and in the end I turned it around, from absolutely nothing to a big cheer at the end, rather than leaving after four minutes.

I had a lovely heckle the other day that made me corpse for about ten minutes. I do this joke which begins, 'What do we give budgies to eat?' And the answer is, 'Cuttlefish,' but I paused before I said it. And this bloke shouted out, 'Gravel!' I love it when we're all together as a team – rather than me picking on them, and them picking on me. That's not what it's all about.

MARK LAMARR

I've had heckles that have had me in hysterics, and you think, 'Well, that hasn't really helped me because it was my job to think it up,' but it cheered everyone up, and at the end of the day, that's what you're there for. When there's a laugh at your expense, you've no choice but to have a go back. If it's directed against you, you can't leave it, even if it's fantastic and you're laughing inwardly – because if you do leave it, then the heckler has won.

One time at the Red Rose there was a black heckler in the audience and sad as it is to say it, it's very hard to deal with black hecklers – not because of them, but because of the audience. People think, 'Hold on – I think there's a racist connotation there,' whether you mean it or not, and whether the black person in the audience thinks so or not. It's a shame that more black people don't come to see comedy, and that's probably why they don't, because everyone else around them is thinking, 'Oh my God, I hope he doesn't speak to the black bloke!' It's a problem that audiences impose upon you: 'Oh no, we really don't think you should talk to him – because you might say something that we don't know how to take.'

I'm very used to people heckling me because I've been on telly. It's a noose around my neck. I was doing 'Late & Live' at the Gilded Balloon. One bloke got more and more frustrated every time I dealt with him. He's well known in Edinburgh as the naked man. He publishes a little magazine of himself naked in different places.

LIVERPOOL JOHN MOORES UNIVERSITY
LEARNING SERVICES

Everyone's aware of him, and so he probably thinks that people admire him. After a long sequence of heckles he said, 'I'm going to kick your fucking head in!'

I found that funny, because he was obviously quite drunk. I thought, 'If that's the boyish game he wants to play, I'll play along with it,' so I said, 'Well, come on then,' because I knew there was no way he'd be able to. So he came towards the stage, and kept turning towards the crowd, and saying, 'I'm going to kick his fucking head in,' and that was when I became convinced he'd have to because you can't show that much bravado and bottle out at the last minute. It's that stupid boyish thing – even if you know you're going to get beaten up, you know you've got to go and do it. I wasn't scared in the slightest. I've been in a lot of fights and I don't think I'm hard or fearless, but I know that if you're in a fight situation, there's no way of getting out of it. If I'd run off the stage he would have run after me and beaten me up if he was going to. So I thought, 'There's going to be a fight, there's going to be a fight,' but I was in such a good mood anyway that I certainly didn't think that any harm was going to come to me. I thought he'd probably swing one punch and fall over.

So eventually, he got up onstage and said, 'I'm going to fucking beat you up,' for about the fifteenth time, and so I said, 'Well do it, so I can get on with the show.' He said, 'No – give me the mike,' and I said, 'No – either you punch me, or you fuck off.' I certainly wasn't going to hit him, but I was convinced that, eventually, he was going to hit me. I turned to the crowd and did a line which got a massive laugh, and when I turned around he was lying prostrate on one of the front tables. I know it was a case of, 'How can I get out of this situation? I've got to pretend that I'm so drunk that I'm going to fall off the stage' – which he obviously wasn't, because he climbed up there in the first place.

HARRY HILL

My favourite heckle put-down is: 'You may heckle me now, but I'm safe in the knowledge that when I get home, I've got a lovely chicken in the oven.' It gets a really big laugh and that's all you need, really. Once you've got the room on your side, then you're away – but if everyone's against you by that stage, you might as well give up.

10. Edinburgh

'Edinburgh's like a great big holiday camp for people of a certain age who are old enough to know better.' – Jenny Eclair

The best definition of the Edinburgh Festival Fringe that I've ever come across came from the comic (unfortunately I can't remember which one) who likened it to twenty-one consecutive New Year's Eves – although what with the week of previews which now precedes each annual three-week jamboree, it's more like twenty-eight. Despite the perennial complaints that Edinburgh's become too commercialised, lost its spark, sold out, etc., this is the comparison that still rings true, because it sums up best of all just how brilliant and horrendous Edinburgh can be.

Both extremes stem from the same source – the fact that for the best part of the hottest month of the year, all but the biggest and smallest comics, plus hundreds of publicity parasites, sadistic hacks, phonies, wannabees and hangers-on all migrate several hundred miles north, far from the fake security of their metropolitan squalor, to the hub of a foreign country that few of them even attempt to understand. There they requisition a few makeshift theatres, several bars and half a dozen restaurants where, but for a few catastrophic annual exceptions, they have the time of their lives.

Like those mill towns of the Industrial Revolution whose entire economies revolve around a single product, throughout the brief breezy respite which the Scots call summer, Edinburgh becomes comedy's capital city. Despite the growing significance and neglected reputations of Glasgow's Mayfest and Laughing Gas, the comedy component of the Brighton Festival, Edinburgh remains the world's most important comedy trade fair (with the possible exception of Just for Laughs in Montreal) and the most unconventional showbusiness convention in the UK.

Comedy on the Edinburgh Festival Fringe revolves around three venues – which last summer joined forces to form the Stella Artois Comedy Festival. The flagship venue is the Assembly Rooms, managed by William Burdett Coutts (artistic director of London's Riverside Studios). This imposing old mausoleum scarcely qualifies as a fringe venue at all – in fact, it's often hard to believe that it's not an offshoot of London's West End. However, it hosts many of the most established comedians on the Fringe and is an annual springboard to television. Indeed, it's perfectly located for media moguls, merely a swift hundred-yard stagger from the George Hotel – site of that perennial shmoozefest also known as the Television Festival. The Assembly Rooms club bar is a watering hole for gossip columnists: imagine several hundred second-rate celebs – and even the occasional first-rate one – crammed into a tiny Traveller's Fare.

A better bet for unearthing new talent is the Gilded Balloon in Cowgate – a dark subterranean alley that curls around the foot of the castle like a sleeping dragon's tail. Whereas the Assembly Rooms epitomise Georgian New Town gentility, the Gilded Balloon sums up the seductive grime and gloom of the medieval Old Town. Run by Norwegian Scot Karen Koren, it attracts a far higher ratio of Scottish comics and punters, and hosts the notorious Late & Live – the nearest thing I've encountered to a stand-up comedy nightclub. Its annexe is the Stepping Stones – formerly the Traverse Theatre, which recently graduated upmarket to plush new premises in Edinburgh's West End.

Christopher Richardson runs the Pleasance – a ramshackle crow's nest of studios clustered around a quaint courtyard, perched on a hill overlooking Arthur's Seat. Outside of the Festival, this windswept quadrangle is a mundane storehouse for canoes, but in August it becomes a pseudo-continental piazza, awful Scots weather permitting, and the focus for the Festival's most innovative comedy. Richardson is always prepared to take risks and put his money where his mouth is (a few years ago he had to sell his car, while Koren remortgaged her house). Richardson's done a great deal to launch that dramatic mongrel artform – sit-down plays written by stand-up comics. Ben Miller's *Huge* and *Live Bed Show* by Arthur Smith both premiered here.

And as for those folk who claim Edinburgh ain't what it used to be? Well, they're the same people who say *Top of the Pops* is rubbish nowadays. They're not talking about Edinburgh or *TOTP*. They're talking about themselves. In the words of Johnny Rotten: if it's too loud, you're too old.

Jeremy Hardy claims that Edinburgh is called the Athens of the North because every summer it's full of students throwing up everywhere, and when I'm too old to hack the pace, I won't go to Edinburgh and moan about it. I'll wrap up warm, back home in Hammersmith, and watch that nice Mr Elton on the telly. Because, despite the bullshit, for comedy fans, Edinburgh is still the business. See you up there.

STEVE COOGAN

I had a bad time last Edinburgh – I had a very bad time. I took a lot of cocaine up there, and I went to hospital a week before I won the Perrier. I collapsed after too many late nights. It was the first time I'd ever taken it. Someone had some and gave it to me, and I took it for a few nights on the trot. I didn't eat much, I didn't sleep, and my blood sugar level was really low. At breakfast, I thought was having a heart attack. Patrick [*Marber, his director and writing partner*] drove me to hospital. It was the worst experience of my life, ever. I was convinced I was going to die. A lot of it was hyperventilation. It was a panic attack, which made it worse. Hyperventilating makes your brain go odd, so they kept me in for observation and put me in a bed and wired me up to an ECG.

I was doing another show in Edinburgh, as well as my own, and the manager came in to see me in hospital. He said, 'D'you think you'll be well enough to do the show tonight?' I said, 'No! I thought I was going to die!' I'd just come out of this panic attack, and I was so relieved to be alive. He said, 'It'd be really good if you could do the show.' He said, 'D'you think you'll be well enough to do your show?' His show was at six, and mine was at ten. I said, 'Well I might be well enough to do mine. I'm starting to feel a lot better now. It's all passed, it's over.' And he said, 'Well if you did your show, and didn't do our show, it might be a good thing – it might be good publicity.' I said, 'What d'you mean?' He said, 'You know, "TOP COMEDIAN COLLAPSES". Might sell a few more tickets.' I said, 'What?' And he said, 'But if you just did the show, there wouldn't be any need for that.' So I said, 'Well, I'll try.' He said, 'It'd be really good if you could do the show, but it can work both ways.' I felt a bit better, and Patrick said, 'I think you'd better do it.' So I got out of bed and got dressed. They said, 'Are you all right?' I said, 'Yeah,' and signed myself out and went and did the show at six o'clock that evening.

For the rest of Edinburgh I was having panic attacks. I had some therapy last year because even when I hadn't taken anything, I had these panic attacks when I thought I was going to die. Throughout Edinburgh I was having them quite a lot. I started not going out in the evening, so that I could relax and do the show. I managed to work hard on the show in spite of that – but I don't touch anything now.

I see a lot of comics who take it regularly. I don't feel that I want it. It was only peer pressure at the time and the fact that it seemed like a good crack. I don't have a craving for drugs. I'm not puritanical or moralistic about it, but I do say to friends, 'Be careful. It can really screw you up. I thought I was going to die.' I did all that thing of seeing my whole life, thinking what I'd achieved and trying to imagine my mother being told of my impending death. It was a horrendous experience.

FRANK SKINNER

There were no gigs in Birmingham at the time but I knew a place called Tic Toc [*Theatre In Coventry Theatre Of Coventry*], which was about as near as it got, so I phoned them up and said, 'I want to book a slot in Edinburgh next year.' They said, 'How long d'you want to do?' I said, 'I dunno – a couple of hours.' They said, 'People don't normally do that long.' I said, 'Well, how long do people do?' They said, 'The top stars only do about an hour.' I said, 'OK, I'll do an hour then – how much is it?' They said, 'Two hundred pounds a week.' I said, 'I'll do a couple of weeks.' I sent them my life savings, which was four hundred pounds, and booked a lunchtime spot in Edinburgh, having never done a gig.

Me and Malcolm decided to pool our resources. He was going down to London clubs and booking anybody he saw – he didn't know who was good and who was bad. We were both flying blind. He'd put together the gigs and I'd compere them. I wrote twenty minutes of new material every week. A lot of it was shit, but some of it wasn't, and I did an hour at Edinburgh with that material. The highest audience was twelve. I played to two on a couple of occasions and one day nobody turned up at all. But I did my hour every day and lost about twelve hundred quid. At this point, my approach was to ingratiate myself with the audience – but while I was up there, I did the Fringe Club [*an impromptu, late night gig at Heriot Watt University Students Union that welcomes all comers, and then slaughters them*]. It was fucking rough. Before I went on, blokes were tipping beer on to comics from the balcony. It was a nightmare – I was shitting myself. But then I thought, 'Bastards!' I went onstage and abused the audience for about fifteen minutes and absolutely stormed it, and I thought, 'That's it! I've found it!'

Edinburgh is a comedy trade fair. When I went there with Steve Coogan in 1990 nobody had heard of me at all. That was a very important year for me, but I only got in on an off chance. Steve needed a support act and he suggested me, but the woman who worked at the Pleasance at the time said, 'Frank Skinner will play at the Pleasance over my dead body!' because she'd seen me at some club and thought I was offensive. But I did play there without needing to kill her, and in fact we did incredibly well.

Winning the Perrier Award is one of the most exciting things that has ever happened to me. That night I went offstage and into the back room – and then the stage manager came in and said, 'They want you back onstage.' At that point, I'd written off the Perrier because I'd been told the announcement was made earlier in the evening and I'd heard nothing. Then I heard this voice over the microphone saying, 'Ladies and gentlemen, I have a very pleasant duty to perform.' I went back on, and the crowd went barmy. They gave me a bouquet of flowers and a bottle of champagne. There was a bloke in the front row who I'd been taking the piss out of all night and so, in a grand showbiz gesture, I leant down and gave him the bottle of champagne and said, 'Here you are – drink this,' and the crowd applauded. It was fantastic – I was so chuffed.

When I started to get gigs at the Comedy Store, there were some comics who could walk into the dressing room without feeling edgy. The bloke on the door would say hello to them. They were really established. People knew them and respected what they did, and I really envied them. I never felt completely at home there, and I thought, 'These are the big guys on the circuit and I'd love to be like that. They really look at home. They look like they've got the right to be here.' When I won the Perrier, I felt I had the right to call myself a comedian.

RICHARD MORTON

The first time I did the Assembly Rooms was in 1991, with Jenny Lecoat [*acerbic stand-up comedienne*]. Addison Cresswell asked me to compere the Assembly Rooms preview, where everyone does five minutes of their act for the international press. He said, 'It'll be brilliant exposure for you!' It was one of the grimmest gigs ever. It was at eleven-thirty a.m., on the first day of the Festival. I went out there and did all my jokes, and they just wrote them all down – there was no laughter at all. Dying as the compere is the worst, because you have to keep coming back out onstage and dying some more – it was never-ending. Worse than that, Channel 4 sent a camera crew in, and filmed the whole thing. I was on Channel 4 news that night. They were saying, 'The Edinburgh Festival starts today!' and there were clips of me doing my act. My girlfriend rang up and said, 'Quick! Put Channel 4 news on. It's brilliant! They've filmed you doing a rehearsal! That's how big you are now!' And I said, 'No, you don't understand. That was live – there was just no laughter!' Of all the times that you want the television to be there! After that I never really pushed for telly. I thought, 'I'll let it come to me.'

JENNY ECLAIR

Last year I did twenty-four gigs on the trot – and I had three dodgy ones. Two were just slightly off, but at one of them they had an allergic reaction to me as soon as I came on. That was very hard to deal with. There was nothing I could do. I tried charming, I tried light, I tried aggressive, I tried every which fucking way. I worked my butt off and there was nothing.

Sometimes you say something and it's misconstrued. In 1992 I suddenly became aware that the front row consisted of tiny people in wheelchairs – torso people. I found myself mentally flicking through my material, and I realised that there was a line which could be deemed offensive to small people – it contained the word dwarf, and I changed it to pixie. I felt a fraud, though. I thought, 'Why are you so crap, Jenny?'

Last year was my best Edinburgh. I had a bloody good laugh, but for the first week, I was the most unhappy person in the world. I couldn't eat. I lost six pounds in a week. I was so frightened. I was really ill with it. I was so scared of failing. I was terrified.

Edinburgh is still a big loss. Last year I did a one-woman show and sold out every night. I haven't even got the money yet – I won't have made anything. I won't have lost much, but publicity and costs are so massive, and you've got to be in one of the three main venues.

ARNOLD BROWN

The Gilded Balloon studio theatre is a great venue for me. It's small, intimate and there are a lot of Scottish people around – and the night I won the Perrier Award was very exciting. There was that same unreality that I felt when I supported Frank Sinatra. I don't like ostentation or hype – I almost felt as if I was caught up in a parody of showbusiness. It was tremendously nerve-wracking, but I knew we were on to the winner, because we'd done a preview in the Third Eye in Glasgow, and it all clicked. I felt under pressure, but the atmosphere was great.

I'm usually very cynical about thrusting for showbiz success, but I went with it. I remember walking around afterwards with Nick Revell and his woman friend, in a nice artistic daze. There was great goodwill towards me. During other years there's rivalry – but I'd already been performing for seven years. I'd done my apprenticeship, and although everybody wants to win, if I was going to win, they were quite happy.

DONNA McPHAIL

The Perrier Award makes your Edinburgh or breaks it. If you don't get a nomination, your audience drops off – and once the winner is announced, it's all over. Apart from the Perrier winner and the nominees, everyone else's audiences drop off and it's a waste of time being there. If you're not included in that, there's no other reason for being there. In 1992 the last week of my show with Jeff Green was miserable. There is no one who gets on to the shortlist who doesn't deserve it, but you are putting money into it – and although that's not all you go up for, that tends to be all that counts. Everyone moans about Perrier but everyone would love to be nominated for it. I don't know one comic in the world who would turn it down.

RICHARD HERRING

The first gig I can remember was when I was with the Oxford University Revue. It was at Late & Live at the Gilded Balloon but it had been set up as a joke to get us, because we were from Oxford. It had been organised specially. All the stand-up comedians were there, and it was all prepared, so that the minute we came on, they booed us off – it was like a wall of sound. They didn't care what happened. It was quite funny, because there was nothing we could do. We knew it wasn't because we were shit – which we probably were – but because they'd decided they didn't like us.

The irony was that we thought, 'Great!' because we were going to get ten quid each – and everyone was heckling us for being rich bastards from Oxford. But we stuck it out and we got paid. The girls who were in it got a bit scared, and hid at the back, but I thought it was quite fun. We decided we'd do it again, so we went back again the next week. We also got slagged off by Keith Allen on *Edinburgh Nights* [*the Edinburgh Festival edition of* The Late Show *on BBC2*]. I don't think we deserved their criticism, that we were posh wankers. Actually, none of us were posh. We were wankers, but we'd just got better 'A' level results than them. I can laugh about it now, but it was so horrible at the time that I almost gave up doing comedy altogether. I felt there was so much resentment there, which I didn't think I deserved. The reason is that in the sixties, everyone from Oxford and Cambridge got on to the telly, so now everyone on the circuit has reacted against that. I thought, 'If I want to do this, I'm going to really have to want to.'

Coming to Edinburgh is all highs and lows – there's very little in between. I don't think it's much use in career terms. I think Edinburgh should be about trying out new ideas – coming up with something new or different in an environment where everyone else is doing the same thing. It's a place to try things out and make friends. On the circuit, it's very hard to make friends with the people you're working with. It's more competitive when you're in front of the same audience as everyone else and you're all trying to get another gig. Comedians are all a bit paranoid, so it's nice to meet them in a more relaxed atmosphere.

JEREMY HARDY

Edinburgh is a very closed environment and it's hard not to get things completely out of proportion. 1993 was the first year I hadn't been there for a decade, and it's a very strange feeling. You're sitting at home, you get the papers in the morning, you read a review of somebody, and you know how utterly devastated or utterly insufferable they'll be that day – because of a hundred words that have been written about them. You do go a bit mental in Edinburgh. For three weeks you're in an intense environment. The press are everywhere – it's an entirely artificial atmosphere, and if you get singled out, it gets even more weird. You're doing interviews all over the place and hundreds and hundreds of people are coming to see you.

Huge arguments blow up about absolutely nothing. People end up in fights about something stupid, because you're feeling nervous and vulnerable. Things get out of hand. I know people who've hated each other for years because of something that happened in Edinburgh when they were in a bar in a hyped-up state, a bit drunk. I've almost had fights with people, and got completely upset about things that are of no consequence at all. In London it wouldn't bother you. It'd be over and done with.

I did enjoy winning the Perrier Award. Either there was goodwill or they were being two-faced, but people were very nice to me about it. The guy who does the pavement drawings on Princes Street did a chalk picture of me and I was so thrilled. But Edinburgh is very unnatural, and you have to understand it for what it is. It's a one off, it's not like any other gig.

Winning the Perrier does make you go a bit mad. You expect far too much to happen afterwards. You really think, 'This is it now!' I remember when I won it, for a couple days I was thinking, 'Oh shit, I am going to be really famous now – and I can't deal with this!' Looking back, I think, 'What a deluded and arrogant little twat.'

The year after I won the Perrier Award, I was completely ignored. I went up again, and I thought I had a better show than the year before. I was in a bigger venue, which sold out, because I was the holder of the title at the time – and it was completely ignored. Two years ago, I went up again and did what I thought was the best show I've ever done – certainly the most personal. People still came to see it, but there was no interest in it at all from the media. I found it quite chastening to go there a couple of months later, after the Festival had finished, and do a normal gig. They were really nice gigs – but, only a couple of hundred people came along, because the English aren't there.

HARRY HILL

The first time I went up as Harry Hill, I did half an hour with Alistair McGowan [*post-alternative impressionist*]. It was the first time I'd done half an hour, and it was the first time I'd done twelve nights in a row. At the time, I hoped I'd get a good review to put on my CV. But in fact, reviews don't make an awful lot of difference as far as getting bookings are concerned – it's really word of mouth. The whole thing is so intense. Comedians know what comics are good. You can't really lie to a comedian about a show or how it's going. I always try something different, but one of the bugbears is those comics who come up and do the same thing.

DOMINIC HOLLAND

You've got a whole bunch of performers in the same place for three weeks. Everyone's competing with each other – it's exciting. After the show, everyone meets up. You have a drink and relate your stories, good and bad. There's a real sense of camaraderie but I never told anyone I sold out. I just said it was going well. My show sold out on the third night, and then every night for the entire run. But I didn't tell people that because a lot of people were playing to empty houses, and so I didn't want to rub their noses in it. I expected to lose two and a half grand, and get one review. That was the best I could have hoped for. In fact, it was an absolute dream for me.

DAVID BADDIEL

When I was supporting Denis Leary, I got one or two really bad reviews. And you know that every other comic has read the review because everyone – despite professing to despise reviews – punches both fists in the air and shouts, 'Yabadabadoo!' when someone else gets a bad one. I remember being very upset by the review of Denis. Although he's a fantastic comic, I used to get as many laughs as him and I think I did pretty well because that Edinburgh [*1991*], there was an enormous buzz about Denis – and so supporting him was quite a tough job, because people had just come to see him. And then the review came out. It was all about Denis, and at the end it said, 'The support is David Baddiel. Well, a cat may look at a king.' I remember being incredibly upset about that. It's difficult for me to talk about low points in terms of bad reviews because I've had so many. It is astounding. I'm such a badly reviewed comic and yet amazingly successful.

When I did Footlights in Edinburgh, on the first night we absolutely stormed it. The next day, Owen Dudley Edwards [*Irish academic and critic*] wrote a review in the *Scotsman* which was a complete slag-off. The last sentence was: 'On this basis, the Cam is an open sewer.'

I almost had a fight with Ian McPherson [*surrealist Irish comic who lives in Edinburgh*]. He had this habit, a couple of Edinburghs ago, of getting very drunk in the Gilded Balloon and going up to anyone who was at all successful on TV – and that included me, Denis Leary, Frank Skinner and Jack Dee – and saying, 'You're rubbish! I'm much better than you!' He came up to me, and started off by doing this over the top sarcasm: 'It's the great David Baddiel! Let me bow to you!' And then he started saying, 'You're shit! You're shit!' And after a while I said, 'No. You're shit,' which isn't a fantastic response, but about the level that it deserved. He looked at me like, where did that come from? What on earth has prompted you to say that?

BOB MORTIMER

We didn't need to do Edinburgh, but we'd been the year before – and we thought it was cracking. We thought, 'It'd be great to be involved in this!' We didn't want any payment – just the price of a nice flat for the three weeks we were up there. There's a pleasant non-violent atmosphere there which is nice. It's not a threatening place, which makes a change. There are plenty of places to go and booze, and there's also that chance of seeing an unexpected cracker. That's where we first saw Charlie Chuck. The night we went to see him, he'd just cancelled the gig because there was no one in. But because there were about seven of us, he said, 'I'll do it, then.' So out comes Charlie Chuck, and we get our own private performance.

CHARLIE CHUCK

I knew nothing about Edinburgh. I took myself up there. Vic and Bob saw me when there were four people in the audience – nobody knew I was up there. The second time, Malcolm Hardee took me up there, and I had bigger audiences. I knew nothing about the Festival Fringe, but it's the best gig I've ever done. It's got everything. Whatever anybody wants, it's on – the firework display, the Tattoo, Edinburgh itself. I'd go up there even if I wasn't performing – the whole thing is absolutely great. It isn't just shows – it just buzzes. It's something else.

JOHN HEGLEY

Edinburgh punctuates the year, and gives it a cycle. Doing your show on your own, you get a bit isolated – so it's nice to see people. It's nice to be forced to be sociable, because I'm not someone who seeks out social contexts, and so it's nice to be put into one, because I enjoy it when I'm there. It's about the joy of being in the bar together. It isn't just a show – it's about the whole process. It's a touchstone, it's a yardstick. It's the biggest thing in the year. It's the harvest.

EDDIE IZZARD

Last year The Uncles [street double-act] did something beautiful in Edinburgh. It was one of the most moving things I've ever seen on the street. There was a woman looking out from the house behind the street where they were doing the show. They waved to her and got all the audience to wave to her. They said, 'What's your name?' 'Bridget.' 'Hello, Bridget.' On the last night but one, they said, 'Come down tomorrow and see the show,' and she came. Everyone was there, and they said, 'Here's Bridget!' They sat her on a chair in a prime position and she watched the whole show. At the end of the show they gave her some flowers and she was crying. It was great.

ROB NEWMAN

I'd just read *American Psycho* and so I started doing all these routines about all the things I could do with a coathanger to the kids in the National Youth Music Theatre who I thought had stolen all my props. Actually, I think I'd just mislaid them. I remember being booed in the street by some suffragettes after that. They were dressed as suffragettes because they were doing some play. To be honest, that was the reason I stopped doing Comedy of Hate. I thought, 'You don't know who I am – you've got no idea what I'm like.' And then I thought, 'Well, I don't make it easy for people by doing this stuff.' I was such a big fan of Denis Leary and Sam Kinison. That's why I was doing it. The thing that I like most is that warmth from an audience and that warmth on the street. Being booed in the street made it my purpose to be as true to myself onstage as I could be.

Of the four best things I've ever seen in Edinburgh, three of them were by Arthur Smith. Incredible performances. *Arthur Smith Sings Andy Williams* is one of the best things I've ever seen in my life. Also *Live Bed Show* and *An Evening With Gary Lineker*. Then it was Bill Hicks in the Wildcat Tent, which I saw five times running. Then I went to see him at the Queen's Theatre and that was the only time I felt green, because he'd written forty minutes' new material since I'd seen him three months before and it was brilliant. He was so charming – he had this twinkly rapport with the audience. My jaw just dropped – I thought, 'I can't compete.' I was wiped out by it.

The list of people who Edinburgh's missed is a list you want to be on – because it reads like a roll call of what's happened in comedy. The Assembly Rooms bar thinks it's at the hub of things – it's like some bizarre Graham Greene novel. They think they're having an effect on events but they're not – they're just talking to themselves. Edinburgh's as out of touch as a Sunday supplement. It's very much a Sunday supplement idea of what comedy is. It's a middle-brow, middle-aged thing. I'm flattered that when I do Edinburgh, I'm one of the few acts that Scottish people come and see.

ARTHUR SMITH

I was at a really disgusting little club in Edinburgh. Everyone was on acid or heroin. People's eyes were shooting round their heads and no one knew what the fuck was going on. They were all out of their trees. It had a reputation – it still does. The funny thing was, I'd been doing a TV show beforehand – I'd been doing a bit of stand-up on STV. I had a new suit on that'd been given to me by my new girlfriend. Of course, at TV gigs everyone's looking after you, and then I got down to this disgusting little club in me new suit, and I was doing this gig and a bloke chucked a pint glass, about two-thirds full. It was warm and it stank of urine – all over my new suit. I said, 'Oh, fuck this,' and I walked off. They were all screaming at me to come back – and in the end I did. I said, 'Well, I don't know. I've had such a fucking night here. I started off being fêted and pampered in a TV studio, and I've ended up covered in piss – and in a way I've enjoyed this one more.' It was quite funny in a way – though it didn't do the suit much good.

My finest moment in Edinburgh was actually me heckling. There was a bloke onstage who wasn't doing very well so people started heckling him, and he came up with the anti-heckle line, 'Does your mouth bleed once a month?' That made me angry so I started heckling – and I have to say I really was heckling rather well. I was pitching it just right – coming in with the right line at a quiet moment, everyone hears you, big laugh. This bloke could see he was losing it. He didn't know who I was, and he said, 'Oh yeah, it's easy for you down there – you try coming up here and doing it, then.' So I said, 'All right!' And I went up onstage and did twenty minutes. And I ended that with, 'And if you think you can get away with lines like, "Does your mouth bleed twice a month," then forget it pal. Fuck you.'

My favourite gig was one of my alternative tours of the Royal Mile. It was at four o'clock in the morning, with two hundred people following me down the road. That in itself was a remarkable event. Firstly, I offered a joint to the squaddie who was guarding the castle and he took it! I said, 'I'll give you a joint if you do some slow marching,' and he did – so that was a brilliant opening. Then I nearly got involved in a fight with these two Scottish guys, who were walking up the hill. I said, 'Now here are two typical Scottish men coming home from the pub,' and one guy got really wound up and was just about to hit me. I talked him down from that and then he started heckling and joining in. He was a brilliant natural comedian – I don't know what happened to him before or since, but he was really funny. Somebody tipped a bucket of water out of a window over the crowd, then I got a policeman doing a dance – and then we all ended up in the back of a lorry. There was a Scots bloke quietly having a piss against a wall – we all crept up around him, and he looked up and saw two hundred people watching him. Then people started taking their clothes off and climbing up flagpoles and singing 'Scotland the Brave'. The police broke it up in the end, but it had been a real laugh and people were trying to give me money. I said, 'Oh no, I don't need the money – if you want to give me money, put it in this bloke's hat.' There was this old, pissed, homeless bloke, lying there asleep by the cathedral. Fifty quid must have gone into that bloke's hat. I love the thought of him waking up the next morning. What I liked about that gig was that there was a sense of danger and spontaneity. That's what live comedy has over telly or theatre, because at any moment the script can change, and on this occasion I ad-libbed the whole thing anyway. I remember thinking at the end of it, 'I could retire now – I don't think I'll ever cap this.' There was no great artistry or subtlety or satire. It was more the uniqueness of the event.

11. On the Telly

'I don't like them blacks, Len, but you're all right 'cos you're on the telly.' – Cab driver, to Lenny Henry

TV is king – and like all absolute monarchies, it divides its subjects into two categories: In and Out. Nowhere is this division more acute than amongst comedians. Jack Dee, Julian Clary, Reeves and Mortimer and Newman and Baddiel are household names – not because they've played 3000-seater barns across the country year after year, but because they've done their own TV series. Arnold Brown has had two series on Radio 4, but none on telly – so the number of people who've heard of him remains pitifully small. The sole exception to this televisual rule is Eddie Izzard, who has stubbornly resisted virtually every TV offer, but still sold out the Ambassadors and then the Albery Theatre on word of mouth, slick PR and ecstatic press coverage alone.

Telly's comedy hegemony is especially ironic, since live stand-up translates notoriously badly on to the idiot box – as is borne out by BBC 2's ill-fated *Paramount City*. This is because comedy, more than any other artform, is a communal experience. Laughter unites an audience, transforming an untidy hotch-potch of strangers into a single entity. We laugh in recognition of something that we share. At a stand-up gig, a lone laugh is an embarrassment far worse than silence – an unwanted error that most comedians feel duty bound to explain away. An actor can perform a play before a single spectator (and on the Edinburgh Festival Fringe, many do) but a stand-up routine is rendered meaningless in front of an audience of one. The opposite of Fine Art, comedy only thrives in crowded rooms. Conversely, television is a solitary pursuit. We may watch it in tandem with another mute spectator, but we relate to the medium in private. As a leisure activity, it's strictly one to one.

The comics who transfer successfully to TV are those who find a new format which suits the one-eyed god, and adapt their act to fit it. The comedians who fail are those who try to transplant their stand-up set straight on to the small screen. It's significant that the most prolific new telly comics have maintained editorial control, either through owning their own production companies, or building close relationships with their producers. TV has an insatiable hunger for comedians – but it also has an alarming habit of chewing them up and spitting them back out again. Apart from Channel 4, where Seamus Cassidy has developed his own stable, where comics are nurtured and encouraged, comedians flirt with the small screen entirely at their own risk – when the fourth wall that they strive so hard to pull down is replaced by an invisible, bullet-proof glass panel.

BRUCE MORTON

Television is like a great big key that opens a big door. Not only does it open a door of opportunity for you to go into a room and meet people who can further your career, but it also opens another door so that a lot of people out there can come into your room. They all want to come in because they know you, and they've got the key.

You can go about your life with a self-image of what you look like and what you are. Then suddenly someone holds up a picture of you and from then on, your self-image has changed. In comparative terms I've had very small TV exposure, but if I'm walking down the road I see people glance. I've got accustomed to it now, and from about fifty feet I can lipread people muttering my name.

At first, it's very flattering – but after a while it becomes irritating. I've started getting an awful lot of paranoia. If I'm walking down the street and someone glances at me, and I think, 'Was that an ordinary glance? Did they just glance at me, or did they glance at me because I'm Bruce Morton?' I find myself in a constant state of readiness, so it's difficult to go down the street for a packet of fags.

On Monday of this week, I was in a really foul black mood. I was really down. Sally and I came out of Woolworths and there was a young man standing there who said, 'Oh, you're that comedian guy, aren't you?' which is what I get. People know me, but they don't know my name, so it's like I'm famous but I'm not, which is confusing too. I glowered and Sally moved in and said, 'Yes, sometimes – but not today.' Then for some reason he asked me what school I went to. I thought, 'Christ! What's all this about? Is it going to be a Protestant/Catholic thing? I'm not in the mood for it today. Leave me alone!'

DAVID BADDIEL

Your identity is created in strange ways. I'm experiencing this at the moment because of the *Spitting Image* puppet. It's recreating my identity for me. My identity is now completely out of control, because there is an effigy of me on television that's telling people what I am. The puppet says everything's crap, and now people are coming up to me and asking me to say or write 'crap', and I don't want to because it's not my catchphrase. I'm quite flattered to be on *Spitting Image*, but I don't really like what the puppet does – it is quite a strong attack on what I do. And yet there are fans who've taken it to their hearts as something that I do and that's very weird. You're on TV, and then suddenly your identity is defined in ways that are nothing to do with you.

It's a very stressful relationship that I have with Rob – but apart from that both of us get an awful lot of flack from all sides. Sometimes there's an internal and an external battle going on and sometimes – particularly recently – I've thought, 'Stop! Stop all this fucking nonsense! I never thought I'd have to get into some sort of bunker mentality in order to do this!' Then I often yearn for the British Library and think I should have been an academic after all. Sometimes I pass people's houses, the lights are on and they're watching telly, and the concept of that stress-free existence seems so appealing – even though I'd probably hate it after a week. It's not fear. It's not that I'm frightened. It's a yearning for anonymity.

MARK LAMARR

I always felt incredibly successful before I got on telly. I thought, 'I'm really good at this, I really enjoy doing it – and there's not really any pressure, either. I can die at a gig and nobody's going to know. I'll get another one tomorrow night and I'll do well.' But as soon as you do anything in the public eye it's a fact of life that there are going to be some people who hate you for no reason and some people who love you for no reason. I've got many fans who write to me who I know don't understand what I'm talking about. They just write to me because I'm on telly. On the other hand I meet lots of people who completely hate me because I'm on telly. I ask them why, and they can't work it out. The scary thing is that I know that every single thing I ever do for the rest of my life from now on, somebody's going to give it a really big slagging, and that's very hard to deal with. When you're onstage, and the whole crowd's laughing and only one person isn't, they're the only person you can see. That's probably the classic insecurity of the comedian. I hate all those clichés, but it's true. We are all very bad at taking criticism because we're all so good at taking the glory. That's why we do it – that moment of glory, that buzz when you're up there and there are hundreds of people sat in front of you thinking, 'You're fucking brilliant!' There's nothing like that on earth – there really isn't. It's all ego. So as soon as someone says, 'No you're not!' you think, 'Oh my God, they're right!' And whether you agree with them or not, it brings you straight back down to earth.

When people first came up and asked me for my autograph, I'd nearly always say no – because I thought, 'I'm not one of those people with special lives who I used to read about when I was a kid!' When I was a kid, there were big stars on telly and their lives were so separate from yours that you'd never dream of meeting them – and if you did, it would be the most exciting thing that had happened in your whole life. If Rolf Harris was filming in my street when I was a kid, I'd be talking about it for years because he was a telly star. When people started treating me like that, I felt, 'Oh no, don't be silly. You're wasting your time here – you should find out where Sean Connery lives. *He's* a star.' And then you realise that, because you're on telly, they're going to see you in the same light as whoever you thought was famous as a kid. When you're a big fan of someone, when they do something you don't like then suddenly you hate them. I also get letters from people saying, 'I can't cope with my life – what shall I do?' Having to face that pressure is very strange.

HUGH DENNIS

On *Carrott Confidential*, we'd sometimes turn up on a Saturday and Steve would have given them the vaguest of ideas about what we were going to do. Then the audience would turn up and we'd say, 'Oh yes, er, we're just off to the canteen for something to eat,' where we'd finish it off. Quite often, they wouldn't see it until the first run through. It wasn't important enough to them, because it was a filler. We were like the Comedy A A.

There is a nervousness about going out the next morning because you feel that everybody you walk past will have watched it and have a view of it. The biggest fear for everyone is of someone coming up to you and saying, 'You're the bloke off of whatsit, aren't you?' You go, 'Yeah,' and they say, 'You're shit!' I take that far more to heart than someone coming up and saying, 'That was very funny.'

JENNY ECLAIR

I haven't done well on television. That's my fault. *Packing Them In* and *Packet of Three* did nothing for me. It wasn't any good. It was my fault as much as anybody else's. I don't think the format was right. I also don't think you can put disparate people in a group and expect them to come up with comedy together. Writing groups evolve naturally, not through a producer's choice. I found the whole thing quite humiliating. I do remember some of the reviews: 'May God forgive all these people involved in this Texas-sized turkey.' I used to reel back from newspaper stands every week – *Time Out* would devote an inch every week to slag it off. I found it very wounding, but it was a kick up the butt. I'll get back down and do it and get it right – I'll be a lot more wary next time round.

RICHARD MORTON

I was warming up for Jack Dee's TV Christmas Special – it's a shit job. I don't like doing it, but Jack said, 'Rich, you're my mate – will you do this for me?' There'd been a big bomb scare, and the crowd had been kept outside waiting. When I walked out, I could feel the bad temper and anger in the room. You can't get round that just with comedy. It's like a kid who's fallen over and scuffed their knee. To make them feel better, you've got to bribe them, with a sweet or a toy or something. I had to massage them into a nice state before I brought Jack out. I had to warm them up – literally. Somebody who's physically cold isn't going to laugh, and they'd been standing outside in Tottenham Court Road for half an hour. You have to be as persuasive and coercive as you possibly can.

The big danger about doing warm-ups is that even if you become a good warm-up act, that's all you're ever seen as. TV people think, 'Well, he's good at warming a crowd up,' but they won't actually see you in the context of a TV star in your own show – so you've got to be very careful. But this time around, I don't really care. I've just done two tours with Jack – about a hundred dates, in big fuck-off theatres. The smallest one was a thousand-seater, and it went well nearly every night. So by the time I get into a TV studio, it doesn't impress me any more. If they sense you're intimidated by TV, they've got the upper hand with you. It hurt me last time to think they weren't going to like me, so I had to work me tabs off to get their respect, but right now I think, 'Naah, it doesn't matter.'

I remember doing five minutes on *Wogan* – which was my biggest ever gig. That was so intimidating. When I turned up in the afternoon, the production team made me go through my material in a giant empty studio, just in front of the cameramen, and nobody laughs. You do your best jokes and they're all going, 'Yeah? We've seen the greats, mate. We don't laugh in the afternoon.' If you can make the crew laugh, you're on a winner – but I didn't. The production team were so scathing about my material. They kept coming in every five minutes up until the show saying, 'We're not sure about that second joke.' They kept changing it around and asking me to alter punchlines. In the end, I was almost distraught. I said, 'Look, trust me! This stuff works every night of the week! This is my job!' And I went out there, and I absolutely stormed. It went brilliantly! It was so wonderful! I was only allowed three and a half minutes, but it over-ran, because the laughs were so big, that I had to wait. The joke they didn't want me to use – a very innocuous gag about cockroaches, which they thought might be a bit weird for early evening – got the biggest laugh, but they cut it out. That was their way of saying, 'We told you so.'

I did lots of odd TV spots, because I got offered a lot – and I thought, 'This is good, because it raises your profile. It's good for your CV, and you get out of town gigs when people see that you've done *Friday Night Live* or *Wogan*,' but not that many people see you. Jack Dee did one series which got repeated twice, and now he can sell out big theatres. But the key to it is that all his stuff was quality. He looked great on the telly and he did exactly what he wanted to do, in his own context. I've seen other comics who I know are great live comedians, but they didn't look right on telly. They didn't come across right. They choose the wrong vehicle, the wrong material – and it just goes. People think, 'Oh I saw them, and they weren't very good.' That's how easy it is to be sucked up and spat back out. So in the last year, I've taken nothing on the telly, because it's too much like Russian roulette. You choose the wrong chamber and people are going to say, 'I saw Richard Morton – he wasn't that hot.' You could say, 'But his shows are great live,' and it just wouldn't matter. Jack's done the right thing but other comics I know have chosen badly. TV knows it's got you, really – because that's where it's all going to be.

DONNA McPHAIL

About four years ago, TV realised that stand-up was cheap entertainment. They got a lot of very young comics with no experience and probably no agents, to do shows like *First Exposure* and *Paramount City*. The producers would seduce the performer, and make them think that this was *it*. And of course, as soon as they'd done that five minutes, it was over with, that act was jettisoned, and they were on to someone else. When you're inexperienced, you don't realise that's going to happen. I've seen comics thinking, 'I've made it! I've made it!' because a producer has been so seductive – and then they've been terribly hurt afterwards. Not only have they been paid fuck all for their best five minutes, but no one saw it anyway and now the big television bubble has burst.

I was in a programme called *Stand Up*, which usually used people like Steve Coogan and Bob Dillinger. Steve couldn't do it that week, so they phoned me up. I didn't realise it was live TV. It was a debate programme, on 'Do Women Really Mean No When They Say No?' Judge Pickles was on it as well, and they asked me to do some comedy. I didn't know any better, and my agent was encouraging me that this would be a good idea. After that, I realised that my agent doesn't know everything, and I should listen to myself, because at the time I thought, 'I'm not sure about this,' but I thought he knew better. I opened with these Judge Pickles jokes but the problem was that during the debate, Judge Pickles turned out to be totally reasonable – so that cut my first lines to pieces. I shouldn't have done it but I was too inexperienced. They said, 'Do something else,' so I did, and the whole thing went down very badly on live television. I was humiliated and totally devastated. No one spoke to me afterwards – neither the presenters or the producers and none of the audience. I asked for a cab and they said, 'Yeah, all right,' and then didn't get it for me, and I nearly missed my train. I was just standing there. It was horrible. I thought, 'Never again am I going to let myself be manipulated in this way when I know it isn't right for me.'

GRAHAM FELLOWS

You have to use TV very carefully. It should play second fiddle to stage performance, because it's a far more potent medium – and it's far more dangerous if you come a cropper. You can have a bad gig onstage and it's OK really, because not that many people saw you. But on TV, if the whole nation sees you die, then that could be it. Also, you use up material much quicker on TV. You can do the same act onstage for years – and in fact, very often, that's what people want. They want to hear the old gags and the old songs – whereas on TV, if you're seen to do the same thing twice, people think, 'I saw this before!' Also, it changes the frame of mind of the punter. When people are watching TV, they're far more cynical. It's far more, 'Well, come on then – make me laugh.' Whereas if people have taken the trouble to buy a ticket and go and sit in a theatre, they're far more ready to be entertained, and far more ready to like you – they'll do some work.

JULIAN CLARY

In Trick or Treat [Clary's first TV series], I remember the producer saying to me, 'I want to start a new national catchphrase. I want you to come out and say, "I'm a happy bunny this evening! Are you a happy bunny?" This will really catch on, and the nation will be saying it.' I found out in the end that it was easier to say yes to him and not do it and then say, 'Oh, I knew I'd forgotten something!'

STEVE COOGAN

The myth of television has been completely debunked for me. I'm still learning, but I know the pitfalls, and I think I know enough about it to see people who don't know what they're doing. Lots of people can recognise talent, but it's very rare to find a producer who understands how to handle that talent. You've got to get into a position where you can work with people who do understand it.

I don't want to get into slagging off individual producers, but I'm happy to say that I don't think *Saturday Zoo* [*Jonathan Ross's Channel 4 chat show cum comedy showcase*] was a very good show. It tried to be adventurous at first, and when that didn't work, they cut their losses by going back to what they knew how to do, which was having a presenter chatting to guests and a couple of stand-ups. I adopted a bunker mentality. I've grown up a bit, basically. On *Paramount City* I thought, 'Do what you're told.'

JACK DEE

When you've been on telly you get this huge roar when you walk onstage, but I still maintain that if you don't cut it, they won't be fooled. They don't think, 'He's not funny, but I'll laugh anyway because I've paid. They're not stupid. Just because they've seen you on telly, they're not taken in by it, any more than if you went and bought something you'd seen an advert for on telly and got it home and found out it didn't work. You're not going to say, 'Well, it was on telly so it must be OK. I'll keep it anyway – I won't ask for my money back.' I don't have a lot of patience with people who say it's easy now, because it's not – there are two thousand people and you've got to keep them roaring throughout the show. You've still got to come up with the goods.

JEREMY HARDY

The TV pilot scenario gets so strung out. It's in discussion for a very long time, then it's finally commissioned, then it's scripted, then it's finally made. Then it's talked about for a very long time, and you've lost a year or two years through all this mucking about with a TV company, which probably isn't that interested anyway, and by the time they finally record it someone else has won the Perrier Award.

I made the mistake of getting involved with TV people who hadn't been following me. They hadn't been thinking about me for some time and what I might do. They wanted the person who'd won the Perrier Award to make a TV pilot for them and had no understanding of what I was doing. They wanted the studio to look like *Top of the Pops*, they wanted ridiculous stuff happening with the cameras. I was working with a good director who I trust. His head was in his hands dealing with these people. He was trying to make a show that suited me, and the producer was trying to turn it into some sort of Nuremberg Rally.

Stupid things happened. They sent all the tickets to my show to people who hadn't been able to get tickets for *The Price is Right*, because it was done at the same studios. Some of them, God love them, actually warmed to it – but everything about the show was sabotaged by the stupidity of that TV company.

I went along with people who weren't in sympathy with me, and didn't appreciate what I wanted to do. They said, 'We really want to do this – we really think you're great!' And they didn't. They had a lot of other stuff. They were recording pilots all over the place with a load of different people. You spend a lot of time writing and in meetings – and then you sit around waiting, because you start thinking, 'Well, there's no point in me organising a tour until this show's on the air.' A lot of people I know have got stuck like that. You wait and you wait – and you get into pilot hell. I spent two or three years doing that – writing different pilots, for TV and radio, doing treatments, and going to lunches and recordings. You're working, and you're earning money, but nobody in the country knows that you're still alive.

If you don't do the live stuff, people aren't going to come and see you time and time again. If you only grace a town with your presence every three years, you're not going to have a following there. What stands Jack Dee and Julian Clary in such good stead is that they keep on doing live stuff. Jack can't wait to get back out on the road. After a successful TV series, he just wants to get out there and do the gigs. That's what builds up goodwill. Television doesn't, because it's ephemeral and superficial.

Comedians have to take responsibility. If you agree to do television, you know the risks that are involved – that you'll blow it in front of a lot of people, and there's no way of recovering it, and you can't dodge the responsibility for what happens. If it's all going in the can you've got no chance to blow something and then win them back. If you're onstage in front of a live audience, you can screw up for five minutes and die and then recover it. But if you're on for five minutes and then that's you gone, a million or more have seen you die on your arse and think that you're crap. That's the risk you take.

ARTHUR SMITH

Paramount City was awful for me. I was really miserable during that, for a whole heap of reasons. They wanted to make me Mr BBC1. They dressed me up in clothes that I felt uncomfortable in, and the clothes were a symptom of the whole thing. I had people at every level doctoring my material, until I lost all confidence in what I was doing there. I'd have Janet Street-Porter on my back saying, 'You gotta try to appeal to women more, Arthur!' The place was neither one thing nor the other. It wasn't a pub, it wasn't a TV studio, it wasn't a club, it wasn't anything. The whole show was manufactured to try to create the experience of being at a live gig and it missed at every point. There's nothing more depressing than doing the same bit of stand-up in front of the same audience three times – you lose your rhythm – they wanted me to be something I wasn't. I felt manipulated.

It wasn't entirely their fault. It was my fault as well, because I'd done two series of *First Exposure*, and I'd run out of material. I had writers giving me material I wasn't sure about. It didn't do me any good at all – or maybe it did, in a sense. Maybe I wouldn't have started writing plays if it hadn't been for *Paramount City*. Nobody in telly wanted to touch me after that – which wasn't such a bad thing, because there is a world outside telly, as I discovered.

I rubbed Janet Street-Porter up the wrong way before it even started. I was third choice after Alexei Sayle and Ade Edmondson. I admire Janet Street-Porter in a way. I think she's pretty formidable, I wouldn't wish there not to be a Janet Street-Porter. I just don't want there to be one in anything I've got anything to do with.

People have sold their souls to be on the telly. Remember that the reason you're doing the show is because you know about comedy, because you've been doing it for years. And if there's some twat in a jacket and a pair of glasses who's just stepped straight out of Cambridge, however much public school chutzpah the guy has, you've got to remember that he knows fuck all. I'm inclined to believe that those people know what they're talking about, and half the time they don't. They're pissing in the dark even more than you are.

EDDIE IZZARD

I tried to set up my career in such a way that no one thing was important – no one person's point of view. It wasn't necessary to get the television series – you could do it in other ways. I'm quite happy making my own mistakes. If I say, 'I'll do it this way. It's a gut feeling – I feel this is right,' and it fucks up, I'm happy to live with that. But if someone says, 'Do it this way!' And you think, 'Shit! I don't think so,' but you say, 'Well, you're the producer,' and you do it that way, and it fails, they'll hate you for it. They'll say, 'You just fucked it up!' 'But I did it your way!' Control it yourself. About five per cent of television producers are worth their salt. Ninety-five per cent are just cruising. They don't know about comedy – they don't understand. On some LWT show, somebody was doing a joke which was all about somebody's legs. The guy was saying, 'I want a close up here,' – but all the comedy was happening in the legs!

I wanted to engineer a position where I was in control. Now my production company is making the pilot [*of his bovine sit-com*, The Cows, *for Channel 4*]. I'm writing it, and I'm creative producer. I've taken so fucking long to get here. A lot of people started doing stand-up and got through after two or three years. I started pushing like crazy when I was eighteen, and now I'm thirty-one. If I get something going, I'm going to hold on to the bugger. I want to do the inverse of the classic band thing, where the band sign away everything. In fact, I've kept everything. I've just taken ages to get here.

12. The Management

'There's a pecking order. It's like being back at school. There's a
best fighter, a second-best fighter – and the kid they all beat up.
Get out of the fucking business if you don't like it. – Addison
Cresswell

Behind every great comedian, there's a cliché about a great manager
who made it happen – but in the case of the current crop of comics, it
happens to be true. The post-alternative boom has spawned a crop
of proactive managers, who mastermind and activate their comics'
careers – rather than copying the old-school approach of sitting by
the phone all day and creaming ten per cent off the top of whatever
call comes in. Avalon and Off the Kerb are the most significant
agencies in the field, chiefly responsible for the current blitz of
comics on TV. Because of their starkly contrasting tastes and styles,
they compliment each other perfectly – and although they're often
cast as adversaries, they're actually batting for the same side (give or
take the occasional tiff) against far bigger opposition.

At first glance, the men behind these agencies look like polar
opposites. Jonathan Thoday (of Avalon) is a laconic Cambridge
graduate – Addison Cresswell (Off the Kerb), a street-wise Millwall
fan. Thoday's office is in Leicester Square, Cresswell's is in
Peckham. Incongruously, they're both the sons of academics – but
their comedic backgrounds couldn't be more diverse.

Thoday stumbled into stand-up after losing four hundred thousand pounds on a West End musical called *Nightclub Confidential*.
He raised the last hundred thousand over one weekend, by forking
out ten thousand on a mailing list of the home addresses of the ten
thousand richest individuals in the country. He wrote an investment
proposal and stuffed ten thousand envelopes in forty-eight hours.
The postage alone cost several thousand pounds. The first day's post
brought nothing, but by day two, the cheques were flooding in.

If any showbiz yarn deserved a happy ending, then surely it was
this one. Unfortunately *Nightclub Confidential* was a turkey – and

Thoday only saved his skin by summoning up sufficient courage to close while there was still some money in the kitty. He repaid a token sum to each investor, salvaging his reputation for the future. It had taken him two years to raise the money. He was twenty-seven at the time. Yet Thoday's initial loss was comedy's (and his) eventual gain – for without any funds, he was forced to chance his arm in the fly-by-night fleapit of stand-up. After spurning the chance to manage Harry Enfield, he stumbled on Rob Newman and David Baddiel. His acts now include Frank Skinner, Harry Hill, Stewart Lee and Richard Herring.

After selling Kiss Me Quick hats on Brighton beach from the age of fourteen, Cresswell entered comedy via a sabbatical as Social Secretary at Brighton Polytechnic where he booked a band called U2 for a hundred pounds. The deal almost fell through because he was loath to pay them fifteen pounds VAT – at the time, he didn't know what VAT was. His first big signing was John Hegley, and he now manages Julian Clary, Jack Dee, Jeff Green, Mark Thomas and Richard Morton, as well as promoting Jo Brand, Jeremy Hardy and Arnold Brown.

Thoday and Cresswell were born within a year of each other. However, while Cresswell (aged thirty-four) has been taking comedians to Edinburgh since 1983 (the high water mark of agit-prop stand-up), Thoday (thirty-three) didn't hit the Fringe until 1989, when politically correct comedy was already on the wane. Cresswell (a Labour Party member and Red Wedge founder) handles a range of benefit-friendly comics like Brand, Brown and Hardy, whereas Thoday specialises in apolitical acts. Indeed, Avalon's only political comedian – Alan Parker Urban Warrior – is actually a parody of a left-wing comic.

Style follows content – Thoday prefers comedians who write (for the stage and in the press), while Cresswell opts for comics who can think on their feet. Avalon displays a preference for character-based, musical and novelty acts – ('I like my acts to have a life outside of stand-up,' says Thoday) – whereas Off the Kerb tends to opt for traditional stand-ups – ('Don't fuck around with the artform. It's been working since Max Miller,' parries Cresswell).

Ironically, it's precisely these aesthetic differences than enable Thoday and Cresswell to co-exist. Their armed truce is lifted for three weeks each August as Edinburgh becomes the battleground in a frantic poster war. From their rival base camps at the Pleasance (Avalon) and the Assembly Rooms (Cresswell), Avalon and Off the Kerb engage in a sticky struggle for prime sites, often obliterating one set of artwork with another while the paste is still wet.

Thoday has made him name by saying no to TV producers – often securing lucrative contracts by holding back scripts from commissioning editors. Thoday has recently moved into television production with Avalon TV (makers of BBC 2's *Fantasy Football League*), while, in a variation on this theme, Cresswell has secured his place in the media meat-market by setting up separate production companies for each of his stars – Julian Clary and Jack Dee. But the biggest gift (and one they share) is their flair for unearthing new comedians, often on obscure bills at remote out-of-town venues. Thoday's talent-spotting reputation is so awesome that he reputedly duped a rival agent into signing up a dud act, merely by feigning a casual interest when he bumped into his foe at a comedy club. Cresswell's punchy vernacular often ruffles feathers but softly spoken Thoday has far more enemies. However, in this line of work, that's probably the biggest compliment of all.

Seamus Cassidy is one of the few telly moguls with an intimate knowledge of the comedy circuit and the patience and insight to guide comics from live gigging on to TV. Kim Kinnie has run the Comedy Store – the unofficial National Theatre of Alternative Comedy, from its earliest incarnation above a Soho strip club, through its formative years in a Leicester Square cellar to its present comparatively palatial home near Piccadilly Circus. Malcolm Hardee is the manager of comedy's rowdiest clubs, the Tunnel (RIP) and Up the Creek, a pioneering performer, and all-round prankster. A brief summary of his incredible CV appears among the biographies at the front of this book.

THE PROMOTER: ADDISON CRESSWELL

I went to Brighton Polytechnic to do a degree in graphic design and started off as their entertainments officer. I ran a dingy little club that the student union owned called The Basement – it held about two hundred people. We built a stage out of old fork-lift palettes, across the fire exit of course because we never knew about fire exits in those days. I bought two anglepoise lamps from British Home

Stores and screwed them into the ceiling – and that was our lighting rig. U2 couldn't get their mixing desk through the front door. They were fucking mad. They said, 'Where are the lights?' I said, 'There's the red one and there's the white one.' I did Echo and the Bunnymen, New Order and Killing Joke. I contacted the record companies, rather than going though the agents – I did the deals with them.

Then I started running a club called Club Savannah, which was underneath the Queen's Hotel. It was just before the New Romantics. I called it 'the walking wardrobe club'. You couldn't get in unless you looked right – the whole art of it was not to let anybody in the club, but have them all queuing outside. I made about a grand, and decided to fuck off to New York for a while. I bummed around, blew all my money, got completely smashed out of my head, and stuck all sorts of things down my neck. I don't remember very much about that period, but I had a fucking good time. I came back with fuck all, decided to move to London, and bumped into an old mate of mine, Roy Hutchins. He said, 'Look – there's this comedy thing happening and I need someone to look after me.' I'll be honest with you: I looked at all this comedy, and I thought, 'What a load of middle-class twits!' It was everything I hated about college, but the thing I had which I was good at was that I could hustle on the phone. I got Roy six gigs at student unions, for fifty quid each, in one day on the phone. Nobody was looking after any of these guys. It was really early days. The only person who was working was Ivor Dembina. He was sending people to do pranks, hiring people like Julian Clary, dressing him up as Gay Tarzan. Me and Ivor were big rivals at the time. He doesn't do it any more. He got out – he wanted to become a comedian, which I always thought was a bad move.

Then we put together the Off the Kerb roadshow – complete mad acts. There was a guy called Andrew Bailey who used to dress up as a businessman, with a bowler hat on, but he only spoke Russian – he'd finish the routine standing on his head, playing the harmonica. We'd close with the Popticians [*John Hegley's busking band*]. There were only four people in the whole show, and everyone was doing four different jobs. It was a pain in the arse, going up and down the motorway at fifty miles an hour to Sheffield and back for fifty quid, but I'd never swap it because it's good training, and half the bastards don't do it any more. They think they can fly straight through to TV.

I went to every student union in the bloody country. I spent two years on the road, in the back of this shitty van, freezing cold, for three hundred quid split between the seven of us. I did it all from a little basement flat in Peckham.

I started to build up a stable and then I got involved with Red Wedge. I planned all the comedy tours for them, It was great at the time. It wouldn't work these days. It was fairly naive, but we had some wild times. We were out for the Labour Party, but after a while it became irrelevant. We were all getting pissed in the hotel. What a great line-up: Ben Elton, Robbie Coltrane, Harry Enfield, Julian Clary, and Arthur Smith compering. Billy Bragg wanted to do our tour more than the rock tour, because the rock tour was always very po-faced: 'I'm not going on before you . . .' whereas the comedy tour was a fucking good laugh. There was this political unit full of mad S W P-type people following us around saying, 'We've got to go to the factories from eleven in the morning, and talk to the people!' 'Fuck off ! We're all on the razzle tonight!' We never used to go to those political rallies in the morning. We always got hammered. We lost six seats out of seven – it was a fucking disaster! We were losing them votes, but it was good fun. After that, I became more of a capitalist and got on with it.

There's quite a few I haven't taken on – and probably regretted it. Gerry Sadowitz asked me to manage him three times before he went to Avalon, and I said no. I thought he was too much trouble. He'd rock the whole fucking firm. They're such a bunch of egomaniacs, comedians. They never like the next guy, really. They all say they get on well, but they don't really. They all monitor each other like mad. It's such a lonely business. They're on their own all the time, and they all just think about themselves. They get very paranoid – they're the most paranoid people I've ever come across. I have to ring my comedians once a day, or they think I don't love them any more.

I've got to like them – I like to think they're a good laugh. I like to think they're real. It sounds like I work for a dating firm, but it is a bit like that. You've got to think, 'Is this guy going to be bit of a laugh?' I've got four fucking teetotallers on the firm so that's quite difficult. You can't exactly take them down the pub and have a bit of a piss-up with them. Jack Dee, Lee Evans, Mark Thomas and Mark Lamarr don't touch a drop and Julian rarely drinks these days. There's only me and Jeff Green holding the fort – we have to drink on their behalf. I've got to think they're going to get on with everybody else, because I try to run it like a family. Most of the people I've been with, I've been with a long time.

The first time I saw Julian was at one of Ivor Dembina's gigs – up the Grays Inn Road in Kings Cross. In those days, he wore stiletto heels. It wasn't brilliant, but I thought, 'This guy's got something else about him.' I made an approach, and he said, 'Yeah, all right. When do we start?' A lot of people said to me, 'It's not going to last – it's just one joke. He'll get fed up with it, and he can't take it anywhere.' That's why we changed the name. It was a pain in the arse being the Joan Collins Fan Club, but it was really hard to shake off that name. We lost a few ticket sales when we finally took it off the poster.

Jack Dee came to do a fifty-quid spot for me when I was running the Tramshed [*in Woolwich*]. I thought he was a right miserable son of a bitch when I first met him. He used to ride a motorbike – he came in dressed in black leathers. He looked really mean. I thought 'Fucking hell! We're going to pay this one on time!' He didn't say much backstage, went on, knocked them dead and fucked off! I made a decision there and then. I thought, 'I'll have some of that!'

The first time I saw Jo Brand was as the Sea Monster at the Tunnel – she was going out with Malcolm Hardee at the time. The first time I met her was in the back of a van. We were driving somewhere with Malcolm and she bit my head off. She was very quick with her tongue – she always has been. I was very wary of her, but she was always good, I always had a feeling. I'm not being sexist but she was as good as the blokes and that's the big difference. Nobody ever says that but that's the truth – a lot of the girls ain't. They suffer, they get heckled and then they go to pieces.

I've never really let anyone go – we've normally parted over a row, actually. I normally feel they've got to the end of their tether anyway. Acts tend to have a five-year life, unless they're really going places. I'm a hyper – I can get them up there, but where they go from there is down to them. They've got to keep coming up with the goods, and a lot of them don't. They get used to a certain lifestyle, and it starts to soften up the act – or they get very bitter about other acts.

I make it my business to get really involved with them, right down to when they're buying a house. I know everything about them. I do real personal management. I know them – I know what makes them fucking tick. I know their act back to front. I feel I can talk to them harshly. I'm like a brother to them – that's how I feel about them. We have rows but it's all kept in-house.

I've seen a few people die. Julian doesn't really die – he goes through the motions. He always says, 'Start the car!' He cruises along and it gets a bit quiet. If I'm squeaking doors, you can hear it – and then he picks up again. I've seen then all lose it a bit, and it's not very comfortable. It makes me fucking squirm. I can't face anyone after a bad gig. I find it very hard to talk to someone, to look them in the eye. I want to fuck off and have a drink somewhere, especially if there's a lot of people there, and I've been hyping it all day, saying, 'Come and see this guy!' and he dies on his arse. It hurts. I'm not liked by everybody, so certain people love it: 'This is going to be fun! How's he going to get out of this one?'

It was a lifetime dream to do the Palladium – we did two nights there with Julian. It was brilliant – we booked the Royal Box for his mum. Nowadays I'm blasé, but then it was, 'Six grand a fucking night? Are you sure about this?' He said, 'Yeah! Book it!' We did a run in the West End [*Camping at the Aldwych*] and the fucking Gulf War broke out. It snowed, we had bombs and he was stuck in New York. I had a hundred grand of my own money tied up in it, and fifteen grand's worth of ticket sales, with about a month to go. I said 'You'd better get your arse back here!' I threw some more money at it. We bought a Capital Radio campaign, and that turned it around. I was fucking shitting myself, but we made about a hundred grand out of it in the end.

Another time, a promoter who I'd done a tour with bounced two twenty-five grand cheques on me and I'd just paid Julian. I sat and stared at those for a long time.

I do feel responsible when things go badly wrong. I move people very quickly once they come with me. I don't take any prisoners and I don't hang around. I have set plans – I know where I want to be by the end of the year, without a doubt. I'm very channelled, and if the comic doesn't want to go along with it, that can cause me a bit of a problem. I say, 'You want to have a go at this? Come on then, let's do it! We're a team, and we're going to go all the way on this!'

I can't work with comics who say, 'I don't want to be famous.'
Fuck off, then. Why get on the stage in the first place if you don't
want to be famous? I've go no time for these idiots. You can be
famous for five minutes at the Comedy Store, or you can get yourself
on the fucking telly, and do the business. You can do big tours round
the country, or you can be a very big fish in a tiny little pond, and do
what I call the merry-go-round. You can stay on it or you can get off,
but the trouble is once you've got off, you shouldn't go back. Comics
are used to having cash in hand, and suddenly they've got to rely on a
cheque from me. It's very difficult to pull them off – it's a bit like
weaning them off heroin.

Basically, the comedy clubs are dives. Compared to theatres,
they're fairly ropy places. Jongleurs and the Comedy Store are
O K – the rest of them are pub rooms, and they're fucking awful.
You're preaching to the converted half the time. If you go to
Jongleurs nowadays, you see the same fucking set every three
weeks. It's the same old mob. They go round doing the same set, but
they're not going anywhere. I don't have any sympathy. I think
they're fucking cowards. He gets onstage – he wants to be famous.
Let's go for it, then.

We've had shit all the way along the line. When Julian's boyfriend
died it was terrible, but he fronted that out. The worst thing would
have been to go into hiding. He was out there, saying, 'Yeah, I'm
gay. I'm happy to be a fucking homosexual!' Good on him. Nobody
ever calls Julian a poof in front of me. I'd knock them out if they did
that – I've threatened to punch a few people in the past. I take real
exception when people have a go at him. I don't mind the papers. I
ignore that. But nobody slags him off in the pub . . . but he's big
enough to sort himself out – he's quite a tough old boot.

Jack suffers from terrible nerves. We played Caroline's [*comedy
club in New York*], and he threw up, walking round the block. He
went on, and didn't do particularly well. He was really upset about
the gig. It wasn't the right place for him and I felt the crowd weren't
very fair on him. I said, 'We're going to go and do another one.' He
didn't want to, but I said, 'No! We're going to go and do another gig!'
So I took him to Stand Up America. The guy said, 'You're too late.' I
said, 'What d'you mean, we're too late?' He was a real flash Italian
guy. He said, 'I'll deal with you in a minute.' I said, 'Oi! You deal
with me now!' I started losing my rag, we got the bouncers over and

Jack was going, 'I don't want to go on!' I said, 'What is it about us Brits? You always give us a bad time! This fucking guy is the business! I only want five poxy minutes!' He said, 'Put him on, then.' I said, 'I want a fucking table and I ain't paying for it either.' I sat down, he went on, and he stormed it. That was a proud moment. He went out there and did it for me – I'm sure he did. And you know what the guy said? 'Come back in two days and I'll put you on again.'

Jeff Green's had two fucking awful years in Edinburgh, and this year he did really well. He sold out every night – I couldn't believe it. This guy hated Edinburgh. I have to drag him back every year. But he loves it now. He can't wait to get back next year. Things have turned round for him. That's lovely when that happens. Everybody said, 'What the fuck did Addison do taking on Jeff Green?' Lots of people didn't rate him. They said, 'I don't know what he sees in him.' Now he's coming through for me. He's doing well, and people are talking about him. It's been a long hard slog though. He's been with me a long time. I was more worried for him than I was for me. I'll always survive, but it could have broken him if I hadn't been with him – it would have hurt him. The whole art of it is to make your act look good. You've got to get the buzz going – I don't care how I do it. It's all part of the game.

Less is more. The more you turn down, the better it is. Every agent in this business takes on too much, and there are certain agents who don't say no to anything. I'm fed up of seeing acts on the telly. They waste them – they burn them out. Jack don't do fucking stand-up on no one else's show. He'll do a sit-down chat and that's it. You want to see Jack Dee do stand-up? You either watch him on the TV on his own show, you buy his video, or you go and see him live – that's it.

I don't do *Dial Midnight*, I don't do *James Whale*, I don't do *Raw Soup* – I don't do any of those shows, because I think they're cheap TV. *Paramount City* drained the acts of any confidence before they went on the telly. The acts were so fucked off with all the script changes. Arthur Smith was completely fucked after that show. He didn't know what he was wearing, what he was doing, it was a fucking disaster – the guy was lost. He had to go into playwrighting. His fucking career was fucked! You try to sell Arthur Smith as a compere for a TV show now, they'll say, 'I saw him on *Paramount City* – he fucked it.' Arthur Smith was the best man for the job at the time, by a long chalk. He was storming it round the clubs. What went wrong? He was not the same guy! What the fuck had they done to him? They put him in some horrible pastel colours. He looked a right fucking lemon! Being good on the telly is all about confidence. I say, 'You're the best in the fucking world, mate! Nobody's better than you! You're going to knock 'em out!' And they go out there feeling great. The whole art of it is to have as much control as you can before you give your act away.

The first time I saw Lee Evans was on the Craig Ferguson tour at the Assembly Rooms in Edinburgh, and I thought he was shite! I went to see Ferguson and Lee came on looking like some spiv from the East End. He had a dreadful outfit on, with braces and white socks, and he looked shit. He was doing all this mime stuff with no gags. It was awful – I thought he was a terrible Northern club act. I walked out after five minutes and went back to the bar. I said to Craig, 'He's shit, that act – you want to get rid of him!' And would you believe it – I fucking look after him now!

THE BOOKER: KIM KINNIE

I was born in Scotland, left school and did lots of variety – I was a comic's feed. Then I went to drama school and got a job at the Citizen's Theatre [*in Glasgow*]. I worked as a jobbing actor for seven or eight years, and woke up one morning in a play at the Empress Theatre in Glasgow, and realised I couldn't fucking do it, basically – it was a total crisis of confidence. I'd been cast in this play late, because they'd sacked someone, and I'd been brought up from London to do it. I couldn't get a laugh. I tried everything. It was a nightmare. I thought, 'What are you doing with your life?'

I started doing directing and choreography and ended up working round nightclubs in Soho at the same time that the Comedy Store started. I was actually working in the same building, doing various bits of choreography, and I thought, 'This is interesting,' so I started working as their stage manager.

The opening night was very long. There were thirty-six acts on. There was every conceivable kind of act from people who'd replied to the adverts in the paper. We got some weird acts: a guy who hit his head with a tray, old variety acts, a strange woman who sat onstage with a bird cage doing nothing. Alexei Sayle compered, and the audience was wild. It was a raucous night. It was riotous – it went on and on and on.

I thought it was the beginning of a trend, and I thought there was a hell of a lot of good young talent there, but coming from a very traditional background, variety and summer season, there was a certain amateurism about it which was appealing but sometimes aggravating. Tony Allen and Malcolm Hardee had been doing Alternative Comedy before the Comedy Store opened. What the Store did was form a central focus and give them a platform. The greatest difference between then and now is that now it's much more professional. Most of those first performers came from theatre companies which were folding because government grants were being withdrawn. A cheaper way to do it was to write your own stuff, and do it in front of a microphone.

The Comedy Store is about hard stand-up. Certainly in the early days it was about being able to control that mob – things are much quieter these days. We started off doing a midnight show on a Saturday, and we didn't have any security. People used to throw things – it was like the Tunnel. I used to throw people out. There are an awful lot of comics who I like dearly, but who aren't Comedy Store acts – they're too gentle and discursive.

One time, two guys were being lippy, and all five foot two of me went over and said, 'Shut your fucking mouth or you're out the door!' They quietened down, but at the end of the night, they came up to me and said, 'You're out of order.' Maybe two years later, I was in a pub in the East End that I'd never been in before, waiting to meet a friend. It was one of those great big barns, full of guys in working clothes. I'd been to a meeting earlier, so I had a suit on, and I was feeling slightly out of place. This guy didn't turn up and I was standing at the bar, when I was aware of somebody clocking me. And then a bloke came up and said, 'Comedy Store!' I said, 'Yeah?' He said, 'Gary, it is him! It fucking is! I fucking told you! You threw us out, you cunt!' I had my back to the wall, but they were great. They bought me drinks! I got pissed with them all night!

There were times when nobody got a chance, when I thought, 'This is too mental!' But there were times when it worked. I think audiences have got very timid. On occasions, I've started the heckling down at the Comedy Store, when we get a really crap open spot, and God knows I've seen enough of them. I do it from the back, and it starts other people off. I have been known to do that. Hecklers can be fun, but I hate an audience that won't give an act a chance. The worst hecklers are the ones we never hear. They sit in the front row and mutter, 'You're not fucking funny,' and there's nothing that anybody can do about it. But I also hate the polite audiences, who sit through stuff that I don't think they should be sitting through, given the nature of the place. Comedy has become a more conventional form of entertainment. Now people make up their minds to come to a comedy club like they make up their minds to go to the theatre. Audiences have also become much more right wing. A few years ago, a comic did a gag about the Royal Family and there was an audible gasp. I thought, 'What is happening here?'

I see an awful lot of new material, and if I have any value, it is encouraging it. What makes me laugh is individual voices. I see an awful lot of people standing up there being copies of other people, who haven't thought through why a gag works. You look for a certain authority, and some originality. A comedian must be in control of their space. I always try to talk to the open spot and say, 'I thought that worked, I thought that didn't work. Phone me in a couple of weeks and let me look at it again in front of a different kind of audience.' That way, you build up to giving them a half spot, where they come and do ten minutes and get paid for it, and then a full spot, and then a full weekend. If I find stuff really offensive, I say, 'I don't think you should be in this end of the game . . .' but I can be a sucker and do sentimental bookings.

The joy of the job is to watch people over a period of three or four years, getting better and better – and finally finding it. Jack Dee came for eighteen months, doing open spots. There was a little bit of Jeremy Hardy and a little bit of Paul Merton and then – wallop! He came in one night, and he had the attitude – comedy is all about having the right attitude. I always know when there's something there. Sometimes I see somebody who might not make it for two years, but I say, 'Keep coming back.' Another one who spent a long time dying at the Store was Eddie Izzard. He couldn't get it right but he kept going off and compering smaller gigs. Then he'd phone me and say, 'Can I come back?' I'd say, 'Oh, Eddie – you know you're not a Store act! Why d'you want to do it?'

It's always wonderful watching Robin Williams stepping off the street and going straight on. If he's in town, he'll just ring the doorbell. You never know when he'll turn up. The first time he came in with Art Garfunkel. 'Can we come in?' 'Sure, Robin! Can I get you a drink?' 'No, can someone make me a cup of tea?' I said, 'Are you going to go on?' He said, 'No, I just want to sit here and watch the show,' by which time, I'd said to everybody, 'Keep it tight, because I think we're going to need space at the end for Williams!' Each time he does that. He protests that he doesn't want to go on, and then he says, 'D'you want me to do five minutes?' and goes on and does thirty-five.

There was a comic who lives in Manchester who came down and did an open spot. He was very good – it was one of those open spots when I thought, 'Yeah! You can do this!' So I said, 'Come back in a couple of weeks and do another five minutes for me.' He did – it was great, and so I said, 'That was really good. I'm going to give you a half spot.' He tore the place apart. Two months later, I gave him a full spot on a Thursday night, and he went enormously well. Another couple of months passed, and I gave him two shows on a Saturday. It went well, and so I gave him a weekend and every show was worse than the last. He lost it – he totally lost belief in himself. In the first show on the Friday he did a line which should have got a laugh and didn't, the panic came into the eyes – and those two hundred and fifty bodies can smell fear in a comic. The worst thing you can do to an audience is to make them feel uncomfortable for you. They need to feel that you're in control, so that they can relax.

I watched this guy get destroyed and at the end of the Saturday night show, I saw him sitting in the dressing room crying, with his head in his hands. I said, 'Come on, it's not that bad! It's only comedy! I know it didn't work, but you know you can do it. You've done it before. You just have to think why it didn't work for you this weekend.' He lost faith. He went on each time thinking, 'They're not going to like me.' Of course he'll bounce back, and he's not a comic if he doesn't, but I felt for him. I knew that guy was going to be shattered for a month.

I get to the stage when I don't want to see any more comics – I also have more and more of a short attention span. I think very few comics should be doing an hour. I think it's a self-indulgent piece of nonsense that they all want to do an hour, after a year in the business – why should I pay six quid to hear twenty minutes of good material within an hour? If there's anything wrong with the business at the moment, it's that there are too many stand-ups, most of whom aren't going to make it. Some of them will make a reasonable living, but there will only ever be room for five nationwide stand-ups.

I laugh a lot. I probably laugh too much sometimes. I roar. I have a distinctive laugh, and the comedians know when I'm there. Laughter is an energy – it's the best energy in the world. I've never done stand-up and I never would, because it's too frightening – but it must be magic to do it. When you see a comic on a roll, it's a joy to watch – because he can't do anything wrong.

THE PRODUCER: SEAMUS CASSIDY

The difference between us [*Channel 4*] and the BBC and ITV is that they tend to see it as, 'Let's put this person on television,' whereas I'm very interested to see what kind of television programme a person would make. I don't like the way TV tends to pick people up and stick them in front of a camera, and then hoick them off to the green room. Whenever somebody has the ability to pursue a line of thought, I think, 'Here's an interesting mind at work! They might be able to make a TV programme!'

There are certain comedians who I'm always perfectly happy to watch in a club who I would never think of doing anything with, because they lack a genuinely original point of view, an original vision. There's a thing that comedians do, and it always feels to me that they've graduated when they get it, which is the signed joke that nobody else could have minted. There was a moment for Eddie Izzard when, suddenly, people liked him. Suddenly all the material pulled together like a drawstring. It became his own material. There was a dramatic point when Jack Dee got a point of view. I remember seeing him years and years ago. He was like a slightly more animated Paul Merton. It was only when I saw him again – when he was very good – that I thought, 'Fuck me! That's the guy I saw! I remember seeing him!' You can sometimes see in less experienced comics that the material is coming from a really interesting comic mind which hasn't been focused. That does take time, but I try to see it as a whole because I don't think viewers analyse comedy. You have to rely on instinct a lot of the time.

Newman and Baddiel are a perfect illustration of the generation gap in comedy for me. I don't understand what's funny – you see that

History Today? That's your only good joke, that is. I just don't find them funny. I really like David – I've met him a few times and chatted to him – but I just want to slap him when I see him on TV, and I'm very disappointed when I meet him and discover that he's a nice intelligent bloke. A lot of people I know think that Chris Lynam [*anarchic alternative clown, whose speciality is sticking a firework up his backside*] is the funniest person ever. I don't know the man, but I suspect that he thinks I've got a personal vendetta against him, because it's fairly well known that I don't like his act very much. Who knows? Maybe Chris Lynam would have been a huge star. I wish someone knew the right thing to do with Gerry Sadowitz. I certainly don't, but I think he's a genius.

I prefer comedians to be prolific. One of the things that really attracted me to Reeves and Mortimer was that you could go and see them a month later and they had a completely different two-hour show – it was so inventive. There are other acts on the circuit who've been peddling the same perfectly adequate fifteen minutes for the last five years. Initially, Vic and Bob weren't actually that popular on the circuit, but their natural charm won them through.

I don't like stand-up showcase shows. *Saturday Live* was a great ensemble show, and there will always be a need for a show like that, but I think there have been a number of pallid imitations since then, like *Paramount City*. It's not so much that it chews up performers' material. It doesn't treat it with any love and care and attention. They just wheel them on and wheel them off. I don't think you can do great comedy without precision, but you can attract more attention by taking a risk. It's about being able to turn over material and look like you've got ideas.

When you put a comedian on television, they think that they've arrived, and you know that it's the start of a long, long road. It actually takes a long time for comedians to hit on television in this country – the shows that get the biggest ratings have all been there for a while. It's taken Jennifer Saunders ten years to get to *Absolutely Fabulous*.

THE PRANKSTER: MALCOLM HARDEE

I was in prison for most of the seventies. In 1970 I was twenty, and I stole Peter Walker's Rolls Royce. He was an MP at the time. That was basically my first offence – apart from a couple of minor shoplifting things. I got three years for that because it was at the same time as the Angry Brigade, but it wasn't political at all – I just went down to Cornwall and found a Rolls Royce with the keys in. Previously, in the sixties, when I was coming through my teenage years, I dabbled in being a disc jockey for a bit. I was the first mobile disc jockey. At least, I was the first one to advertise in the *Melody Maker*. I was in a band for a bit, the Bonzo Dog Doodah Band [*with Neil Innes*].

I did three years and came out, and got another three years for cheque fraud. While I was inside, I met the original Bernie the Bolt [*from the classic ITV game show*, the Golden Shot, *starring Bob Monkhouse*]. Bernie didn't want to be in showbiz. He was a nice bloke – he was very shy – but Bob Monkhouse made a feature of him. Bernie was just a studio technician, getting a hundred and twelve pounds a week. Overnight, he became a personality. He was asked to open supermarkets and he had to join Equity. It all went to his head. He ended up in the same nick as me, and I teamed up with him. For the first three years I was in the same cell as him, in Exeter. When I came out, I met a postman who sold me cheque books and cheque cards – straight from the post. It's a very good crime, because the owner of the cheque book is only slightly inconvenienced; I bought loads of stuff from shops that they probably wouldn't have sold anyway; the banks don't lose out because they're insured; and the insurance companies don't really lose a lot, because they're owned by the banks anyway. So really, I was just keeping the wheels of commerce flowing. Well, that's what I told the judge. I did it for a year. In those days, there was a thirty pound limit – so I could only buy stuff under thirty quid. You just buy rubbish. I bought loads of clothes, which became unfashionable by the time I came out. I got three years. Then I got another two years for stealing cars again.

All the time I was inside, I was in the prison dramatic group – and when I came out I read in the local paper that some performers wanted to form a theatre group. It was Goldsmiths' College, which is just up the road. So I went along to the audition, and I got in. At the time, I thought it was because of my enormous talent, but now I think it was because I had a driving licence. They wanted someone to drive the van.

The show was dreadful. It was called *Put It All in the Pot* – going round scaring schoolkids during the summer holidays. But Martin Soan was in it. He was a Punch and Judy man with a show called *The Greatest Show on Legs*. The reason for that was because the booth was actually strapped on to his shoulders. Hence if the show went badly, he could run off – which did happen on a couple of occasions. It was a really good Punch and Judy show – it was traditional, not like the weak old stuff you see at the seaside. I said, 'We should change the script a bit, and do it for adults.' But there weren't the venues in those days. No Comedy Store. Nothing. So we set off in a van, and went down to Brighton. We went all around the country, up to Wales and Scotland, and ended up in the West Country, where there was a thriving hippy fair and theatre scene – which is where the Alternative Comedy movement came out of.

We used to go round pubs, doing a parody Punch and Judy and going round with the hat and living off of that. At that time, there were a lot of people who'd decided to give it all up. A lot of them went to Norfolk, some went to Wales, and some went down to the West Country. There was a big influx of middle-class people living in places like Totnes with nothing to do, so they set up their own entertainment. There were fairs like Festival of Fools. I remember seeing Rik Mayall on a hay bale, and Alexei Sayle in a theatre troupe performing Bertolt Brecht. We played a few universities, but we weren't that successful. Because it was a Punch and Judy show, we were accused of sexism – wrongly so, because it was very much a parody. Essex University wouldn't let us go on.

The first time I saw the term Alternative Cabaret was in Salcombe. We were in competition with the Salcombe Yacht Club, who had a mainstream cabaret on a Saturday at a rival pub called the Ferry Inn, so we put up a sign saying 'Alternative Cabaret' – we were performing in the courtyard of a pub. Nobody used to see Martin, because he was stuck in the booth – while I was the front man, going round with the hat. But this pub in Salcombe was in a beautiful spot. There was an estuary at the front of the patio, going out to the sea, so I said to Martin, 'Why don't you take the booth off and dive into the sea? You can swim round, climb up the steps, and get more money.' So at the end of the show, he took the booth off, dived into the sea, and came round with the hat. It worked. We got about forty quid, which was a lot in those days. So we went back there the next day, and I said, 'Do the same thing again,' but the tide had gone out – and there was a fifteen-foot drop into two foot of water. He came out covered in blood and seaweed and we only got about three quid.

The next summer I got arrested again, for something I didn't do. I was cab driving in my spare time, and I picked up a bloke who'd done a burglary. He got arrested, and said I'd picked him up from it, which I had. In law, you're as guilty if you aid and abet. I got two years for that – which was a godsend in a way, because I was sick of the Punch and Judy show, and I started writing my own material. I got released on appeal after seven months, came out and got a job with Martin, down at the [Woolwich] Tramshed. We were called the New Fundation.

The old Fundation included Hale and Pace. They were extremely popular, but the council put in a new manager who didn't think they were arty enough. Perhaps they weren't. They were fairly mainstream, as Hale and Pace are. So they sacked them all, and put us lot in. At the time I didn't know about any of this, because I'd just come out of the nick. We did the Punch and Judy show for the first week, and they said, 'Can you do another hour next week?' So I dug out all these sketches that I'd written when I was inside. We had to write a whole new show each week, between me and Martin, and Rik and Ade [Rik Mayall and Adrian Edmondson], who were then called Twentieth Century Coyote.

It was sketch-based and circus stuff – most of it was rubbish. It only lasted for about two months. The audience weren't happy with it. They wanted the old lot back – and quite rightly. One of the old Fundation was a bloke called Phil Skinner. I'd actually been at school with him in Lewisham but I didn't know he'd been in the old Fundation, because I'd been in the nick at the time. One night someone in the audience shouted out, 'Bring back Phil Skinner!' I didn't know what they were talking about. I said, 'I'd love to, but I can't. I haven't seen him since I was about nine.'

Phil actually turned up at the Tunnel once. He was very mainstream. He did some sexist gags, and someone shouted out, 'Sexist!' And then he did something that touched on racism, so someone shouted out, 'Racist!' He could see it was all going tragically wrong, so he thought he'd go into some safe material. He did a parody of a weatherman. He said, 'Now for the weather . . .' and somebody shouted out, 'Meteorologist!'

Around that time, the Comedy Store started. Rik and Ade told us about it – they'd been at the first show. We used to go along every week. The unwritten agreement used to be that if you did three acts and didn't get gonged off, then you were a booked act and you got fifteen quid.

We ended up doing the famous balloon dance which wasn't as wordy or as articulate as Rik and Ade so there was a split up. We became associated with more mainstream entertainment. In actual fact, we wrote it as a parody of a play called *Romans in Britain* [*controversial play by Howard Brenton*]. It wasn't meant to be the Chippendales, but we got an agent, and we ended up doing end-of-the-pier shows, and Northern nightclubs – which had some value at the time because it taught us a bit of craft, and how to get up in front of rough crowds. At the same time, Rik and Ade moved off with their university chums, and ended up doing *The Young Ones*.

The Greatest Show On Legs split up in 1983, but every year we used to do a pub crawl. Because we started in a pub, we selected five local pubs, and did five free shows. One of those pubs was the Mitre, which became the Tunnel. We did it on a Sunday, and there were three hundred people there. It was the only one we had to charge to get in. I had to go back the next Sunday to pick up some props. There was a heavy metal band onstage, and four people in the audience. So I said to the manager, 'This'd be a good place to have a comedy club,' and he agreed. The opening gig was the first Sunday in January '84. On the bill was John Hegley, Skint Video and Ronnie Golden. It was full up. The next week, the compere didn't turn up, so I thought, 'Fuck it – I'll do it,' and so I compered it every Sunday until it closed in 1989.

It was in a very rough area. It was on the M2, and we used to get the Eltham brigade turning up. I got accused of stirring it up. That wasn't strictly true, but it was really rough. It finished at the right time really – because it was getting even rougher. The landlord was probably one of the worst pub landlords in the world. He put on Acid House raves on Saturday nights – he was one of the first to do it. He used to open the pub at six in the morning. It was all quite legal, apparently – he didn't sell alcohol. But some of the kids who came along were only about fourteen or fifteen. They all flooded in. There were about seven hundred people in there. Eventually, it got raided. It was the first big raid. The police closed off the Blackwall Tunnel, they had helicopters, they were coming through the roof. They spent half a million pounds and all they found was a lump of cannabis in the landlady's handbag. That's why it closed. It had nothing to do with me. I said to him, 'They're not going to let you carry on like this,' particularly as they were quite young kids. He didn't get his licence back, so that was the end of it.

The worst night was when I wasn't there. They were throwing glasses at Clarence and Joy Pickles. Arthur Smith was compering. He got up again, did another five minutes, got the audience in the palm of his hand, and then said, 'They're mates of mine,' and walked off. It was about that time that I thought, 'Enough's enough.' But there was some excellent heckling – some of the best I've ever heard. Jo Brand got one of the best ones: 'Don't show us your tits!' One time, I said to the audience, 'I think the heckling's getting a bit much,' so the next week, the whole audience decided to hum the acts off. I always encouraged open spots. If anyone phoned up, I always gave them a booking – I let the audience decide.

I put Vic Reeves on at Blackwall Arts Centre, only about a year before the television series. It was a really easy gig, in a small place – only about ninety people. I think they got eighty pounds. They did the gig, and the audience actually signed a petition, saying they never wanted to see Vic or Bob in the building ever again. A year later, the bloke from the Blackwall Arts Centre rang me up, and offered me four thousand quid to put them on in the big theatre next door.

Up the Creek is like the Tunnel with 'A' levels. Sunday night is the heckly night, but all the heckling's witty now. If anybody's just shouting, 'Fuck off!' they get chucked out. Generally, I agree with the audience. The bad acts get the bad times and the good acts don't. I saw Norman Lovett have a bad time once when he shouldn't have done, and I did get up and intervene – it wasn't the whole audience, just a group of lads sitting round one table. I went on and shut them up and brought him back on again, and he went down really well. But that's the only time I've ever done it.

I got knocked out in a nightclub called Joanna's in Glasgow. We were doing The Greatest Show On Legs and we used to do a Scottish sword dance. Instead of using swords, we'd use someone out of the audience. I hadn't done Scotland before, and I stupidly did a Glaswegian accent. I said, 'I need a volunteer – you!' and pointed to a bloke, pretending I was some hard Glaswegian. He stood up and knocked me out. I came to onstage and got up. Eventually, his brother got up and did a sketch.

I did a gig at Newcastle Poly. We got there about four o'clock, and as I was talking to the social secretary, this bloke ran past with a girl over his shoulder. I said, 'Who's that, then?' She said, 'Oh, that's all right. That's the agricultural students. They have their beer Olympics on a Thursday.' We carried on talking, and then another one came past. I said, 'They're not going to be in the show, are they? We're not on till eight, and look what they're like now.' She said, 'No.' So we went on, and it was really nice. There were about a hundred in and I was doing all the right things. Then just before the end, I heard about a hundred and fifty people singing – all blokes by the sound of it. There were some massive oak doors leading to the adjoining room. All of a sudden, they came off their hinges, and the agricultural students came charging through. We'd just started the balloon dance. I was standing there naked, with two balloons. There was a moment when they looked at us, and we looked at them – and then they charged the stage. They went berserk – luckily, we had a cricket bat as one of the props and we fled into the dressing room.

It's a very odd area round here. If you turn right, you're into Greenwich and Blackheath, which is trendy and middle class, but if you turn left, you're in Deptford with the rougher element – and there's always a lot more of them. If you went over the road and asked anyone who Eddie Izzard was, they wouldn't know. But if you asked them who Jim Davidson was, they would. I try to attract a mixed audience. I don't like preaching to the converted.

Political comedy didn't work. I did a gig in Edinburgh with a lot of right-on political acts. The landlord's wife used to sit in and watch the gigs and she used to laugh like a drain. She'd been watching it for about a week when she came up to me and said, 'Can't you tell this joke . . .' And she told me a joke about a nigger with a parrot on his shoulder. She'd sat through all those acts for a week, and she still didn't realise I couldn't get up onstage and tell that joke.

The right-on political stuff has more or less gone. Even John Maloney has changed his act to fit the mood of the times. He used to go on and spout quite left-wing stuff, and then he realised it wasn't really getting anywhere – and he deliberately wrote an act that would go down well at Jongleurs. Now it's veering towards silly stuff, rather than the clever wordy stuff – acts like Harry Hill. Nostalgic acts like Tommy Cockles are also on the way up.

The audiences are bigger now, and because there's more of them, you do get *Sun* readers and the general public coming to see it. There's more of them, because there's more of it being shown on telly. The old mainstream's dying out rapidly, as are the comedians themselves. I wouldn't bring in a frilly-shirted Northern comic doing old Paki jokes, but some mainstream comics can be very good, although lots of them would still die a death on the circuit because of the attitudes they've got. But the big difference between alternative and mainstream is that mainstream comics all do other people's material, with the odd idea thrown in – whereas Alternative Comedy is all written by the people who are up onstage. Prior to 1979, there wasn't any circuit, so there was nowhere for young comics to go and perform. The only place you could have gone was to go and do a stint at Butlins. When Alternative Comedy started, they didn't do racist and sexist stuff for political reasons. But the other reason they didn't do it was because people were fed up with it. It had become boring. It was old hat and dated more than anything else. There was an ideological element, but Alexei Sayle and that lot were like a breath of fresh air. Alternative Comedy should be about being rebellious and sending up pomposity.

The Edinburgh Festival sums it up. The first year we were there was with The Greatest Show On Legs. We filled a seven hundred seat tent. They were making a fortune, but we were only on five hundred pounds a week between us. There was a press conference at the end of the first week with a feminist theatre troupe called Monstrous Regiment. One of the women was very fat. I said, 'Where are you from?' She said, 'The Isle of Wight.' I said, 'I thought you *were* the Isle of Wight!' So when it came to the press conference, they wouldn't let us in.

We were sleeping in tents, next to the tent we were performing in. I was actually sleeping next to a pigsty, because there was a German opera lot in there who had a pig. We all looked a bit rough. Eventually, we got in. Monstrous Regiment were doing a show about people in prison, how it's not their fault, it's society's fault. But one woman had her handbag nicked by some Herbert and she went fucking mad. She was saying, 'Call the police!' I said, 'Don't worry, it's not his fault. It's our fault!' She didn't laugh at that.

At the end of the press conference, someone from each company had to get up and say something about their show to the assembled members of the press, who were all pissed as rats. By this time, this woman had recovered her composure, and was saying, 'We're doing this show about prison. It's not their fault – it's our fault.' I was getting bitter and cynical about the whole thing so I said to Martin, 'Pass me that newspaper.' I got up and said, 'We're The Greatest Show On Legs. We're doing a comedy show, but it's not a moment for levity because I've just read in this newspaper that the great Glenda Jackson has died of a heart attack, and in the spirit of the Fringe, I'd like to ask for a minute's silence.' And then I took another look at the paper, and said, 'Oh, sorry! It wasn't Glenda Jackson. It was Wendy Jackson, a pensioner from Sydenham. Well that doesn't matter, does it?' They all went mad. A bloke at the front shouted, 'Bad taste!' He had an orange and yellow shirt on, if I remember rightly.

We went back up the year after. We were in a tent with Emma Thompson on one side and a bloke called Eric Bogosian [*American stand-up, star of the feature film* Talk Radio] on the other. The problem was that all three shows were going on at the same time, and you could hear the show next door. In Eric Bogosian's show he had a tape of a heavy metal group playing, which came right out in the middle of a quiet bit of our show. I asked him if he could either make it five minutes earlier or five minutes later, but he said no.

We had a tractor in our show. My entrance was coming on in this tractor, going up a ramp and over some toy cars. I'd done about a week of this and you could hear this heavy metal every bloody night. In the end, I got fed up with it, and I said, 'Let's go and see Eric!' I was naked at the time. I got on the tractor, and our whole audience followed me out of our tent and into his. There he was, with a broom, miming to A C/D C. His show was called *Funhouse*. I read a review which said it was an anarchistic look at the American way of life, so I thought, 'He won't mind.' I drove through and said, 'Hello, Eric!' and came back into our tent. The next thing I heard was the sound of a tractor being smashed up, and then Eric came storming in. We were just about to do the balloon dance, so Martin was naked, and because he was naked, Eric thought he was me.

The organisation went mad. They fined us eight hundred quid. We had to repay the money for the tickets he had to refund, damage to the dressing rooms, and I had to go round with a letter of apology [*several years later, Hardee was watching late night television at home in Deptford, when it was announced that Bogosian would be performing live on TV at the Albany Empire – a few hundred yards from where Hardee lived. Hardee drove his tractor to the Albany Empire, to repeat this impromptu entrance on TV – but, sadly, it was too big to fit through the door*].

I managed Gerry Sadowitz for three years, which nearly drove me up the wall. He doesn't sleep at night, so he used to ring me up at three in the morning and scream down the phone that someone had nicked one of his lines. When I put him on in Edinburgh, his advert in the Fringe programme said, 'He's had his act ripped off by Bing Hitler,' who was Craig Ferguson. He hadn't at all, and Craig decided to sue Gerry for libel. All Ferguson had was a similar style, but not one line was the same. Bing Hitler hated everything, and so did Gerry, they were both Glaswegians and that was where the similarity ended. In the end, we settled out of court. The Fringe club kept all Gerry's ticket money and handed it to Craig Ferguson – about twelve hundred pounds, which was quite a lot at that time.

When the balloon dance was at its peak, we got invited by this agent to do Freddie Mercury's fortieth birthday in a place called Club Zenon in Piccadilly. When we got there, they wouldn't let us mix with the party. We had to sit in the dressing room. There was about twelve speciality acts on, each doing five minutes. There was a midget and a Russian acrobat. We were all stuck in this dressing room looking out at Freddie Mercury, Elton John, Rod Stewart and Princess Margaret.

Just before we were due to go on, when we were all naked and ready, the manager came in and said, 'You can't go on.' I said, 'Why not?' He said, 'The press are all here, and we don't want Freddie Mercury to be associated with anything that might be considered gay.' I said, 'Well he is gay. It's obvious he's gay. His band's called Queen. Everyone knows, don't they?' He said, 'It doesn't matter. You're not doing it,' and he paid us – six hundred quid. I said, 'Oh, all right. Can we go to the party?' He said, 'Not until he's cut the cake.' So we sat in this dressing room, and then this massive cake came in – it was a pink Rolls Royce, with a number plate on – FM1. Four blokes walked it in, put it over a couple of tables, and all he did was pose for the press with a big knife and stabbed it. Then they all buggered off into another room round the back. I said, 'Can we go out now and party?' He said, 'You can, but you can't go in that room out there.' So we ended up with all the liggers. It was about three pound for half a pint of lager.

I was pissed off because we'd gone all that way, they wouldn't let us do the sketch and we couldn't meet any people, so I said, 'We'll fuck off, shall we?' So we went out, and in the corridor was the cake. I said, 'We'll have that!' So we picked it up. We had a Luton transit van at the time. We put in it but there was still about three foot of cake sticking out the back. I drove it home, but I used to live on the top floor and I couldn't get it in the door. So I said to Martin, 'We'll put it in your flat,' because he had an old Victorian flat on the ground floor. It was about half two in the morning by then. We went round to his house and we had to take the window out to get the cake in, but we got it in his front room and there it was – pride of place. I went home and went to bed.

Nine o'clock the next morning, the agent who booked us was on the phone. He said, 'You've stolen Freddie Mercury's birthday cake!' I said, 'I haven't.' Apparently some teenagers saw us coming out with it and called the police. It was worth four thousand quid. So I went whizzing back round to Martin's house. I said, 'They've sussed it! What are we going to do? We can't eat it!' But it was coming up to Christmas, so Martin said, 'I know! We'll phone up the old people's home and ask them if they want a cake for Christmas!' So we got the window out, and got the cake in the transit – three foot out the back again. And as I was driving off, a police car came the other way. They were going slowly – you could tell they were looking for his house. I thought, 'They're going to look in the mirror and see this.' But they didn't, although I saw them in my mirror, getting out to go and question him. I'd missed them by about two minutes. So I gave the cake to the old people's home. They loved it.

I went home and thought, 'Fuck it, I'm going to get some sleep!' I'd had about two hours sleep when at about four o'clock in the afternoon, there was a ring on the bell – two detectives turned up. They said, 'You've stolen Freddie Mercury's birthday cake!' I said, 'No.' They said, 'Well, we've got reason to believe you have.' They came in and they had magnifying glasses. They were looking around for crumbs! But they didn't find any, and I never heard anything else after that.

13. The Last Laugh

'Comedians are the worst people to ask, because they talk such bollocks.' – Jeremy Hardy

JACK DEE

Stand-up comedy is the logical conclusion of a personality defect. It's an extension of a behaviour pattern that we've all picked up at some point. I've always been able to make people laugh. Looking back, I realise that that was as important to me as anything else ever was. If I knew a good joke, I'd know exactly who to go and tell it to to get the best laugh. Likewise, I knew exactly who not to tell. My way into people was by tapping into their sense of humour, by finding out what makes them laugh and being able to relate to them on that level.

You want to make people laugh, but you almost want to hurt them with what you're saying. There's a lot of frustration: 'Fuck you, I am good, I can do this! You're going to accept this whether you like it or not!'

DAVID BADDIEL

At the moment, I'm having an enormous row with my comedy partner and it's a magnified version of the whole thing, of getting very nervous, and not really wanting to do the gig – and having to go on, and suddenly being all right when you get onstage. Last night, I was really fucked off, and I really didn't want to do the gig. I felt like pulling it out of spite and hatred. Then when I went on, I think I was pretty good and that was probably to do with that. Once I was onstage, I had to do it – and that energy transformed itself into something else.

But that doesn't mean the problems aren't there when you come offstage. That's one of the things that's frustrating about it. It's so cathartic being onstage, when you're doing well, that you feel you should have come to some other point at the end of it, but your problems are still there at the end of the day. That can be one of the reasons why I think comics end up killing themselves – because your body and you whole psyche feel, 'I've come somewhere now!' But you haven't really – not in your own life. It's a phantom.

I don't think that I come offstage having grown as a person, or having healed any scars. However, I think that's true of therapy as well. I don't actually think that therapy solves problems. It's a Freudian notion that if you repress something, that's the problem – and as soon as you talk about it, hey!, it's fine. I think that's wrong. I've never been to a therapist. Maybe I should do or maybe that's why I do this instead – because it is true that while I'm doing it onstage, I feel much better. Rob's much more of a depressive than I am. I'm not generally that depressed. I've got my own neuroses, but I'm not somebody who goes around being really miserable all the time. Being onstage gives you a certain clarity of thought.

I'm always tired, because I never sleep – so normally my brain is here, there and everywhere. Sometimes, when I'm onstage, I feel, to use a horrible American word, 'focused' for the hour or so that I'm on. You can get a buzz from doing really well at a gig, but I don't think that you come away feeling that the healing process has begun – and I think it'd be quite bad if you did.

JENNY ECLAIR

I'm very strict with myself about drink before a gig. For five or six years now, I've never touched a drop of alcohol before I go onstage. I've learnt that. About eight years ago, I used to drink before I went onstage – and one night, I was pissed and I was hopeless. My boyfriend picked me up after the gig and I threw up all over the dashboard of his Mark Ten Jaguar. It got behind the original radio – and clogged it up, and broke it. He was really angry with me so I cleaned up my act there and then. I hosed myself down and had a good think. You drink because of the fear. You think that it's going to relax you but it doesn't – it just fucks up your timing.

I've lived with the same man for eleven years, and he's never seen me do stand-up comedy. He's seen me in plays, and he'll watch me on telly and listen to me on the radio. He's incredibly supportive – I couldn't do it if he wasn't that supportive. There aren't many men who are prepared to babysit, four or five nights a week, but he can't cope with seeing me live onstage.

Having a kid made me get my arse into gear. I had to get professional about it. I had to start making proper money, because if I was going to work, I had to pay for a nanny – so there was a financial thing to keep up. When you've got a child to feed and clothe, serious money has to be made. You've got to be good – you can't be doing try-out spots or working for thirty quid. I had a goal to achieve. I had to get up to a certain level, to be able to do the gigs that paid good money. I didn't want my daughter to be embarrassed of me. It did focus me a lot. As soon as I brought her home from hospital, I realised that I couldn't stay at home and be a mother. I have no respect for anybody who isn't a working mother. They're the only people who I have any admiration for. I've got to get to Newcastle, and she's got to be picked up from school. Everybody else is just busking it. Nobody else knows shit.

I'm talking from the viewpoint of a thirty-two-year-old woman with a child, with food problems and body-image problems. Sometimes, I have to remember when I do college gigs, 'Hold on, these people are fourteen years younger than me. They're not interested in this side of me.' I have a section about depression, which I've stopped doing at universities because they're not really interested. I sometimes worry that there's a new generation of comedy audiences. That's why I would never stop gigging, because if you stop gigging, your comedy becomes archaic.

You have to be slightly flawed to want to do something so daft. I've been in and out of therapy for years, mostly for food problems and death phobia. I don't pay for it – I get in on the National Health, because I have got a personality disorder. I wouldn't dare do my act in front of my mother. She'd drag me off the stage by my ear and give me a real smack. I've done it in front of my brother and sister. My mother's very worried about whether I can do this when I'm forty. I don't see why not. Nobody's embarrassed about Billy Connolly getting up on stage. Comedy is a licence to be silly. It's a form of escapism from everyday mundanity. I'd far rather be onstage than unpacking a supermarket trolley, which is what life can come down to.

ARTHUR SMITH

Anybody who does stand-up has had experience, albeit in the pub or at a dinner party, of making people laugh. You probably have a reputation among your friends of being a bit of a wag. You must have enormous self-confidence in the first place – even to consider it. But within that self-confidence is self-delusion. You're thinking you'll do your three one-liners, they'll all go superbly well and everyone'll love you. You'll just say whatever comes into your head – any old bullshit – and you'll be hilarious, just like you are in the pub. You think, 'I'll go up and be funny because I can be,' and you get a bit of a shock because it isn't like that at all.

EDDIE IZZARD

I felt I could do it from really small, but everything I was doing was saying, 'No you can't – you're a complete shite. There's no chance.' A lot of people have that madness – and they either decide to kill it, or they hold on to it and carry on. When things opened up, after such a lot of struggling, I relaxed – I became really calm, and suddenly thought, 'Shit! I'm not mad!' Because you do think, 'Perhaps I'm mad because I think I can do this and it's not coming out.' I thought, 'Thank fuck for that!' I was twenty-seven when I started stand-up. That's when it started to click. I thought talent was number one – but it's actually determination. Madonna is a classic example. The first show I took up to Edinburgh was in 1981. I had three years of taking up shows which weren't getting anywhere. I had a year of being despondent, and then street performing for three years, and then another five years of stand-up – but I wouldn't give up. I was on the dole for four or five years and came out as a transvestite. But I'm a ridiculous optimist. I can positivise any fucking thing in the world. Coming out as being TV was traumatic – but it was positive.

BRUCE MORTON

I always work best when I'm tense, and when things aren't going well. That's then I write the best stuff. I don't try to create situations of tension in the hope that I'll get a good routine out of it, but in those situations are the real raw things which are the most fertile ground for humour.

I don't think I've ever thought, 'If I go out and do a routine about this, that'll help me to understand my situation and deal with it better,' but it has happened in retrospect. The classic example is the tale I tell about that awkwardness of going into a public toilet and trying to pee in front of other men. I thought, 'That's quite funny,' so I wrote a routine about it and after I'd done the routine a dozen times, I was getting so much laughter, and so many nods of recognition, from men in the audience, that I realised that it's a common absurdism, and so now I've got a perspective on it.

I used to talk about my fascination with high-heeled shoes, which formed a big routine in the *Shoe Fetishist's Guide* that I did [*his first TV show, on Channel 4*]. I was trying to work out what this was all about. Is it innate or is it learned that high-heeled shoes are sexy? That was the thrust of the routine, and it was only after I'd done it a few times that I got the answer to it, and the answer was very simple. It was simply that in all the porny mags you look at when you're growing up, the women in them will be almost entirely naked – but they almost invariably have high-heeled shoes on, so it's learned. There's a process of discovery that goes on, but it's usually by accident.

LEE EVANS

It could be making up for the attention that you haven't had. If I stand up there and say, 'I've locked my car keys in my car,' I'm picking up on a hostility that everybody's suffered at one time and offloading their foolishness, so they feel a release because I'm the idiot. They think, 'Phew! He's the idiot and it's not happening to me!' It's a pack thing. If everybody's walking down the street normally, and then one bloke starts limping really strangely, they all think, 'He's strange and I'm glad it ain't me!' That's the whole thing about picking on the audience – let's all laugh at him. I'm glad it ain't me. It's a release.

Angry comedy is another release. Everybody's pissed off with something, and someone comes out with it. It's like a rally. That's what political comedy is. You say, 'Isn't it fucking terrible?' And the audience all shout, 'Yeah!'

People are very important, and there are too many people in the world who don't respect other people, and other people's space.

Where I came from in Avonmouth was fucking shit. I did a few talent contests until I started to get good. Sometimes I got some prize money – which kept me going for a couple of weeks. And I've gone from there to living all right with the missus, and getting a good wedge in. I can't do anything else. There's nothing else I can do. That's it. Full stop. If I actually give this up now, what do I do? I've got no exams or anything. I never took any. I ain't got no 'O' levels, no CSEs – nothing. So I can't do another job. I've done loads of jobs but never stuck at one. So that's it. That's my only motivation.

RICHARD HERRING

It must be to do with being liked – it must be to do with being seen as popular. Throughout my life, I've always viewed myself as being unpopular in some way with certain types of people. At college, the rugby players in the bar took a real dislike to me – probably justifiably, because I was a bit cocky when I first went up to Oxford, and a bit odd, so it gave me a lot of pleasure to be successful and make people laugh. It's probably to do with being accepted. Women tend to find it attractive if someone's funny, and in any case it's sexy for yourself to have people enjoying you being funny. If you're in a group of friends and you're cracking jokes and everyone's laughing, that feels good, because you're accepted by them. If you can take it one stage further and do that with a group of strangers, it adds an extra element to it. There is a certain amount of selfishness about it, but it is nice to cheer people up as well. The annoying thing with comedy is that I partly do it to look cool and appeal to girls, and then I attract all these people who are like me when I was thirteen.

A lot of comedians have a desire to be loved. There are quite a few adopted comedians: Stewart Lee is an adopted only child, and Rob Newman is adopted. I'm always worried about everyone hating me because I was the headmaster's son. I think you carry those things through. Lots of comedians concentrate on adolescent things. Some of them talk about adolescent toys and TV programmes, but the better ones talk about things that have happened to them which they haven't shaken off.

I've reached a stage in my life where I've got over that teenage thing of always worrying about being popular, when it always seems to matter if someone slags you off, but I still hark back to it, and it's something that a lot of people find impossible to shake off. Wanting to be liked by everyone else is the central thing for most adolescents, and for lots of comics. Adolescents also don't want to be seen as different, so using your difference as a way of becoming accepted is a form of revenge. You're saying, 'Aha! You all hated me when I was fifteen because of this, but now everyone likes me because of it.' Stewart Lee is the ultimate revenge comedian. He loves to get back at people in very trivial ways. You laugh at him for being so trivial about his ex-girlfriend's mother, but it actually gives him pleasure.

Most comedians are people who haven't been accepted at some point in some way. There's a pleasure in being accepted by people who didn't accept you before, and if all the blokes at college who used to make my life hell, because they thought I was stupid, said to their friends, 'I was at college with him,' and were proud to be associated with me, then that would give me pleasure. To make really good comedy, there has got to be an element of anger and unpleasant emotion beneath it, and we allow that to rebound on us, so we look like idiots. For Stewart that's quite a big deal, because he doesn't like looking like an idiot. He doesn't like fooling around and pulling funny faces because he thinks it makes him look stupid, but he allows his personality to be picked apart. I guess we all do that.

MARK LAMARR

You never know where the peak of a joke is. There are times when you're building on something and doing such a good job, and then you realise that you've gone too far – not necessarily that it's disgusting or evil, just that it ceases to be funny. You never know where that point is, and it's just as bad to stop before you get to it. In Edinburgh, I was compering a gig at the Gilded Balloon in front of a really tough audience. It took me ten minutes to get a laugh out of them – and then, for the next five minutes, they were pissing themselves. But instead of thinking, 'I've got them laughing – now I should get off,' I thought, 'I've got them laughing – and that's the way they'll stay!' In retrospect, I should have stopped there and got someone else on – but I didn't and it went straight back downhill.

The whole art of comedy is to seem as if you're funny all the time, as if when you get offstage you're going to be as funny at the bar.

When I first saw Arthur Smith I thought, 'Wow! That bloke is the funniest man who ever lived!' I didn't feel as if he'd gone on and done an act. It felt like he'd been called from the bar for half an hour to take over the show, and that he was by far the best at it, but that he couldn't really be bothered because he wasn't that interested. Most comedians are quite funny people, but we're not the funniest people we know. The funniest person you know is always the bloke down the pub who's always funny, because he isn't under pressure to be funny. None of us can match that.

DOMINIC HOLLAND

There's a huge amount of jealousy stand-up comedy, because everyone wants to be a star. There's not a stand-up on the circuit who doesn't want to be a star – and yet maybe only two per cent will do it. And if you start doing well, you become the brunt of some bad jibes. Friends of mine say, 'There's a big backlash against you after Edinburgh.' When I went to Edinburgh, people said, 'You shouldn't be doing an hour. You're too young. You'll die on your arse.' People said, 'Everyone's waiting for you to take a fall.' The camaraderie is there until someone starts making moves – and when you start getting a bit of daylight between yourself and your peers, you can feel the resentment. It's not very nice and I'm really sensitive to it. I get a lot of shit.

I practise Catholicism – obviously not rigidly, because I live with my girlfriend and I do things which the Church wouldn't agree with. I believe in contraception, but I'm proud to be a Catholic, and I have faith in the Church. I like going to Mass. I don't go to confession. I haven't been for years. I should go – but maybe I'd go in there funny and come out sensible, saying, 'He's got all my jokes – I can't do it any more!'

For a while, my girlfriend didn't want me to mention her name during the show, or talk about our sex life. She said, 'I don't want you to talk about blow jobs,' and I respect that, because it's very personal. A lot of comics go on about it: 'My girlfriend was giving me a blow job . . .' She said, 'I'd be personally offended. I don't want you talking about oral sex, or any kind of sexual deviancy.' I understand that, so I don't do it. She'd be offended if I was going on about crude stuff.

My girlfriend is the only person who's fully aware of what I can do. I can make her laugh like a drain, so she says, 'If you can do this on stage, Dominic, the sky's your limit.' She knows that what I do onstage is maybe a fifth of what I could do. I can do a cracking show and she'll say, 'Look, you've got a great theme here, and you just do three gags on it and then piss off. Eddie Izzard would do ten minutes on that.' She's very hard but brilliantly constructive. She'll say, 'That was a shit gag,' and I'll get angry. I'll say, 'Look, Nick, there were twelve hundred people in there! I can't just go on and ad-lib!' She saw me the other night in Southend. It was a good gig – they had a good time, but Nicky knew it was pretty regimented. She's the first one to praise me if it's gone well, because she wants to see me become as good as I can be.

She's my biggest fan – she's really concerned that there's lots of groupies in comedy, and that's bullshit. I don't get involved in that at all. There are some silly little girls who come up to you after a gig and give you a phone number. That happened to me the other night, but I'm not interested in that at all. She's worried about that, but I'm not. I don't care how successful I get. I'd much rather have a successful relationship than a spate of young blondes.

I didn't want to tell you about my convictions, because you might think it would be arrogant. I was thinking, 'I can't tell him that I think I'm going to make it,' because however you say that, you're going to get covered in mud. But I'm so passionate about comedy that I immediately lose all my reticence and start talking completely honestly and candidly. And all the while, I'm thinking. 'What are you doing? You said you weren't going to say this!'

When I'm in my lounge, I can do stuff which I think, 'If only I could do this on stage!' It's only a matter of time. I will get there. People who see me don't see anything like what I can do.

VIC REEVES

We always go around looking for acts and attempting to assist them. The last time I really buckled was watching John Shuttleworth about three years ago. I suggested to various people that they should have him on television. He hasn't really done as well as he could have done, but that's not his fault – he's been given short spots. He's one of those people who you need to look at for half an hour before you get what's going on.

Tommy Cockles had only spoken once on stage, and we took him on a national tour. He didn't even have a name. He was called Simon Day. We said his name was shit, so on the first night of the tour, we said we'd put a note under his hotel door with a name on it. So he was waiting in his hotel room while we sat in our hotel room coming up will all these names. It was down to Tommy Cockles or Peter Peanuts. So we wrote Tommy Cockles on a little note and put it under his door. When he came out, he was quite happy to be Tommy Cockles. He could have been Peter Peanuts, but it wouldn't have had quite the same ring to it. Perhaps he would have been a different character.

GRAHAM FELLOWS

It's nice to receive laughter, but it can leave you feeling a bit lonely at the end of the gig. You feel a bit paranoid after the laughter's died down. The pressure of making people laugh empties you. It should fill you up, shouldn't it? But I find it can empty me a bit, perhaps because deep down, I want to be taken seriously. I can see why comedians can end up as very lonely, disenchanted people.

I moved out of London to a quiet little market town in Lincolnshire. My girlfriend's parents live there and I've got two little daughters. That puts things in perspective – it makes me feel that it's not quite as important. My kids are the most important thing, but it helps me to keep at it, because I need to make a living to look after them. Now I have to fight for time to work. I feel I want to spend a lot of time with them.

It's very hard to sustain one character who's so all consuming. John Shuttleworth has quite a powerful hold on me. There are elements of my father in there and an uncle – various people that I've met. John Shuttleworth sits on his emotions. He inhabits a lonely world. He used to get me down when I inhabited a similar world. He can get depressive. I can feel that I'm turning into him. It doesn't happen so much now. Because I've got the kids, I feel a bit more centred about it.

My girlfriend likes it, but she doesn't get it all. Men seem to find it funnier than women. She listened to the radio series, and the last

one was quite a dark one. There weren't really any jokes in it at all –
no punchlines, not that there are many anyway. I was very proud of
it, because the whole thing spirals into itself. John's at the halfway
house, waiting for the proprietress to come back and open up, so
John can get in and get a power source to mow the lawn. But she
doesn't turn up, and John gets more and more upset, as less and less
happens. At the end, she said, 'It's not funny.' She was right. It
wasn't funny – but it was the best thing I'd done.

I suspect I'll kill him off eventually. The heartening thing for me is
that Dame Edna Everage was actually created in the year I was
born, 1959. Barry Humphries has got a couple of other characters he
does as well, but I'm no Steve Coogan. I'm not as versatile as that.
I'm not so interested in characterisation per se. I want to talk about
the things that are important to me in life. I don't have any interest in
talking about politics or international affairs, because other people
do it far better. My particular interest tends to be people – the truth
of people's lives and the way they inter-react.

My favourite lines are the ones that are true. About the second
week after we moved to Lincolnshire, there was a car boot sale in the
car park of Gateway. There was a family there in a van – they were
very poor and they were selling everything. There was a Spirograph,
which I was going to buy, but their little girl looked like she didn't
want it to be sold. I took that experience and made it into a little
story onstage. John wants to buy the Spirograph and the little girl
says, 'Oh no, Dad – not that one!' The dad says, 'No, everything's
got to go.' John says, 'It was only 50p but I didn't buy it – there were a
few bits missing.' It paints a very sad picture – of John, and this
family. When I can take things from real life, it's so much better than
making them up. If you get a laugh off something that's true, that
really happened, that's wonderful.

DONNA McPHAIL

Because most of my comedy is based on me, I feel quite happy to
take the piss out of myself. I did use a story that happened with me
and another comic. I used his first name for a while. I used it in
Edinburgh because I knew that no one knew who it was, but I
wouldn't do it in London. Most jokes are sad or cruel. We only laugh
out of relief that someone else has said it, so when people put

themselves down, everybody likes that. They like one person to take the risk of saying things that they'd never say.

JO BRAND

I try to put across this attitude that I don't care what blokes think of me because I think a lot of blokes know that it's actually quite important to women how blokes see them. It would have worried me when I was eighteen, but it doesn't any more – I don't make an effort for them. If they say, 'You're fat and unattractive,' I don't really care that they think that. When you get older, you realise that those sorts of things aren't important any more. I couldn't have done this when I was a teenager. I would have been too humiliated, because it was important to me then.

STEWART LEE

Topical comedy is the same old themes with the words changed over and over again. A lot of people don't even do jokes – they just say things that everyone's noticed. I've seen someone go on and open a set by saying, 'What about those bloody Pop Tarts?' I thought, 'You're going to elaborate on that now, aren't you? You're going to tell us some sort of story about Pop Tarts,' but that was all he did. He was just reminding people that Pop Tarts weren't very nice – and it got a laugh. I was standing in the wings, thinking, 'Surely you've said this to each other by now? Don't you have any friends to talk to? Why do you need to pay someone to tell you that when you already know!' Those kind of acts appeal to people who need to have their own stupid opinions confirmed.

A lot of comedians are the friends you never had. They're that witty bloke who you wished was in your group, who could say, 'What about those bloody Pop Tarts?' and everyone would laugh. They're that witty bloke who you wished was you. When someone goes on and says, 'What about those Pop Tarts? Aren't they horrible?' you see people saying to each other, 'You said that yesterday!' It's as if they're as good as that person onstage. But I'm not interested in them wanting to be me. I don't want them to be me, and I don't want to be them. I don't want to have shared experiences with them. If they've paid, I should be giving them something different and special that they wouldn't have experienced or thought of. Otherwise they might as well go to the pub and talk about Pop Tarts.

Last year, I had a bit of a mental breakdown and a sexually transmitted disease, and I've been doing stuff about it onstage. I put in enough detail for audiences to know it's true. I want to see how low you can go in terms of status, but still be of a higher status than the audience. Onstage, you've got the power to confess these things in a really nonchalant way. I like to freak them out a bit, because they don't expect it at all. They are really embarrassed by it, and it's interesting to see if you can still keep them laughing when they feel uncomfortable. I could sit in a room and write topical jokes all day long, but what I like to try and do is get a laugh out of something that is as far away from being recognisable as funny as I can find.

JOHN HEGLEY

Sometimes I have to remind myself how fantastic it is to make people laugh. I find it very difficult to laugh. I rarely laugh at someone, even if I think they're really funny. I sometimes forget what it's like to laugh. It would be very good for me to laugh more, because I love laughing. I've got a friend in Bristol, and when I was eighteen, we used to make up mad routines and perform them into a tape recorder. We never performed them for anyone else, and a lot of the stuff on the tape is us laughing at the performance. There was no audience, so we laughed – now somebody else does the laughing. If you go onstage, say something funny and start laughing yourself, it isn't going to help. I don't laugh very much at other people, but fortunately this mate of mine in Bristol still makes me laugh. So when I go and see him, he says funny things and I'm glad he's not on the stage because that would ruin it.

JULIAN CLARY

Sometimes I'm not quite sure why people are laughing so much – that's a very strange feeling. Because I do a lot of innuendo, people sometimes read an innuendo into something – and I've got no idea what they're laughing at. I did a routine about my ex-boyfriend – about the volume and velocity of his orgasm. I only talk about things which are true – which have actually happened. I said, 'I can't remember what he looked like – I know there was hair involved and a certain number of eyes.' I couldn't work out why that was funny.

Laughter is a very addictive feeling. It's an instant response – you've said the right thing in the right way. It's an animal thing about baying at someone who's standing outside, who's not conforming. It's a way of banishing you from the group. That's the meaning of life in a nutshell, I think.

FRANK SKINNER

I was a blank page when I arrived on the circuit, and to some extent, the audiences wrote my act for me. I found out pretty early on what they liked, and what they didn't. I had no interest in educating them or being prescriptive about what I did, but it took me a long time to realise that I could say things onstage that I found funny and I'd say to my mates, and that it was O K and I could get away with it. For a long time I couldn't do that in London. London audiences were a bit tight-arsed, but in Birmingham I was doing jokes which weren't quite politically correct. We've done the racism and sexism stuff – comics aren't racist or sexist on the circuit so we can relax, and I was surprised how honest I could be. Most of the things I found funny, they found funny – because most of them were ordinary people like me. I'd think, 'They won't laugh at this, it's too strong for them,' but they'd laugh at it and I'd think, 'This is great! It's just like me mates in the pub!'

I've never been a professional Brummie. I make the odd reference to it. Some people, all they talk about is where they come from – and they're inclined to slag it off. The main thing that Birmingham gave me comedy-wise wasn't a sense of where I was, but of where I wasn't.

There's one joke that I really like that's an old Max Miller. I don't know why I like it so much. It's about the bloke who goes to buy a car, but he hardly has any money. He's offered a car – can't afford it, motorbike – hasn't got enough, push bike – hasn't got enough for that, and in the end all he can afford is a hoop and stick. So he buys the hoop and stick, for about five bob, and he goes off into the countryside with it. And he goes for miles up hill and down dale until he gets a bit thirsty, so he stops outside this pub and puts his hoop and stick in the car park. He goes inside and has a half of mild but when he comes out it's gone. He says to the landlord, 'Someone's nicked me hoop and stick.' The landlord says, 'Oh, I'm sorry about that – how much did you pay for it?' 'Five bob,' says the bloke. 'Well that's all right,' says the landlord. 'I'll reimburse you.' 'It's no use reimbursing me!' says the bloke. 'How am I going to get home?'

HARRY HILL

My favourite joke is quite a long one, and you probably won't laugh at it – but when I first heard it in the playground, I cried with laughter. There are these three businessmen who go out and have a really successful business lunch, have some drinks and go and see a top West End show. They think, 'How can we top this night off?' And one of them says, 'Let's go and see a prostitute.' So they go to Soho, and go in the first place they come to. They ask the woman behind the desk, 'How much is it?' 'Three prices,' she says. 'Twenty-five pounds, fifty pounds and seventy-five pounds. So the first bloke goes upstairs. Ten minutes later, he comes back down – smiling all over his face. The other two say, 'What happened?' He says, 'I went upstairs, paid twenty-five pounds, she took my trousers down, put a pineapple ring on my John Thomas and ate it off. Best experience I've had in my life.' So the second bloke says, 'Right! I'll pay fifty pounds!' and runs upstairs. Fifteen minutes later, he comes back down with a great big smile on his face. The other two say, 'What happened?' He says, 'I went upstairs, paid fifty pounds, she took my trousers down, put two pineapple rings on my John Thomas and ate them off. Best experience I've ever had in my life!' So the third one says, 'Right! I'll pay seventy-five pounds!' and he runs upstairs. Twenty minutes later, he comes back down with a really long face. 'What happened?' say the other two. 'You should be happy!' He says, 'Well, I went upstairs, paid my seventy-five pounds, she took my trousers down, put one, two, three pineapple rings on my John Thomas, covered it with cream, put a cherry on top, looked so good I ate it myself.'

HUGH DENNIS

It's always difficult when people come up to you in the street and say, 'You're a comedian – tell us a joke.' I say, 'Well, I am a comedian –

but I don't really do that kind of thing.' They think you're a bit of a
wanker because you won't tell them a joke – but, generally, I can't
remember any.

The Knowledge

TOMMY COCKLES

Stage name of Simon Day's seaside showbiz caricature, who lampoons the whimsical nostalgia of vaudeville's old guard. Cockles is a retired old-time all-round entertainer, whose dewy-eyed, rose-tinted reminiscences about the golden age of Light Ents unwittingly reveal him to be an end-of-the-pier also-ran. Cockles/Day owes his discovery and early development to the talent-spotting talents of Vic Reeves and Bob Mortimer – who took him on a national tour on the strength of his first gig.

THE COMEDY STORE

The unofficial National Theatre of alternative and post-alternative comedy. It was founded above a strip joint in Dean Street, Soho, in May 1979, and owed its early success to the explosive talents of communist Lithuanian Scouser Alexei Sayle, who compered the club throughout its first year. It moved to slightly plusher premises in an L-shaped Leicester Square cellar in 1985 and on to its present location, in an expansive basement on Oxendon Street in 1993. Its capacity has doubled, from 100 to 200 to 400, with each subsequent move upmarket, yet it still sustains the boisterous atmosphere that made it famous, even if its reputation as the first and foremost Alternative Comedy club now owes more to its West End location and familiarity with tourists and out-of-towners than its early innovation. Nevertheless world famous comedians such as Robin Williams have been known to drop in and perform unannounced – and the club is a habitual home from home for American agents. Under the ownership of Don Ward, and the management of Kim Kinnie, it has launched the careers of Ben Elton, Rik Mayall, Adrian Edmondson, Dawn French and Jennifer Saunders, to name a few, and is responsible for blooding virtually every comic in this book.

THE COMEDY STORE PLAYERS

Improvisation troupe with a constantly changing cast who play a twice weekly residency at the Comedy Store. Among its pioneering participants were Josie Lawrence, Tony Slattery and Paul Merton, although its backbone and unsung hero is pianist Richard Vranch. It transferred to BBC Radio 4 as *Whose Line Is It Anyway?*, before being poached by Channel 4. Responsible for introducing 'Impro' to the nation, although most comics seem to feel that this popular yet formulaic and repetitious ragbag of drama-school parlour games actually owes much more to sit-down theatre than it does to stand-up comedy.

THE COMIC STRIP

Innovative comic sketch troupe, the core of which was a comedic mixed marriage of two Comedy Store double acts, Rik Mayall and Ade Edmondson, and Dawn French and Jennifer Saunders. First performed at the Boulevard, a comedy club cum fringe theatre, incongruously housed in a studio annex adjoining the celebrated Soho strip club, Raymond's Revuebar. The Comic Strip subsequently found fame on television in a series of self contained feature films (including *Five Go Mad in Dorset*, *Strike* and *Didn't You Kill My Brother?*). They went on to work successfully apart (Mayall in *The New Statesman*, Mayall and Edmondson in *Bottom*, French and Saunders in *French and Saunders* and Saunders in *Absolutely Fabulous*), while the Boulevard became the home of the Raging Bull comedy club, managed and compered by Eddie Izzard.

KEVIN DAY

Proficient South London stand-up comedian who marries left-wing diatribes against Tory iniquities with accessible street-humour centred on the twentysomething leisure axioms of sex and drugs and rock and roll. His most recent one-man show, *I Was A Teenage Racist*, which premiered at the Edinburgh Festival Fringe in 1993 and toured around the country, was a significant departure from this familiar mix, dovetailing his teenage flirtations with the National Front and the death of his black best friend in police custody. Presented *Loose Talk*, on Radio 1 with Mark Thomas.

FELIX DEXTER

One of the few black comedians to carve out a reputation on the Alternative Comedy circuit, which, despite its anti-racist pretensions, remains almost exclusively caucasian. However, he also plays the smaller but rapidly growing black circuit, and his act is enjoyed at gigs as disparate as the Hackney Empire and Jongleurs. He recently received wider (albeit belated) television exposure in a series of outrageous and hilarious cameos on the BBC2 black sketch series, *The Real McCoy*.

BOB DILLINGER

First-rate Mancunian comic whose humour and appearance both repay debts to pioneering punk poet John Cooper Clarke. His carefully crafted one-liners are wedded to economical comic songs, faultlessly self-accompanied on acoustic guitar, a rich blend of musical stand-up matched only by Richard Morton. His caustic wit, honed in the less effete Northern clubs, has a far broader appeal than most other comedians in his field. However, despite appearances on TV programmes like *Wogan*, he remains woefully underexposed, mainly because of his Northern location, lack of metropolitan management and family commitments.

SIMON FANSHAWE

Fanshawe won the prestigious Perrier Award as recently as 1989, but he blew his Alternative Comedy credibility by presenting *That's Life* alongside Esther Rantzen on BBC1. Subsequently sacked after cracking a lewd joke about condoms, he made a comparatively unsuccessful return to the circuit at the 1990 Edinburgh Festival Fringe. Stranded between two stools, he reinvented himself as the presenter of his own radio chat show, *Fanshawe on Five* (BBC Radio 5), and as producer of Laughing Gas, the comedy component of the annual Brighton Festival. A quintessential Anglo-Scot, he was born in Edinburgh and educated at Marlborough. In 1993 he appeared in the wonderful West End flop *Elegies for Angels, Punks and Raving Queens* at the Criterion Theatre. He lives in Brighton.

The author and publishers accept that the allegation that Simon Fanshawe was sacked from *That's Life* cannot be substantiated in either fact or rumour and they apologise for its inclusion.

CRAIG FERGUSON

Swarthy Glaswegian comedian who started his career using the
stage name Bing Hitler. Although his humour shares more than
geography with Billy Connolly, his huge Glaswegian following has
never been duplicated in London – despite starring in a recent West
End revival of *The Rocky Horror Show*.

FOOTLIGHTS

The Cambridge University Revue, the seedbed for *Monty Python's
Flying Circus* and *Beyond the Fringe* and the inaugural winner of
the Perrier Award in 1981 with a dream line-up that included Emma
Thompson, Tony Slattery, Stephen Fry and Hugh Laurie. From a
cast of six only two failed to become household names. During
subsequent years, its quality has fluctuated dramatically – and
although its name remains extremely useful for filling theatres
throughout the Edinburgh Festival, and Light Entertainment
Producers' posts on Radio 4, its historical cachet has created a
backlash on the circuit, where Footlights luminaries like David
Baddiel have endured the inverted snobbery of alternative comics
committed to positive discrimination.

BILL HICKS

Self-loathing, cynical Texan comic, whose last two live shows –
Dangerous and *Relentless* (both broadcast on Channel 4) – celebrate
sex, pornography, drugs and cigarettes and attack the United States
Republican Party and the National Rifle Association. He died
unexpectedly of pancreatic cancer in March 1994.

SEAN HUGHES

Southern Irish comedian who in 1989 at the age of twenty-four
became the youngest ever winner of the Perrier Award, a distinction
that he still holds to this day. His winning one-man show – *A One
Night Stand With Sean Hughes* – was a stand-up/sit-down hybrid,
performed out front without a fourth wall from a stage set complete
with ringing telephone, etc. He has since branched out into poetry

(*Sean's Book*) and television (*Sean's Show*, two series of which have been broadcast on Channel 4). His most recent work was *Patrick's Day*, another cocktail of cabaret and theatre, co-written and performed with Owen O'Neill, which follows the fluctuating fortunes of two Irish bartenders adrift in the Big Smoke.

JONGLEURS

If the Comedy Store is Alternative Comedy's unofficial National Theatre, then Jongleurs is its Royal Court. Throughout the eighties, this Clapham club was an essential stepping stone for rising stand-up stars – and even TV celebs like Lenny Henry have been known to call in unannounced to try out new material. Last year, it sprouted a twin in Camden Lock, complete with raked seating, air conditioning, waitress service, and (more ominously) an anti-heckling policy – a corporate development which reflects the ambiguous effects of comedy's gradual yet persistent migration upmarket. Nevertheless, this Camden Lock offshoot is one of the finest stand-up venues in the country while the Clapham prototype still enjoys a kudos that's bettered only by the Comedy Store.

PHIL KAY

Scottish comedian, born in Edinburgh but based in Glasgow, who won So You Think You're Funny – an annual talent contest for unknown comics (which was won by fellow Scots Bruce Morton in 1988 and Rhona Cameron in 1992) – at the Edinburgh Festival Fringe in 1989. Kay's apparently instinctive style is actually highly structured and although he still lacks sufficient material to craft a first-class full-length solo show, his quickfire wit and seductive stage persona make him a top rate compere. He was shortlisted for the Perrier Award in 1993.

DENIS LEARY

Cynical Boston-born stand-up, whose nihilistic one-minute monologues have made him a star on MTV. His taboo-busting solo show – *No Cure For Cancer* – was a huge hit at the Edinburgh Festival

Fringe in 1991, and was subsequently broadcast by Channel 4. He took the same show back to the States and has since appeared in several Hollywood movies. His comic style lies somewhere between the Comedy of Hate epitomised by US stand-up Sam Kinison and the bohemian libertarianism of Bill Hicks.

NORMAN LOVETT

Lovable gentle giant whose ponderous stage persona and autistic delivery enhance rather than disguise the insightful surrealism of his wit. Best known for his appearance on BBC2's Sci-Fi comedy series *Red Dwarf*, he still plays occasional gigs on the London comedy circuit. Although his migration to Edinburgh has curtailed these appearances of late, it has added greater poise and perspective to his uniquely conceptual brand of comedy.

FRED MACAULAY

Glaswegian accountant who became a stand-up comedian at the relatively late age of thirty and has since become a rock-solid, if somewhat predictable, stalwart on the London comedy circuit. Remarkably, he still lives in Scotland and commutes to London by plane several weekends every month. In 1988 he founded The Funny Farm, Scotland's only comedy collective, with Bruce Morton and Stu Who.

PAUL MERTON

A veteran alternative comic, Merton trawled the circuit throughout the eighties, but found nationwide fame in *Paul Merton – The Series* on Channel 4, and on BBC1's satirical news quiz, *Have I Got News For You?* He also appeared on Channel 4's *Whose Line Is It Anyway?* Bloke-ish bathos and surreal flights of fancy constitute the key ingredients of Merton's popular appeal, which straddles a wide range of disparate tastes, as his recent sell-out show at the London Palladium attests. His is married to comic actress Caroline Quentin – who appeared in the comedy dramas *An Evening With Gary Lineker* and *Live Bed Show*, by stand-up playwright Arthur Smith.

HENRY NORMAL

Mancunian comic poet, nicknamed the Crumpsall Cowboy, who marries stand-up and verse in the manner of John Hegley. Like Hegley, his influences straddle the punk poems of John Cooper Clarke, the pop ballads of Merseybeat bards like Roger McGough and Brian Patten and the nonsense verses of Victorians like Edward Lear and Lewis Carroll. Yet there's a kitchen sink grit to Normal's couplets which is conspicuous by its absence from Hegley's Lutonite stanzas, and the influence of sixties Northern novelists like Stan Barstow and Alan Sillitoe lurks beneath the surface of his ostensibly matey rhymes. He has written for Steve Coogan, published several slim volumes of verse (including *A Love Like Hell*, *A More Intimate Fame* and *Nude Modelling in the Afterlife*) and appeared on Channel 4 alongside Jenny Eclair and Frank Skinner in the series *Packing Them In* and *Packet of Three*.

NOT THE NINE O'CLOCK NEWS

Immensely popular TV comedy sketch show starring Rowan Atkinson, Mel Smith, Griff Rhys Jones and Pamela Stephenson. Although these four performers were never Alternative Comedians per se, they influenced a generation of post-alternative comics such as Steve Coogan who were growing up in the early eighties when the series was at its zenith. Less revolutionary than *Three of a Kind* (which cemented the Light Ent reputations of Lenny Henry and Tracey Ullman), *Not The Nine O'Clock News* nevertheless liberated TV comedy from the clutches of Dick Emery, Benny Hill and the Two Ronnies – a service to society for which all comedy fans should be eternally grateful. Smith and Jones went on to star in several series of *Alas Smith and Jones* for the BBC. Pamela Stephenson went on to marry Billy Connolly, while Rowan Atkinson has established himself as an international comedian, particularly in the field of popular mime with Mr Bean.

OWEN O'NEILL

Northern Irish Catholic comedian, whose humour deals fearlessly with sectarian problems (such as Protestant girlfriends) in the Ulster of the nineties. More of a raconteur than an out-and-out gagsmith, his humour isn't ideally suited to the one-liner oriented London comedy circuit – although he's a competent enough stand-up to hold his own in the roughest comedy clubs. However, the breadth and depth of O'Neill's wit is better served by his bittersweet plays, like the recent two-hander, *Patrick's Day*, which he co-wrote and performed with Sean Hughes.

ALAN PARKER URBAN WARRIOR

An inspired comic caricature created by Simon Munnery – formerly one half of autistic double-act God and Jesus. Alan Parker is a send-up of anarchic adolescent angst, a trainspotter turned fare-dodger, whose sworn enemies are the DSS, the Conservative Party and British Rail. Informed by Rik Mayall's early alter-egos, Kevin Turvey and Rik (from *The Young Ones*), Munnery pre-empted the 'political correctness' debate by several years, inventing the perfect satirical icon for the current counter-reaction against the sanctimonious comedy of the eighties.

PARROT

Glaswegian stand-up comedian and former shipbuilder, whose gritty humour is informed by the monotonous tyranny of the factory hooter and the fleeting armistice of drunken Friday nights. Parrot was shortlisted for the Perrier Award in 1993 but his poorly attended performances at the subsequent Perrier Pick Of the Fringe season at London's Purcell Room confirmed that Scottish comedians come from, and speak to, a separate nation.

THE PERRIER AWARD

Some comics swear by the Perrier Award – others swear about it. Indifference is a lot rarer. Since its inception in 1981 it's become comedy's unofficial Oscars, with all the attendant hype, bitchery and backstabbing that major awards ceremonies attract. It's been accused of being too conservative (usually by performers who thought they were too radical to win it) and divisiveness (often by those who hoped they weren't). Awarded annually, at the Edinburgh Festival Fringe, the first five winners were all ensembles

(including the Cambridge Footlights and Théâtre de Complicité).
From the mid-eighties, the award followed the trend away from
revue towards stand-up, and with the exception of one double-act,
the last eight winners have all been solo comics. Indeed, as its
exponents experiment with new formats, it's becoming increasingly
difficult to define what's eligible, and what isn't. Arthur Smith's *Live
Bed Show* – a two-handed sit-down/stand-up hybrid which he
performed with Caroline Quentin, was shortlisted in 1989, while
Thirtysomehow – a comic play written and performed by co-
mediennes Julie Balloo, Jenny Eclair and Maria Callous, was
deemed ineligible in 1990.

For several years, there's also been a fierce debate on the panel as
to whether the award is for best comic or the best new comic (it can
seem silly to waste the award on a comic who is already a household
name). This problem has been alleviated if not solved by the
conception of an optional Newcomers' award, though it remains a
moot point who's too big to win the principal prize. Jack Dee and
Eddie Izzard didn't win – and Newman and Baddiel were never even
shortlisted. I should declare an interest – I've been a panellist for the
last three years, and while picking winners in any artform always
seems somewhat spurious, the shortlist at least is a pretty accurate
barometer of which comics are up and coming (who actually wins
appears to be more of a lottery). The winner gets an important leg-
up, and the Perrier Pick of the Fringe season on the South Bank
brings most of Edinburgh's best acts to London every autumn. Love
it or loathe it, no Fringe comic ignores it – and for all its fuss and
bluster, the Festival would be far duller without it.

PERRIER AWARD WINNERS

1981: Cambridge Footlights
1982: Writers Inc
1983: Los Trios Ringbarkus
1984: Brass Band (shortlist included Hank Wangford)
1985: Théâtre de Complicité
1986: Ben Keaton (shortlist included Roy Hutchins, Jenny Lecoat)
1987: Arnold Brown (with Jungr & Parker) (shortlist included
    Simon Fanshawe, Jeremy Hardy, Nick Revell)

1988: Jeremy Hardy (shortlist included Doug Anthony Allstars, Roy Hutchins)
1989: Simon Fanshawe (shortlist included John Hegley, Live Bed Show)
1990: Sean Hughes (shortlist included Dillie Keane)
1991: Frank Skinner (shortlist included Jack Dee, Eddie Izzard, Bruce Morton)
1992: Steve Coogan, with John Thomson (shortlist included Jo Brand, John Shuttleworth, Mark Thomas)
1993: Lee Evans (shortlist included Donna McPhail, Phil Kay, Parrot)

PERRIER MOST PROMISING NEWCOMER AWARD WINNERS

1992: Harry Hill
1993: Dominic Holland

MICHAEL REDMOND

Softly spoken, silver-haired Southern Irish stand-up who worked the London circuit for several years but is now based in Edinburgh. He shares with Celtic comics like Ian McPherson and Arnold Brown a rare compassion fused with an affection for surreal conceptual leaps. He also bears an uncanny resemblance to Mr Rusty, tricycling star of *The Magic Roundabout*.

NICK REVELL

Veteran alternative comedian from the same school of Lambrusco socialist stand-up as Simon Fanshawe and Jeremy Hardy with whom Revell was shortlisted for the Perrier Award at the Edinburgh Festival Fringe in 1987. His stand-up career never quite built on this initial success and after a lacklustre double-bill with Stu Who in Edinburgh in 1991, he grew disillusioned with gag-tied routines that revolved around one-liners. However, since that low-water mark, he has developed a more complex, anecdotal style – an investment which was repaid at the 1993 Festival Fringe in an intriguing and sophisticated one-man show, *The Ghost of John Belushi Flushed My Toilet*, which subsequently transferred to London's Hampstead

Theatre. He has also developed his career on radio, as the star of Radio 4's *The Million Pound Radio Show*.

GERRY SADOWITZ

Abusive and nihilistic, yet incredibly talented Glaswegian-Jewish stand-up animal – whose work is at once the epitome of, and a reaction against, all the basic tenets of Alternative Comedy. He is also a top-rate magician, with an entirely separate, yet equally devoted following among members of the Magic Circle. Confounding all industry predictions, he actually secured a series – *The Pallbearers Revue* – on BBC2 (most insiders felt sure his act was far too offensive for TV) but since then his career hasn't scaled the heights that his undoubted genius deserves. 'Terry Waite, what a bastard,' began one typical gag, 'you lend some people a fiver and you never see them again.'

MARK STEEL

With the possible exception of Mark Thomas, Mark Steel is probably the only left-wing comedian of any substance who still performs regularly on the London comedy circuit. A chirpy cockney and sometime milkman, Steel's unreconstructed hard-left humour is tempered by his affectionate delivery – and the puerile singalong ballads that he hammers out on the piano. His stand-up set is a testament to the inherent strengths and weaknesses of agit-prop Alternative Comedy, but his sardonic socialist wit found its finest forum in *Yeltsin, Trotsky and the Betting Shop* – a hilarious (yet highly informative) one-man re-enactment of the history of Russian Communism, which recast Josef Stalin as a belligerent shop steward.

JIM TAVARE

A comedic gentle giant who transformed his act (and his reputation) when he started using a double-bass as a musical stooge cum straight man. Since then his stage persona has developed into that of a musical Tommy Cooper – performing an inept masterclass whose highlights are its meticulously choreographed cock-ups and inbuilt disasters. He also appears alongside comic guitarist Dave Cohen in a spoof kosher rock band called Guns 'n' Moses. Jim is probably more successful overseas than he is in Britain, since his broad humour translates easily into other comic cultures. He has appeared at comedy festivals in Montreal and Melbourne, and latterly in Cologne – a far cry from his origins as a drama student at RADA and subsequently a support act for Macclesfield pub-rockers, The Macc Ladds – who billed him as 'the lad with spunk dripping out of his arse'.

WEEKENDING

BBC Radio 4's longest running comedy series (since 1970), it trades in satirical sketches that lampoon the events – particularly political – of the previous week, and concludes with a prophetic parodic summary of next week's news. Past performers and writers include Simon Brett, Douglas Adams, Griff Rhys Jones and Tracey Ullman. Rob Newman and David Baddiel met through its weekly writers' meetings, and alternative veteran Arnold Brown cut his teeth writing one-liners for it at £1.50 a time a couple of years before the opening of the Comedy Store. Other old boys include Lee and Herring and Steve Punt. The series had an entirely male cast until 1977 – a tradition that was only terminated by the irresistible rise of Margaret Thatcher, the Madonna of Alternative Comedy.

STU WHO

Abrasive but likeable Scottish stand-up comic, born and bred in Cumbernauld. In 1988, with Bruce Morton and Fred MacAulay he founded The Funny Farm, Scotland's only comedy collective, which now has its own series on STV.

STEVEN WRIGHT

Undisputed doyen of the surreal one-liner, his perfectly formed gags are less like jokes than haikus – displaying an incredible density of cerebral protein within a remarkably compact shell. His perform-ance technique is equally economical, combining a lobotomised tone of voice with a physical style so lethargic that he delivers much of his material sitting down. Although he is American, his humour is truly international and his out-to-lunch witticisms have had a profound influence on the weirder end of U K Alternative Comedy. On his last live appearance in Britain, over three nights at London's Dominion Theatre in 1993, he was supported by one such British disciple, Arnold Brown.

THE YOUNG ONES

Arguably the first Alternative Comedy sit-com to break into the mainstream. Charting the anarchic adventures of four unruly yet thoroughly middle-class undergraduates living in a disgusting student bedsit, its surreal style and abrasive content duplicated the approach and concerns of early Alternative Comedy. It was written by Ben Elton and starred Rik Mayall as a toffee-nosed Marxist, Adrian Edmondson as a plastic punk, Nigel Planer as a pathetic hippy and (in occasional cameos) Alexei Sayle as their lunatic landlord. All five comics were early Comedy Store regulars who went on to become major T V stars.

Acknowledgements

Readers may be puzzled by the selection of comics in this book, and wonder why some names have been included and others omitted. I've confined myself to the new wave of comedians whose careers I've been fortunate enough to follow from live performing (where most of their stories come from) to television or radio (where most readers know them from). I saw little point in approaching any comics whose star had already risen before I'd had a chance to witness any of their ascent at first hand. In such instances, my experience of their comedy is no more intimate than that of the average peaktime television viewer.

There are a few exceptions to this rule, but my overall selection hasn't been based on personal preference. Indeed several of my favourite comics are excluded, simply because they are not well known enough – usually because their live talent hasn't translated successfully on to TV. Several other comedians agreed to participate – even though I had written extremely critically about them in the recent past. To them I'm especially grateful, as I am to all these comics, who gave their time without receiving any payment – even though several of them asked.

Of all the comics I approached, only Sean Hughes and Paul Merton were unwilling to be interviewed. I respect their decision – but I mention their names lest their absence be interpreted as an adverse judgement. It isn't. I would have loved to have included them, and to some extent this book remains incomplete without them. The only other notable absentee is Gerry Sadowitz.

My thanks to Jane Carr, my editor at Fourth Estate; Ian Mayes and Jocelyn Targett, my editors at the *Guardian*; Julie Burchill, Gillian Glover, Cosmo Landesman, David Robinson, Waldemar Januszczak, Allen Wright, Toby Young, and most of all to all those comedians whose performances and reminiscences have given me so many hours of intoxicating pleasure.

PICTURE CREDITS

p. 26 Julian Clary © David Sillitoe; p. 36 Graham Fellows ©
A. Clift; p. 37 Jeff Green © F. Sanjar; p. 46 Harry Hill ©
David Sillitoe, used by kind permission of the *Guardian*; p. 51
Mark Lamarr © F. Sanjar; p. 53 Donna McPhail © F. Sanjar;
p. 55 Bruce Morton © Robert Perry; p. 65 Frank Skinner ©
David Sillitoe, used by kind permission of the *Guardian*; p. 67
Arthur Smith © F. Sanjar.

All photographs used by kind permission of the performers'
managements.

'If there's anything you haven't understood, please regard it as significant.' – Arnold Brown

Index

Mayfest 55, 233
McGough, Roger 42
McPhail, Donna 13
  biography 53–4
  childhood 75
  Edinburgh 239–40
  first gigs 129–30
  great gigs 191
  hecklers 229–30
  last laugh 295–6
  punters 206–8
  TV 254–5
  weird gigs 167, 173–4
· worst gigs 156–7
McPherson, Ian 243
Meccano Comedy Club 98, 140
Mercury, Freddie 283, 284
Merton, Paul 1, 68, 139, 148, 154, 160, 230,
  271, 273, 302, 306
Meuros, Reg 57
Miller, Ben 234
Miller, Max 261, 298–9
Millies, The 129
Milligan, Spike 74
Mills, Bob 13, 138
Monkhouse, Bob 186, 275
Montreal Comedy Festival (aka Just for
  Laughs) 69, 233
Monty Python's Flying Circus 81, 95,
  304
Morecambe, Eric 47, 64
Mortimer, Bob 12, 24
  biography 63–4
  childhood 82
  day job 118–9
  Edinburgh 243–4
  first gigs 132–3
  hecklers 226
  management 274, 279
  punters 197
  schooldays 89, 92
  TV 248
  worst gigs 162
Morton, Bruce 14
  biography 55–6
  day job 107–8
  first gigs 141
  great gigs 182–3
  last laugh 288–9
  punters 198, 200–201
  schooldays 97

  TV 249–50
  weird gigs 167–9
  worst gigs 165
Morton, Richard
  biography 57–8
  childhood 85–7
  Edinburgh 238
  first gigs 144
  great gigs 184
  hecklers 215, 220–21
  management 261
  punters 197–9
  TV 252–4
  weird gigs 180
  worst gigs 154–5
Mummy's Little Girl (Eclair) 33
Munnery, Simon (aka Alan Parker Urban
  Warrior) 10, 147, 196, 261, 308
Murdoch, Rupert 9
Murphy, Eddie 13

National Theatre 190
Newman, Rob 2, 9–11, 18, 19, 28, 40, 45 49
  biography 59–60
  childhood 70
  day job 101
  Edinburgh 245
  first gigs 133–4
  great gigs 181, 183
  hecklers 216, 217
  last laugh 286, 290
  management 261, 273
  punters 196
  schooldays 98
  TV 248, 250
  weird gigs 179
  worst gigs 147–8
Newsnight 125
Newsrevue 133
Nightclub Confidential 260
Norden, Denis 124
Normal, Henry 33, 42, 307
Not Only But Also 82
Not the Nine O'Clock News 23, 95, 307

Off the Kerb 57, 260, 263
Okin, Earl 128
O'Neill, Owen 222, 305, 307
On the Hour 28
Orton, Joe 26
Oxford University 117, 240